Collins

WJEC Eduqas
GCSE 9-1 Revis

English

English

Language & Literature

WJEC Eduqas
GCSE 9-1

Revision Guide

Paul Burns

About this Revision Guide & Workbook

Revise

These pages provide a recap of everything you need to know for each topic.

You should read through all the information before taking the Quick Test at the end. This will test whether you can recall the key facts.

Quick Test

Insert the correct punctuation:

1. Wheres my hamster Leo cried
2. He had gone there was no doubt about it
3. Maureen who lived next door searched her bins
4. Maureens son found Hammy in the kitchen

Practise

These topic-based questions appear shortly after the revision pages for each topic and will test whether you have understood the topic. If you get any of the questions wrong, make sure you read the correct answer carefully.

Review

These topic-based questions appear later in the book, allowing you to revisit the topic and test how well you have remembered the information. If you get any of the questions wrong, make sure you read the correct answer carefully.

Mix it Up

These pages feature a mix of questions for all the different topics, just like you would get in an exam. They will give you more practice answering exam-style questions.

Test Yourself on the Go

Visit our website at www.collins.co.uk/collinsGCSErevision and print off a set of flashcards. These pocket-sized cards feature questions and answers so that you can test yourself on all the key facts anytime and anywhere. You will also find lots more information about the advantages of spaced practice and how to plan for it.

Workbook

This section features even more topic-based questions as well as practice exam papers, providing two further practice opportunities for each topic to guarantee the best results.

ebook 

To access the ebook revision guide visit

www.collins.co.uk/ebooks

and follow the step-by-step instructions.

English Contents

Contents

Spelling

You must be able to:

- Spell basic and regular words
- Spell complex and irregular words.

Spelling Rules

- A lot of English spelling is regular, meaning it follows rules or patterns. Here are some of the most useful rules.

'i' before 'e' except after 'c'

- achieve
- receive

Changing the 'y' to 'ie'

- Change the 'y' to 'ie' when adding 's' to a word ending in 'y'.
  - berry – berries
  - pity – pities

  but only if there is a **consonant** before the 'y'. If there is a **vowel** before the 'y', you just add 's'.
  - boy – boys
  - say – says
- Follow the same rule when you add 'ed'.
  - pity – pitied
  - play – played

- To form the **plural** of words that end in 'o', add 'es' (potatoes), except for words taken from Italian (pianos).
- If a word ends in 's' or a 'buzzing' or 'hissing' sound, add 'es' (glasses, dashes).
- You can also learn when to double a letter before 'ing' or 'ed'.
- Look for other patterns and rules that will help your spelling and learn them.

Key Point

Spelling matters: it helps you to make your meaning clear. You can – and should – work at improving your spelling.

Homophones

- **Homophones** are words that sound the same but have different meanings. These cause a lot of problems. Here are some of the most common:
  - 'Here' means 'in this place': 'It's over here.'
  - You hear with your ears: 'I can hear you.'
  - 'There' means 'in that place': 'I put it over there.' It is also used in phrases such as 'there is' and 'there are'.
  - 'They're' is a **contraction** of 'they are': 'They're not really friends.'
  - 'Their' means 'belonging to them': 'They took all their things with them.'
  - 'Where', like 'here' and 'there', refers to place: 'Where do you think you're going?'

- 'Wear' is used about clothes etc.: 'You wear your earrings on your ears'.
- 'Were' (a **near homophone**) is the past tense of 'are': 'We were very happy there.'
- 'To' indicates direction: 'He went to the cinema.' It is also used as part of a verb: 'I want to do this now.'
- 'Too' means excessively: 'Too much' or 'too many'.
- 'Two' is the number 2: 'There were two questions to choose from.'

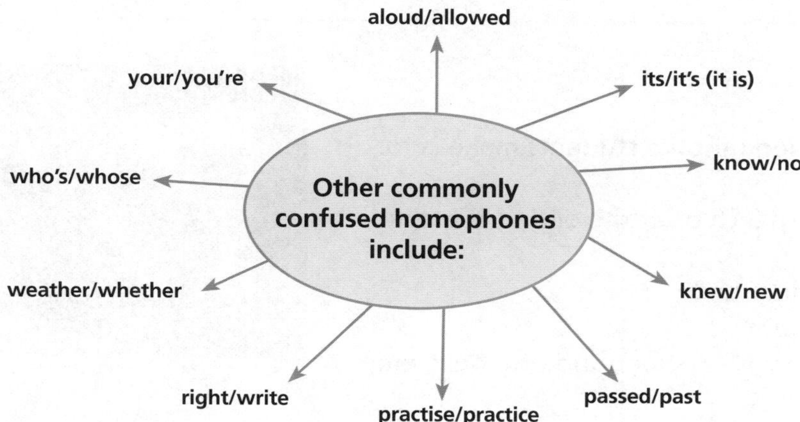

Key Point

Identify the words you tend to get wrong. Make a list of them and set about learning them.

- If you're not sure about any of these, look up their meanings and practise using them in sentences. You might be able to think of others that give you trouble.

Spelling Strategies

- Mnemonics are ways of remembering things. It can be useful to learn a phrase where the first letters of the words spell out the word you are trying to spell:
  - Big Elephants Can Always Upset Small Elephants (**because**).
- Another useful trick is to isolate the part of the word that causes you trouble:
  - There is a **rat** in sepa**rat**e.
- Or you might associate the spelling with the meaning of the word:
  - **Necessary** – it is necessary to wear one **c**ollar, two **s**ocks
- Some letters are not pronounced clearly, if at all (silent letters).
- Try splitting up the word and saying it slowly and carefully to yourself:
  - **en-vir-on-ment**
  - **k-now-ledge**.

Key Words

consonant
vowel
plural
homophone
contraction
past tense
verb
mnemonic
isolate
associate
silent letter

Quick Test

Identify the correct spelling from the alternatives given in the following sentences:

1. We had know/no idea wear/where we were going.
2. Its/It's Monday today.
3. I can't decide weather/whether to/two/too buy it or not.
4. Hurry up or you'll miss football practice/practise.

Punctuation

You must be able to:

- Clearly demarcate sentences
- Accurately use a range of punctuation.

Ending Sentences

- **Full stops** separate sentences. A common mistake students make is to use **commas** instead of full stops.
- **Question marks** can be used in direct speech or at the end of rhetorical questions:
  - 'Do you really want to do that?' she asked.
  - Are we ready to meet the challenge?
- **Exclamation marks** are used to show surprise, shock and other extreme emotions:
  - What a monstrosity!
  - That's amazing!

Commas

- Commas are used to separate subordinate clauses and phrases from main clauses. Subordinate clauses give extra information but are not necessary for the sentence to make sense:
  - Mina, having run the marathon, was exhausted.
  - After eating two puddings, Ali was full.
- They are used in lists:
  - I ordered fish, chips, mushy peas and a fizzy drink.
- Commas are also used to introduce and to end direct speech:
  - He shouted, 'Leave me alone!'
  - 'Nobody move,' ordered the policeman.

'having run the marathon' is the subordinate clause

'After eating two puddings' is the subordinate clause

Key Point

Commas must not be used to link clauses (statements that could stand alone as sentences) unless a connective or relative pronoun is used:

I fed the cat, although it had already eaten.

I fed the cat, which had already eaten.

Colons and Semi-colons

- **Colons** are used before an explanation:
  - It took two hours: it was a difficult job.
- They introduce quotations:
  - Mercutio plays down his injury: 'Ay, ay, a scratch, a scratch.'
- They introduce lists:
  - The collection was wide and varied: historic manuscripts; suits of armour; ancient bones; and hundreds of old coins.
- Note that **semi-colons** are used to separate the items in the list above. Semi-colons separate items in a list that consist of more than one or two words. The semi-colon helps with clarity.
- Semi-colons are also used to show that two clauses are closely related, when the writer does not want to use a connective or a full stop:
  - The flowers are blooming; the trees are green.

Brackets, Dashes and Ellipsis

- Brackets (**parentheses**) go around a bit of extra information:
  - A huge man (he was at least seven feet tall) dashed across the road.
- Dashes can be used to show an interruption in the train of thought:
  - I finished the meal – if you could call it that – and quickly left.
- **Ellipsis** (…) indicates the omission of words from a sentence. It can be used to show a thought trailing off or to make the reader wonder what comes next:
  - I realised that I was not alone…

Inverted Commas

- **Inverted commas** can also be referred to as **speech marks** or **quotation marks**.
- Speech marks surround the actual words spoken:
  - 'Never again!' she cried.
- Similarly, when quoting from a text, you put the inverted commas (quotation marks) around any words taken from the original:
  - Tybalt refers to Romeo as 'that villain'.
- Inverted commas are also used for titles:
  - Shelley's 'Ozymandias' is about power.

Apostrophes

- **Apostrophes** are used to show **omission** (also called contraction), or **possession**.
- Only use apostrophes for omission when writing informally. In formal writing you should write all words in full. When you do use an apostrophe, put it where the missing letter or letters would have been:
  - You **shouldn't** have done that.
  - **Malik's** finished but **Rachel's** still working.
  - **Let's** go home.
- Apostrophes for possession show ownership. If the owner is singular, or a plural that does not end in 's', add an apostrophe and an 's' to the word that indicates the 'owner':
  - the cat's tail
  - the class's teacher
  - the children's toys
  - James's hat.
- The only time you have to do anything different is for a plural ending in 's'. In this case, simply add an apostrophe:
  - the cats' tails
  - the boys' team.

Quick Test

Insert the correct punctuation:

1. Wheres my hamster Leo cried
2. He had gone there was no doubt about it
3. Maureen who lived next door searched her bins
4. Maureens son found Hammy in the kitchen

Key Point

Punctuation matters because writing does not make sense without it. Incorrect punctuation can change the meaning of your writing or even turn it into nonsense, confusing the reader.

Key Words

full stop
comma
question mark
exclamation mark
colon
semi-colon
parenthesis
ellipsis
inverted commas
speech marks
quotation marks
apostrophe
omission
possession

Sentence Structure

You must be able to:

- Use sentence structures accurately
- Use a variety of sentence structures for effect.

Simple Sentences

- Every sentence must contain a **subject** and a main verb. The subject is the person or thing (a **noun**) that the sentence is about. The verb is the doing, feeling or being word:

Ronnie ate

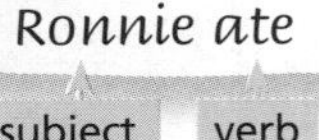

- **Simple sentences** often include an **object** (also a noun).

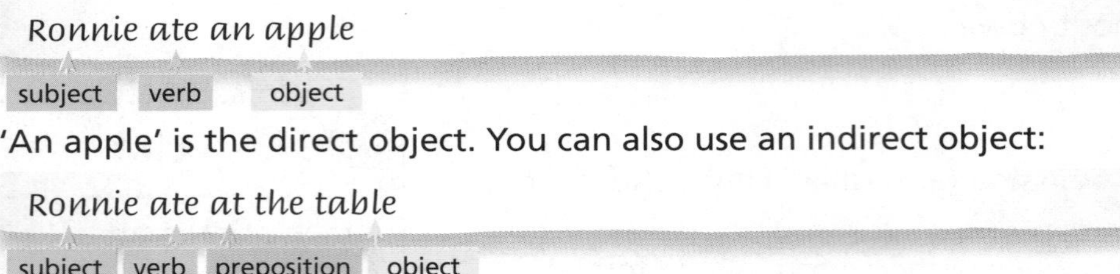

The **preposition** explains Ronnie's relationship to the table.

- You can vary simple sentences, and other sentence forms, by changing the verb from the **active** to the **passive voice**:

The apple was eaten by Ronnie

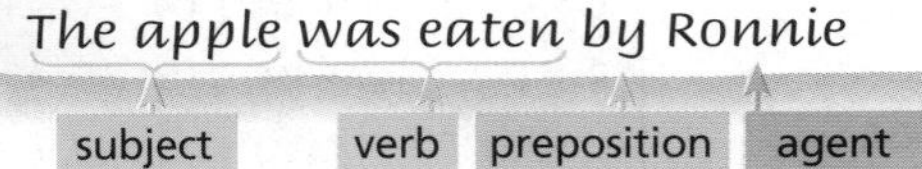

Here the apple, by being put at the start of the sentence, becomes the subject.

Minor Sentences

- A **minor sentence**, also known as a **fragment**, is not really a sentence at all because it does not contain a main verb. Fragments are very short and are used for effect. They are often answers to questions or exclamations:
  - Oh my word!
  - Just another boring day.
- They should be used rarely or they will lose their impact.

Compound Sentences

- To make a **compound sentence** you join together two **clauses** of equal importance using a **conjunction**. Clauses are phrases that could stand alone as simple sentences.
- You can use 'and', 'but' or 'or' to form compound sentences:
  - Lucia left the room and went to the shops.
  - Lucia left the room but stayed in the house.

Key Point

Try to vary the length and type of sentences you use. The examiner is looking for a range of sentence types.

- You can join more than two clauses in this way, though the result often appears clumsy:
  - Lucia left the room and went to the shops and bought a banana.

Complex Sentences

- A **complex sentence** also has two or more clauses joined together. The main clause should make sense on its own but the **subordinate clause**, which adds detail or explanation, does not need to.
- Some complex sentences are formed by joining two clauses with a conjunction. In these sentences the two clauses are not equal. Examples of conjunctions you might use are:

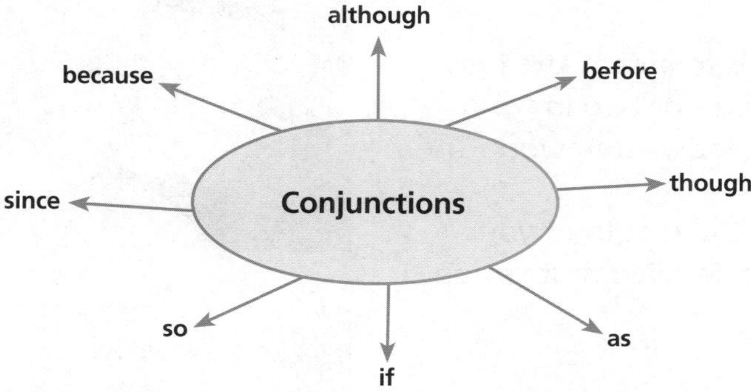

- The conjunction tells you what the relationship between the two clauses is:
  - Charlie left school **because** he had moved house.
  - Charlie left home **after** he had moved house.

  In the first sentence, moving house is the reason for Charlie leaving school, whereas the second simply tells us the order in which the events happened.
- Sometimes the conjunction is placed at the beginning of the sentence rather than between the two clauses:
  - Although he felt ill, Dan ate an apple.
- Conjunctions are not needed to form complex sentences:
  - Maria, who loved shopping, left the house immediately.
  - After she left the house, Maria went shopping.
- The first of these examples uses a **relative pronoun** (who) to connect the clauses, while the second changes the verb form to a past participle (having left).
- You can build even longer sentences by using several clauses and joining them in an appropriate way:
  - Dan was ill for several days so he stayed in bed; sometimes he read and watched television, but mostly he was bored and grumpy.

Quick Test

Which of the following is (a) a simple sentence, (b) a compound sentence, (c) a complex sentence and (d) a minor sentence?

1. Never again.
2. The hamster was found safe and well.
3. She liked sheep but she hated cows.
4. Although she had been there before, the girl could not remember where she was.

Key Point

Complex sentences can give more information and express more complex ideas.

Key Words

subject
noun
simple sentence
object
preposition
active voice
passive voice
minor sentence
fragment
compound sentence
clause
conjunction
complex sentence
subordinate clause
relative pronoun

Text Structure and Organisation

You must be able to:

- Organise your writing in coherent paragraphs
- Use a range of discourse markers.

Paragraphs

- The traditional way of starting a new **paragraph** is to **indent** the first line of the new paragraph, that is, start a centimetre or two in from your margin. This is usual in most books, and in handwritten work. Try to do it in your exams.
- There is no set length for paragraphs. Try to vary the length of your paragraphs. You might use long paragraphs for a detailed description or explanation and short paragraphs for impact.

Key Point

Paragraphs help you to organise your text so that it makes sense, follows a logical order and is easier to read.

Starting a New Paragraph

- When you start writing about something new, you should start a new paragraph. This could be a change of:
  - **speaker** – when using direct speech, start a new paragraph when a new person speaks:

    > 'I didn't see anything,' added Marco.

  - **person** – introducing a new character:

    > Julie was quite the opposite…

  - **place**:

    > Toppington is also worth a visit…

  - **time**:

    > A week later, Roland realised that all was not well…

  - **topic or idea** – moving from one aspect of your subject to another or introducing a different opinion:

    > Another cause of concern is the local bus shelter…
    > Some residents disagree with this view…

- Paragraphs often start with **topic sentences**, which introduce the topic or subject of the paragraph:

  > When we left, there was nobody else on the boat.

  ← The topic of the paragraph is the boat and whether or not it was empty.

  > Laurie Grantham, 17, has her own take on fashion.

  ← This paragraph is about Laurie's attitude to fashion.

Opening and Closing Paragraphs

- Opening and closing paragraphs can make a big difference to the impact of your writing. How you approach them depends on the form and purpose of your writing.
- Beginnings and endings in descriptive and creative writing are dealt with on pages 40–43. Beginnings and endings in non-fiction are dealt with on page 30 and pages 53–55.

Discourse Markers

- **Discourse markers** connect sentences and paragraphs. They guide readers through the text, showing how one sentence relates to another and how one paragraph relates to another.
- They can be single-word **connectives**, such as 'however', or phrases, such as 'in addition to this'. A discourse marker can also be a phrase which picks up on an idea from the previous paragraph:
  - This kind of behaviour is common throughout Europe.
- Not all discourse markers (for example, 'however' and 'therefore') have to be used at the beginning of a sentence. They can be more effective a little way in.
- Discourse markers have many different purposes:

To add information or ideas	In addition; As well as; Furthermore; Moreover	The new building, moreover, will ruin the view from Huntington Hill.
To point out a similarity	Similarly; In the same way	Similarly, the owl hunts at night.
To introduce a contrasting idea or point of view	Nevertheless; On the other hand; In spite of; Alternatively	Some good points have been made in favour of the plan. Nevertheless, I still think it's a bad idea.
To express cause and effect	As a result; Consequently; In order to; Therefore	I have had no objections so far. I will, therefore, continue as planned.
To give order or to sum up	Firstly; Finally; In conclusion; Basically	Finally, I'd like to thank Josh for making all this possible.
To express passing time	Subsequently; Later; As soon as; Meanwhile	The police took an hour to arrive. Meanwhile, Archie had escaped.

Key Point

You do not have to use a discourse marker in every sentence or even every paragraph, especially in descriptive and narrative writing.

Quick Test

Identify the discourse markers in the following sentences and explain their purpose.

1. First, I will consider Ken's proposal.
2. Tom's idea, on the other hand, is ridiculous.
3. Before I continue, I want to talk about the bus shelter.
4. I suggest, therefore, that we demolish the bus shelter.

Key Words

paragraph
indent
topic sentence
discourse marker
connective

Standard English and Grammar

You must be able to:

- Use Standard English
- Use correct grammatical structures.

Standard English

- **Standard English** is the version of English that is widely accepted as being correct.
- You may not always have to write in Standard English. Characters in a story might use **dialect** or **slang**. If you are writing for teenagers or children, you might use the sort of language they would use with their friends.
- For all other purposes write in Standard English, using correct **grammar** and spelling.

Personal Pronouns: First Person

- The most common misuse of **personal pronouns** is the confusion of 'I' and 'me'. 'I' is the subject of the sentence; 'me' is the object:
  - 'Ikram and me were late' is clearly wrong because you would not say: 'Me was late.' You would say: 'I was late.' So, logically, it must be: 'Ikram and I were late.'
  - Similarly you should not say: 'They gave prizes to Lucy and I.' The correct form is: 'They gave prizes to Lucy and me.'

Personal Pronouns: Second Person

- 'You' is both the **singular** and **plural** form of the second person. You could say, 'Thank you for coming' to one person or to hundreds. There is no such word as 'yous'.
- Do not use the Americanism 'you guys'. 'Guys' is not Standard English.

Key Point

Standard English is the form of English that is most widely understood. You need to be able to use it so that your audience can understand what you are saying.

Words and Phrases to Avoid

- Be aware of any words or phrases that are common in your area but are not Standard English, and avoid using them in formal writing.
- The same applies to current slang used by young people (such as 'sick' for 'good') and Americanisms, for example, using 'lay' instead of 'lie' or 'period' rather than 'full stop'.

Modal Verbs

- Do not use the word 'of' instead of 'have' after **modal verbs** such as would, could, should and might:
  - If I'd known, I would **have** told you.

Verbs: Agreement and Tenses

- There are three basic tenses – past, **present** and future. This section focuses on the past tense because that is where most errors occur.
  - A common error is to confuse the first and **third person** of the verb, for example, using 'you was' instead of 'you were'.
  - Another is the confusion of the **simple past tense** and the **perfect tense**, which expresses a completed action (for example, using 'done' instead of 'did' or 'has done'). The perfect tense is formed by adding the past participle to 'have' or 'has'.
- Most verbs follow this pattern:

	Singular	Plural
Simple past	I/you/he/she/it walked.	We/you/they walked.
Perfect	I/you have walked. He/she/it has walked.	We/you/they have walked.

- Many of the most commonly used verbs are irregular, among them the verb 'to be'. These are its correct forms:

	Singular	Plural
Simple past	I was.	We were.
	You were.	You were.
	He/she/it was.	They were.
Perfect	I/you have been.	We/you have been.
	He/she/it has been.	They have been.

- Some other irregular verbs that cause problems are shown here.

Simple Past	Perfect
ate	have/has eaten
did	have/has done
drove	have/has driven
gave	have/has given
got	have/has got
lay	have/has lain

Simple Past	Perfect
sang	has/has sung
saw	have/has seen
spoke	have/has spoken
taught	have/has taught
went	have/has gone
woke	have/has woken

- If you are writing in the past tense and you want to refer to something that happened before the events you are describing, use the **past perfect tense**, which is formed using 'had' and the past participle:
  - She had eaten before she arrived.
- If you are writing about an event in the past, which continued for some time, use the **past continuous**, formed by the past tense of the verb 'to be' and the present participle:
  - She was eating for the whole journey.

Key Point

The subject and verb of your sentence must agree in number and person.

Quick Test

Rewrite the following sentences in Standard English:

1. Me and Jay was put on detention.
2. I seen you guys on Saturday.
3. You was the bestest player we had.
4. After we had sang the first number, we done a dance.

Key Words

Standard English
dialect
slang
grammar
personal pronoun
singular
plural
modal verb
present tense
third person
simple past tense
perfect tense
past perfect tense
past continuous tense

Practice Questions

1 The following paragraph includes 10 incorrect spellings. Find them and rewrite them correctly.

> We where hoping for good whether for Sports Day. Unfortunately, on Friday morning it was poring with rain. Luckily, by ten o'clock it was clear and sunny. I was very exited when I got to the stadium but I had a long weight for my race, the 200 meters. Their were eight of us in the final. I was in the inside lane, witch I don't usually like, but I ran well round the bend and was second comming into the straight. As I crossed the line I was neck and neck with Jo. It wasn't until the teacher congratulated me that I knew I had definately won.

____

______________________________ [10]

2 The following five sentences have been written without punctuation. Insert the correct punctuation.

a) Peter who was the tallest boy in the class easily won the high jump.

____

b) What are you doing in the sand pit shouted Miss O'Connor get out of there at once.

____

c) Francesca won medals for the long jump the high jump and the relay.

____

d) I wasnt entered in any of the races because Im hopeless at running.

____

e) Jonathan finished last however he was pleased with his time.

______________________________ [5]

3 **a)** Change each of the following pairs of sentences into single sentences, using conjunctions.

i) Julia stayed off school. She had a stomach ache.

____

ii) He might be in the changing rooms. He might have already left.

____

b) Change the following pairs of sentences into single sentences using relative pronouns.

i) Michael announced the results. He has a really loud voice.

____

ii) The form with the best results won a cup. The cup was presented by Mr Cadogan.

____

c) Turn the following three sentences into a single sentence.

Maria had won the discus competition. She went home early. She was feeling sick.

______________________________ [5]

4 Rewrite the following sentences using Standard English.

a) Me and Hayley is going to town tomorrow.

____

b) You guys can come wiv us if youse want.

____

c) We was well chuffed with what we bought.

____

d) I don't know nothing about what they done at school.

____

e) I aint skiving off again coz I wanna get my GCSEs.

______________________________ [5]

5 Insert each of the following five connectives or discourse markers in the text below to help it to make sense.

however **as well as** **also** **as a result of** **consequently**

I am disgusted by the plan to close our library. (1)________ having a massive impact on our community, this act shows how little interest the council has in education.
(2) ________ this attitude, our children are being deprived of a wonderful resource.
Adults, especially older people, (3) ________ benefit greatly from the library. The council says we can use Hartington Library, but that is much too far away for most pensioners.
(4) ________, they will lose what has become for many a real lifeline, making them feel part of the community. (5) ________, it does not have to be like this. There are other ways for the council to save money: we could start with cutting down on the Mayor's free trips to America! [5]

6 Rewrite the following paragraph on a separate piece of paper, correcting errors in spelling, punctuation and grammar.

My first experiance of Bingley Park Library was when I was five. My grandmother, who were an avid reader, visitted the library every week and always borrowed four books. She read more or less anything but she especially liked detective story's, gardening books, and film star's biografies. Naturally, she wanted the rest of her family to be as enthusiastic as she was about books therefore, as soon as I could read, me and her marched down to bingley park. It was an imposing and rather frightening edifice for a child of five, the librarian, Miss Maloney, was just as imposing and twice as intimidating. [10]

Identifying Information and Ideas 1

You must be able to:

- Identify and interpret explicit information and ideas

Identifying Information and Ideas in the Exam

- Identifying information is an essential and basic skill. You will use it throughout both the Language and Literature exams.
- The first question of Component 1 and questions A1 and A3 of Component 2 will ask you to find information or ideas in a specified part of a text.
- Question 1 of Component 1 asks you to list five pieces of information. You get a mark for each piece of information correctly identified.
- Both questions A1 and A3 in Component 2 consist of three questions, each of which will ask you to identify a piece of information or an idea from one of the texts provided. There will be one mark for each correct answer.
- Usually, you can gain full marks for these questions by identifying explicit information or ideas. However, you can also get marks for identifying information or ideas that are clearly implied.

Explicit Information

- Explicit information is information that is openly stated. You will find it in the text.
- When answering questions it does not matter whether you think what the writer says is true or plausible. You are required to find the information and repeat it, either in the writer's words or in your own.
- Read the text below and list five things the writer tells us about Griselda the cat:

> There were only two places where Griselda would sit in the garden: in the middle of the lawn (to catch the sun) and (if the sun was too hot) in the shade of the plum tree. She sometimes hunted at night and would return in the morning with little presents for us, mice or birds, which she always left in the middle of the kitchen floor to make sure we got them.

- You could say:
  - She would only sit in two places in the garden.
  - She liked to sit in the middle of the lawn.
  - If it was hot she sat under the plum tree.
  - She hunted at night.
  - She brought back mice and birds.
  - She left mice and birds in the kitchen.

  There are six points made here. You can get marks for any five of them but if you put more than five you will not get any extra marks.

Key Point

You may be directed to a section of the text. Make sure you take your information only from that part of the text.

- You would not get marks for:
  - She was a cat – you are told this in the question, not in the text.
  - She was friendly – there is no mention of this in the text.
  - There was a plum tree in the garden – true, but it is not about Griselda. It would be a good answer if you were told to 'list five things about the place where Griselda lived'.

Explicit Ideas

- Explicit ideas are ideas and **opinions** that are openly stated.
- You could be asked, for example:
  - List five ways in which people react to the news.
  - List five reasons given for the start of the war.
- Read the text below and **identify** five ideas that, according to the writer, would improve the park:

> Bilberry Recreation Ground is an eyesore. It is time for radical action. Let's start by getting rid of the graffiti – it's not art; it's vandalism. The Victorian benches are also in a sad state – let's restore them. There used to be beautiful flower beds. It's time we planted some new ones. Let's encourage families to return by building a new and exciting playground. What about a kiosk selling cups of tea and ice cream? Finally, may I suggest a change of name? 'Recreation Ground' sounds old-fashioned and dreary. Let's call it Bilberry Park from now on.

- You would get marks for:
  - Get rid of the graffiti.
  - Restore the park benches.
  - Plant new flower beds.
  - Build a playground.
  - Build a refreshment kiosk.
  - Change the name.
- You would not get marks for:
  - It is an eyesore – this is not an idea for improvement.
  - Put a fence round the park – you might think this is a good idea but the writer does not mention it.
  - Take radical action – this is too vague.

Key Point

It does not matter whether you agree with what the writer says. You are being asked to identify the writer's ideas, not yours.

Quick Test

1. What does 'explicit' mean?
2. Can you quote from the text?
3. Can you put the answer in your own words?
4. If you are asked to list five points, do you get an extra mark for giving six?

Key Words

explicit
opinion
identify

Identifying Information and Ideas 2

You must be able to:

- Identify and interpret implicit information and ideas.

Implicit Information

- **Implicit** information is not stated openly. It is **implied**, so you have to 'read between the lines' to **infer** it from the text.
- Sometimes information is implied by saying what is not true:
  - He was not a happy child.

  This implies that he was sad.
- One piece of information can be implied by giving another:
  - They painted their garden shed blue.

  We can infer from this that they had a garden. Otherwise it would not be a 'garden' shed.

Key Point

To imply something means to suggest something without expressly stating it. If you infer something you understand something that has been implied.

Implicit Ideas

- Similarly, writers can make their views and feelings clear without openly stating them:
  - I would rather stick pins in my eyes than sit through another maths lesson.

  This implies that the writer does not like maths.
- When you infer meaning and explain what you have inferred, you are **interpreting** implicit information or ideas.
- Sometimes we infer a writer's views or feelings by putting together a number of pieces of **evidence**. Read the following text:

> One thing that really annoys me is the way they constantly scratch themselves. And every dog I've ever met has had smelly breath. As for the constant barking and yapping! Give me a nice quiet cat or hamster any day.

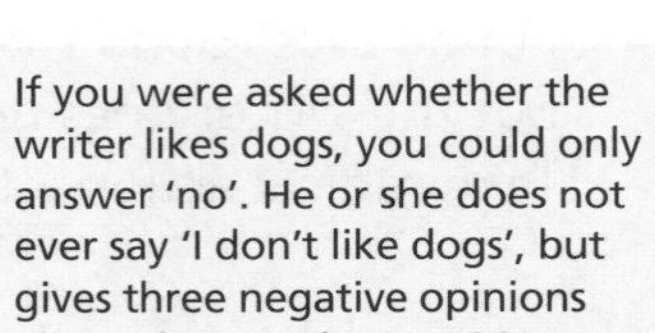

If you were asked whether the writer likes dogs, you could only answer 'no'. He or she does not ever say 'I don't like dogs', but gives three negative opinions about them and no positive ones.

- Read the following passage:

I Left My Heart on Bilberry Rec

by Mary Goodenough

Bilberry Rec is a part of my past. It didn't have wonderful facilities or beautiful vistas. There were no rose gardens or tea shops, no adventure playgrounds and certainly no 'wild meadows'. There were a few trees and hedges, the 'swing park' and a football pitch.

It was what it said it was: a recreation ground, a place where people of all ages went for recreation. Small children played on the swings and didn't often bash their heads on the concrete floor. Bigger children played football or cricket – or just fought. Courting couples walked hand in hand along the muddy paths or snogged on the broken benches. Pensioners walked their dogs and everyone used it as a short cut.

I know times have changed. And my head tells me the new Bilberry Park will be much nicer (and cleaner and safer) than the old Rec, but my heart wants it left just as it is. It's a sure sign of getting older – an attack of illogical nostalgia.

- Answer the following questions:
  1. What sort of memories does Mary Goodenough have about Bilberry Rec?
  2. Did anyone have accidents in the old Bilberry Rec? If so, who?
  3. Why does Goodenough think her feelings are 'a sure sign of getting older'?
- You might answer as follows:
  1. She has happy memories.
     - This is implied by references to her 'heart' and nostalgia.
  2. Children sometimes had accidents.
     - This is implied by saying that it didn't happen 'often'.
  3. Because of her happy memories, she does not want the park to change but she knows it is probably the right thing to happen.
     - This is implied by saying that her 'head' tells her it will be better and that her nostalgia is 'illogical'.

Key Point

You will usually be able to answer question 1 of Component 1 and questions A1 and A3 of Component 2 with explicit ideas or information from the text, but you will get credit if your answers are clearly implied.

Quick Test

1. Who implies, the writer or the reader?
2. Who infers?
3. Should you give your opinion?
4. When you are asked to list points from the text, do you still get credit if these are implied rather than explicitly stated?

Key Words

implicit
imply
infer
interpret
evidence

Synthesis and Summary

You must be able to:
- Select and synthesise evidence from different texts
- Summarise the content of texts.

Synthesis

- **Synthesis** is the bringing together of parts to make a whole. In English exams this usually takes the form of writing about two different texts.
- In Component 2 of the English Language exam you will have to compare the **content** of two non-fiction texts.
- The texts will be about similar subjects but one will have been written in the nineteenth century and one in the twenty-first century, so it is likely that there will be differences in attitudes as well as in the things and people described.

Key Point

Remember to look for both explicit and implicit information and ideas.

Summary

- A **summary** is a shortened version of something, keeping the main points but leaving out unnecessary detail.
- When you write a summary do not add your own thoughts or comment on the writers' style or techniques.
- You should use evidence from the text in the form of short quotations but most of the answer should be in your own words. Do not copy out huge chunks of the text.
- In your exam your ability to summarise will be tested in question A5 of Component 2. It is unlikely that the question will use the word 'summarise', however.
- Remember you are being asked about two texts, so write about them both at equal length.
  - Do not write about one and then the other.
  - Write about both throughout your answer, summarising different aspects of the texts as you go.

Approaching the Question

- Read the question carefully. It will not just ask you to summarise the texts; it will have a particular focus, for example:
  - Using information from both texts, explain how school has changed over time.
  - Explain the different feelings of the two writers about school.
- **Skim read** both texts.
- Underline or highlight the main points in the texts.
- You might want to do a (very quick) plan, listing **differences** (and **similarities** if asked for).
- Focus on the question.
- Don't repeat yourself.
- Write in proper sentences, using connectives.

Example

- Below are two short extracts from texts about sea voyages. Think about what you would include if you were asked to explain the differences between the voyages:

> ***Daily Southern Cross*, 21 October 1859**
>
> The *Mermaid* […] arrived in harbour on Wednesday at 4 a.m. She left Liverpool on 11th July at 5 p.m. Passengers have been very healthy during the voyage; three infants died, and one birth occurred. The passengers speak highly of Captain White and officers.

> ***Southern Star*, 19 July 2014**
>
> After three weeks the luxury liner *Ariadne* finally arrived home and the passengers disembarked from the journey one of them described as 'a floating nightmare'. For the last week almost a quarter of the passengers had been confined to their cabins with mild food poisoning and many are now demanding their money back.

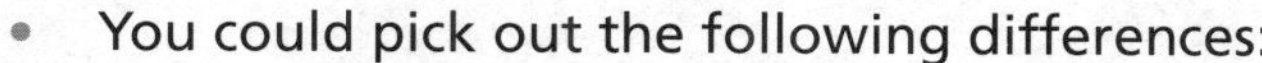

- You could pick out the following differences:

Mermaid	Ariadne
Journey over three months	Three-week journey
Passengers 'healthy' – three infants died	Food poisoning
Passengers praise captain and crew	Passengers demand money back

- A paragraph summarising the differences might read:

> *The **Mermaid's** journey lasted over three months; **Ariadne's** took three weeks. The **Mermaid's** passengers are 'healthy' but the **Ariadne's** have food poisoning. However, 'three infants died' on the **Mermaid**, suggesting that not everyone was healthy. Nevertheless, it would seem that the Victorian passengers were happier than the modern ones, as they 'speak highly' of the crew rather than complaining.*

Key Point

Bear in mind that this is a short answer question, attracting only 4 marks of the total of 40 for the paper, so you should aim to spend no more than 12 minutes on it.

Key Words

synthesis
content
summary
skim read
difference
similarity

Quick Test

1. Should a summary be shorter than the original text?
2. Should you use quotations in your summary?
3. Can you write about just one of the texts?
4. Should you discuss the writers' use of language in your answer?

Referring to the Text

You must be able to:

- Select appropriate and relevant examples from texts
- Use textual references to support and illustrate your interpretation of the texts.

Referring to the Text

- You can **refer** to a text by **paraphrasing** the text or by **quoting** from the text.
- For all Language questions and some Literature questions, you will have a text in front of you from which you can take your examples.
- For other Literature questions you will have to rely on your memory, so it is a good idea to learn some significant quotations.

Paraphrasing

- Paraphrasing means putting something into your own words. It is useful for summing up, for example:

> *The writer gives us a number of examples of cruelty to animals such as neglect and physical violence, which he describes in very vivid terms.*

- When you are writing about a longer text, such as a novel, you might not need to quote because you are writing about events or feelings and the exact wording is not important:

> *Lydia clearly does not think much about her family's reputation. When she returns from London she does not express any shame at her behaviour but boasts about being married.*

Key Point

It is very important to refer to the text in your answers, both in English Language and English Literature exams.

Using Quotations

- A **quotation** is a word or phrase taken directly from the text. Indicate that you are quoting by putting inverted commas (quotation marks) around the quotation.
- There are three main ways to set out your quotations.

  1. If your quotation consists of just a few words (or even one word) and fits naturally into your sentence, you simply put it into inverted commas (quotation marks) within the sentence:

  > *At the start of the soliloquy Juliet refers to 'love-performing night' but later it becomes a 'sober suited matron all in black'.*

  This is called **embedding**. Examiners like you to embed and it should be the method you use most often.

2 If the quotation will not fit easily into your sentence but is fairly short (no more than 40 words of prose or one line of verse), put a colon (:) before it, continue on the same line and use inverted commas:

Benvolio passionately asserts that he is not lying: 'This is the truth or let Benvolio die.'

3 If you want to use a longer quotation, leave a line and indent. You must indent the whole quotation. When quoting verse, end the lines where they end in the original. Do not use inverted commas:

This opposition will inevitably cause problems for the lovers and Juliet expresses her dilemma:

> *My only love sprung from my only hate!*
> *Too early seen unknown and known too late!*

The use of paradox emphasises her confusion.

Key Point

Only put words taken directly from the text inside the quotation marks. Spell and punctuate exactly as in the text.

Using PEE

- Remember to use PEE (Point, Evidence, Explanation).
- First make your **point**, saying what you want to say about the text.
- Then give your **evidence**, either in the form of a paraphrase or a quotation.
- Finally, **explain** or explore the evidence you have given.

The writer is very concerned about what he sees as widespread cruelty to domestic animals. He mentions the 'heartless neglect' of some dogs by their owners. The use of this emotive adjective paints the owners as villains and appeals to the compassion of the readers.

Here the first sentence makes the point, the second gives the evidence in quotation marks, and the third explains/explores the evidence.

Quick Test

1. What are the two different ways of using evidence from the text?
2. When you quote, what goes inside the inverted commas?
3. When should you not 'embed' a quotation?
4. What does PEE stand for?

Key Words

refer
paraphrase
quote (verb)
quotation (noun)
embed

Analysing Language 1

You must be able to:

- Explain, comment on and analyse how writers use language
- Use relevant subject terminology to support your views.

Diction and Register

- Diction and register both refer to the writer's choice of words or vocabulary.
- Most texts you read will be in Standard English. Sometimes, however, you will come across a text that uses a lot of non-standard words, for example slang and dialect words (see pages 14–15).
- Their use can tell you something about the writer, the narrator, certain characters or the audience at which the text is aimed.
- Writers might use specialised diction: for example, a lot of scientific or medical terms. The use of such language shows that the text is aimed at people who are interested in the subject and probably already know quite a lot about it.
- Writers might use words and expressions associated with a particular subject – for example, war or nature – for rhetorical or figurative purposes. Sometimes their word choice is referred to as a semantic field. We can often infer their attitude to the subject from their choice of semantic field.

Key Point

When we talk about 'parts of speech' or 'word class' we are referring to what words do in sentences. It is important that you can identify these so that you can refer easily to them in a way that shows you understand their function: for example, 'The writer uses a lot of adjectives associated with war to describe the scene.'

Parts of Speech (Word Classes)

- Nouns are naming words.
  - Concrete nouns name objects (chair, mountain).
  - Abstract nouns name ideas and feelings (love, suspicion).
  - Proper nouns have capital letters and name individual people (Jelena), places (Warsaw), days of the week (Saturday), months (April) etc.
  - A 'noun phrase' is a group of words built around a noun.
- Adjectives describe nouns (the **red** house; his **undying** love).
- Verbs are doing, feeling and being words. You might comment on whether verbs are:
  - in the past tense (she walked; he was thinking)
  - in the present tense (she is walking; he thinks)
  - or in the future tense (we are going to walk; you will go).
- Adverbs describe verbs, telling us how something is being done, for example, she spoke **slowly**; he writes **carefully**.
- Pronouns stand in for other words, usually nouns. Whether the writer uses first person (I/we), second person (you) or third person (he/she/they) can make a difference to how we read the text. 'I' makes the text more personal to the writer. 'We' and 'you' aim to involve the reader more in the text. There are different types of pronouns.

Personal pronouns	Relative pronouns
I/me	who
we/us	whom
you	whose
he/him	that
she/her	which
it	
they/them	

- **Prepositions** are used to express the relationship between nouns (or noun phrases) and other parts of the sentence or clause:
  - We went **to** the cinema.
  - The cat is **under** the table.
- **Conjunctions** join words, phrases and clauses: for example, 'and', 'but', 'although', 'because'. A conjunction is a type of connective but the two words are not interchangeable. Other types of word and phrase, including relative pronouns and adverbs, can also act as connectives (see Sentence Structure, pages 10–11).
- **Determiners** come before nouns and help to define them. The most common are the definite article (the) and the indefinite article (a/an). Other examples of determiners are 'this', 'both' and 'some'.

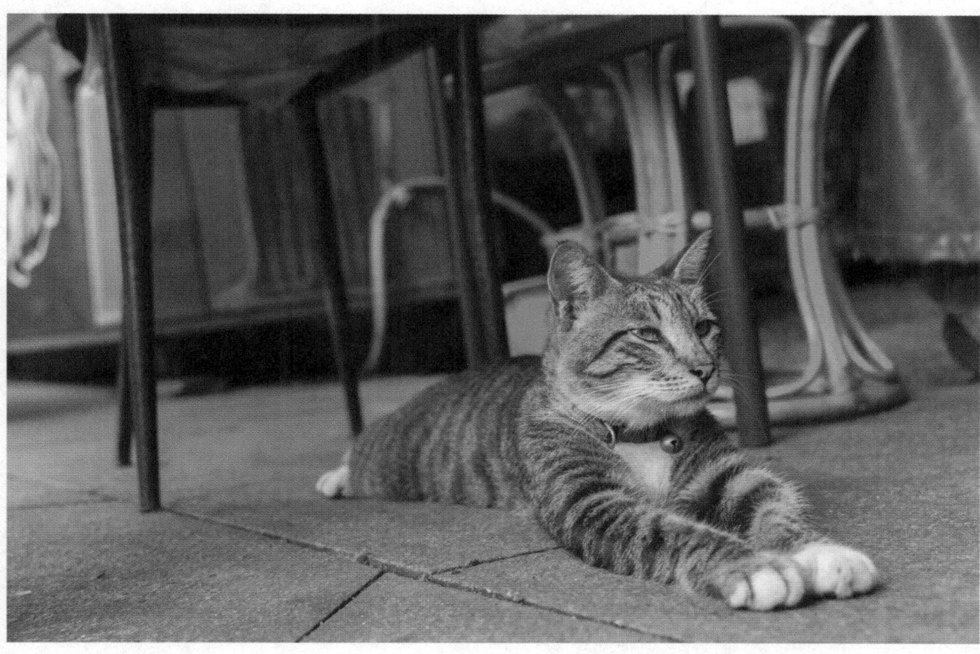

Quick Test

Read this sentence:

The old horse was munching thoughtfully on his oats.

Identify:

1. Two nouns
2. A verb
3. An adjective
4. A preposition
5. An adverb

Key Point

If you are not confident about identifying parts of speech it is better to avoid mentioning them. Using incorrect terminology will not impress the examiner.

Key Words

diction
register
vocabulary
semantic field
noun
concrete noun
abstract noun
proper noun
adjective
verb
adverb
pronoun
preposition
conjunction
determiner

Analysing Language 2

You must be able to:

- Explain, comment on and analyse how writers use language
- Use relevant subject terminology to support your views.

Connotation

- A connotation is an implied meaning. Words can have associations other than their literal meanings. For example, 'red' indicates danger or anger. 'Heart' has connotations of love and sincerity.

Key Point

Writers use language to affect and influence their readers.

Emotive Language

- Writers often seek to arouse certain feelings or emotions in the reader, for example, pity or anger. This can be done by using emotive language: words and phrases that have certain connotations.
- A reporter writing about a crime could write:

> Burglars stole some jewellery from Mr Bolton's house.

This just tells us the facts. A writer who wanted to influence our emotions might write:

> Heartless burglars stole jewellery of great sentimental value from frail pensioner Albert Bolton.

The adjective 'heartless' makes the burglars sound deliberately cruel, and 'frail' emphasises the weakness of the victim, while the phrase 'of great sentimental value' tells us how important the jewellery was to Mr Bolton. This increases our sympathy for him.

Rhetorical Language

- Rhetoric is the art of speaking. Effective speakers have developed ways of influencing their audiences. Writers also use rhetorical techniques to affect readers.
- Hyperbole is another word for exaggeration:

> Councillor Williams is the most obnoxious man ever to disgrace this council chamber.

- Lists of three are used to hammer home a point:

> Friends, Romans, countrymen.

- Repetition is used to emphasise the importance of the point being made:

> Victory at all costs, victory in spite of all terror, victory however long and hard the road may be; for without victory there is no survival.

- Rhetorical questions are questions that do not need an answer. Sometimes the writer gives an answer:

> Can we do this? Yes, we can.

Sometimes they are left unanswered to make the reader think about the answer:

> What kind of people do they think we are?

Sound

- The sound of words can make a difference to their meaning and effect.
- **Onomatopoeia** is the use of words that sound like their meaning:

> The door creaked open and clunked shut.

- **Alliteration**, the use of a series of words starting with the same sound, is common in newspaper headlines as well as in poetry and other literary texts:
  - Brave Bella battles burglars.
  - Storm'd at with shot and shell.
- When you see alliteration, think about why the writer uses a particular sound. Some consonants ('d', 'k', 'g') are hard. Others ('s', 'f') are soft. 'P' and 'b' have an explosive quality.
- The repetition of 's' sounds is also referred to as **sibilance**.
- **Assonance** is the use of a series of similar vowel sounds for effect:

> From the br**o**nzey s**o**ft sky…T**i**pples over and sp**i**lls down.

Imagery

- Literal **imagery** is the use of description to convey a mood or atmosphere. A description of a storm might create an atmosphere of violence and danger.
- Figurative imagery uses an image of one thing to tell us about another.
  - **Similes** compare one thing to another directly, using 'like' or 'as':

    > Straight and slight as a young larch tree.

  - **Metaphors** imply a comparison. Something is written about *as if it were* something else:

    > Beth was a real angel.

  - **Personification** makes a thing, idea or feeling into a person:

    > At my back I always hear
    > Time's winged chariot hurrying near.

  - The personification of nature, giving it human qualities, is also called **pathetic fallacy**:

    > The clouds wept with joy.

    This term can also be applied to a literal description in which nature or the weather reflects the feelings of characters.
  - A **symbol** is an object that represents a feeling or idea, for example a dove to represent peace.

Key Point

Imagery is usually associated with literary texts, such as poems. However, non-fiction texts also use imagery to paint pictures in the readers' minds.

Key Words

connotation
emotive language
rhetoric
hyperbole
repetition
rhetorical question
onomatopoeia
alliteration
sibilance
assonance
imagery
simile
metaphor
personification
pathetic fallacy
symbol

Quick Test

Of which literary techniques are the following examples?

1. Macbeth doth murder sleep.
2. Ill met by moonlight.
3. I wandered lonely as a cloud.
4. You were sunrise to me.

Analysing Form and Structure

You must be able to:

- Explain, comment on and analyse how writers use form and structure
- Use relevant subject terminology to support your views.

Form and Structure

- The structure of a text is the way in which it is organised: for example, the order in which information is given or events described.
- The terms 'structure' and 'form' are both used to describe how a text is set out on the page.

Openings

- The beginning (**opening**) of a text is very important as it has to draw in the readers and encourage them to continue reading.
- Some texts begin by giving an overview of the subject, indicating what the text is going to be about:

> There are thousands of varieties of butterfly. In this article I will discuss some of the most common.

- A writer might explain why he or she has decided to write:

> Lewis's views about youth unemployment are fundamentally wrong.

- Fiction writers can use their openings to introduce characters or settings:

> 'I shall never forget Tony's face,' said the carrier.

- Texts can also start with dramatic statements, designed to shock, surprise or intrigue:

> It was a bright cold day in April, and the clocks were striking thirteen.

Endings

- Fiction writers might give a neat **conclusion**: for example, with the solving of a crime or a marriage:

> Reader, I married him.

- They might prefer to leave us with a sense of mystery or suspense:

> 'Who are they?' asked George […]
> *'Wolves.'*

- Writers of essays and articles usually end by drawing together their main points and reaching a conclusion.
- Some texts end with a question or even an instruction:

> Get out there now and use your vote!

Key Point

You should consider why the writer has decided to arrange things in a particular way and the effect of this on the reader.

Chronological Order

- **Chronological order** gives events in the order in which they happened. This is the most common way of ordering fiction and non-fiction texts such as histories, biographies and travel writing.
- Writers might, however, start at the end of the story or somewhere in the middle before going back to recap previous events in 'flashbacks'.
- **Reverse chronological order** means starting with the latest event and working backwards. You will see this in **blogs** and discussion forums.

Other Ways of Ordering Texts

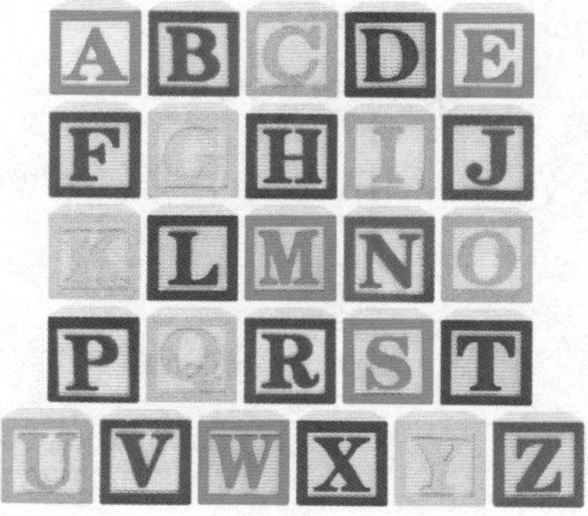

- Some texts start with general information and move on to more detailed information and explanation.
- A text giving a point of view might build up to what the writer thinks are the most persuasive arguments.
- Information can be arranged in **alphabetical order**, as in dictionaries and encyclopaedias.
- Texts sometimes rank things or people in order of importance or popularity, as in a music chart, either starting with the best and working down or starting with the worst and working up.

Divisions

- Books are usually divided into **chapters**, sometimes with titles or numbers.
- Most prose is arranged in **paragraphs** (see pages 12–13), while verse is often divided into **stanzas** (see pages 78–79). Make sure you use the correct terminology.
- Other devices used to divide up text include **bullet points**, numbering and **text boxes**.
- Headlines and subheadings help to guide readers through the text.

Key Point

Texts, especially longer texts, are often divided into sections. These give order to their contents and help readers find their way through the text.

Analysing Structure

- When analysing a short text, or an extract from a longer text, think about how and why the writer changes focus from one paragraph or section to another, perhaps moving from a general description to something more detailed, from a group of people to a particular character, or from description to action or speech.

Quick Test

Put the following in:

1. chronological order
2. reverse chronological order
3. alphabetical order
   a) December 2014
   b) January 2002
   c) April 2011
   d) November 2011

Key Words

opening
conclusion
chronological order
reverse chronological order
blog
alphabetical order
chapter
paragraph
stanza
bullet point
text box

Review Questions

1 Insert the correctly spelled word in each of the following pairs of sentences.

a) except/accept

I did them all ______________ the last one.

I ______________ your apology.

b) affect/effect

The weather seemed to have a bad ______________ on everyone's mood.

I don't think the weather will ______________ the result.

c) aloud/allowed

Nobody is ______________ in here at lunchtime.

Mo really likes reading ______________ in class.

d) write/right

Nobody got the ______________ answer.

I'll ______________ a letter and explain.

e) who's/whose

He couldn't return it because he didn't know ______________ coat it was.

Tell me ______________ going and then I'll decide. [5]

2 Rewrite the following passage on a separate piece of paper using the correct punctuation.

> dont you think we should wait for him asked Eve
> not at all Henry replied he never waits for us
> well that's true Eve said but he doesn't know the way

[10]

3 Rewrite the following passage on a separate piece of paper, using a variety of simple, compound and complex sentences (and adding words if necessary) to make it more effective.

> Henry and Eve waited for another ten minutes. Joel did not arrive. They left without him. They walked to the bus stop. There was no-one there. This suggested they had just missed the bus. Henry was very annoyed with Joel. Eve told him to calm down. She told him to forget about Joel. The journey was uneventful. They got off the bus by the lake. It looked eerie in the moonlight. They sat down on a grassy bank. They took their sandwiches and drinks out of the bag. Henry felt a hand on his shoulder.

[10]

4 Pick the five sentences in which the correct forms of the verb are used.

a) You was really good tonight. ☐

b) Ms Greenall taught me how to boil an egg. ☐

c) They've gotten two more kittens. ☐

d) I knew the song because we had sung it in class. ☐

e) I rung the bell twice but nobody come. ☐

f) She lay on the sofa until she felt better. ☐

g) I done my homework at break. ☐

h) He says he won't come because he's already seen it. ☐

i) I have done what you asked. ☐

j) I'm going to lay down here for a while. ☐ [5]

5 Put the following nouns into their plural forms.

a) pizza ______________________

b) latch ______________________

c) mosquito ______________________

d) sheep ______________________

e) donkey ______________________

f) stadium ______________________

g) quality ______________________

h) church ______________________

i) woman ______________________

j) hypothesis ______________________ [5]

6 Rearrange the following paragraphs so that the whole letter makes sense.

a) The next thing I knew two young girls were leaning over me. I'm sorry to say I thought the worst when I saw the rings through their noses. But they asked me if I was all right and very gently helped me to stand up. One of them stayed with me while the other went into the shop and fetched a chair. Then I noticed there were two boys carefully collecting all my shopping and bagging it up.

b) When it was all collected in, they called a taxi to take me home. I'm sorry to say I didn't ask their names, so I'd like to give them a big thank you through your newspaper. Whoever you are, you're a real credit to Bilberry and to your generation!

c) I was in town on Wednesday to do my usual shop in the supermarket. I got a little more than usual so my bags were rather heavy. As I came out of the shop I lost my balance and keeled over, spilling all my shopping.

d) I wasn't badly hurt but it was quite a shock. I just sat there on the pavement, stunned and not knowing what to do.

e) I am writing to express my thanks to a group of young people I met last week. It isn't often we hear good things about teenagers. We read so much about crime and vandalism, drinking and bad manners that we can easily end up thinking the worst of all teenagers.

a) ☐ b) ☐ c) ☐ d) ☐ e) ☐ [5]

Practice Questions

1. Read the passage below.

   This is a description of Scrooge. List five things you learn about him here. [5]

From *A Christmas Carol* by Charles Dickens

The cold within him froze his old features, nipped his pointed nose, shrivelled his cheek, stiffened his gait; made his eyes red; his thin lips blue; and spoke out shrewdly in his grating voice, A frosty rime was on his head, and on his eyebrows, and his wiry chin,

2. Read the passage below.

   What impressions does Dickens create of Scrooge's character?

   You must refer to the language used in the text to support your answer, using relevant subject terminology where appropriate. [5]

From *A Christmas Carol* by Charles Dickens

Nobody ever stopped him in the street to say, with gladsome looks, 'My dear Scrooge, how are you? When will you come to see me?' No beggars implored him to bestow a trifle;[1] no children asked him what it was o'clock; no man or woman ever once in all his life inquired the way to such and such a place, of Scrooge. Even the blindmen's dogs appeared to know him; and when they saw him coming on, would tug their owners into doorways and up courts; and then would wag their tails as though they said, 'No eye at all is better than an evil eye, dark master!'

[1] *bestow a trifle* – to give a small amount

3 Read the passage below and answer the questions that follow.

From a letter written by Charles Lamb to William Wordsworth

London, January 30, 1801

I ought before this to have replied to your very kind invitation into Cumberland. With you and your sister I could gang[1] anywhere. But I am afraid whether I shall ever be able to afford so desperate a Journey. Separate from the pleasure of your company, I don't much care if I never see a mountain in my life. I have passed all my days in London [...] The lighted shops of the Strand and Fleet Street, the innumerable trades, tradesmen and customers, coaches, waggons, playhouses, all the bustle and wickedness round about Covent Garden, the very women of the Town, the Watchmen, drunken scenes, rattles;[2]—life awake, if you awake, at all hours of the night, the impossibility of being dull in Fleet Street, the crowds, the very dirt & mud, the Sun shining upon houses and pavements, the print shops, the old *Book* stalls, [...] coffee houses, steams of soup from kitchens, the pantomimes, London itself a pantomime and a masquerade, all these things work themselves into my mind and feed me without a power of satiating me. The wonder of these sights impels me into night walks about the crowded streets, and I often shed tears in the motley Strand from fullness of joy at so much *Life*.—All these emotions must be strange to you. So are your rural emotions to me [...]

My attachments are all local, purely local.—I have no passion [...] to groves and valleys.—The rooms where I was born, the furniture which has been before my eyes all my life, a book case which has followed me about (like a faithful dog, only exceeding him in knowledge) wherever I have moved, old tables, streets, squares, where I have sunned myself, my old school,—these are my mistresses. Have I not enough, without your mountains?

---

[1] *gang* – a dialect word for 'go'
[2] *rattles* – constant chatterers

a) Name one place in London that Lamb enjoys. __________ [1]

b) According to Lamb, what is the only attraction of Cumberland for him? [1]

____

c) What emotion makes Lamb cry when he is in London? [1]

____

4 Now read this article and explain the differences between Weston's and Lamb's attitudes to city life. [4]

Write your answer on a separate piece of paper.

I'm a City-Hater – Get Me out of Here!

by Malcolm Weston

I've had enough. I'm leaving. Who was it who said that when a man is tired of London he's tired of life? Well, I don't think I'm tired of life – I'd like to go on living as long as I can – but I'm fed up to the back teeth with London. It's dirty. It's noisy. You can barely move in Oxford Street sometimes. Everything's expensive (how can anyone afford to live here?). And everyone is so bad-tempered. I know it's meant to be terribly lively and exciting but, frankly, I'm bored with it. Sorry, Londoners. It's nothing personal: I don't really like any cities – or towns. So I'm off home. And this time next week you'll find me (if you can – it's a bit off the beaten track) halfway up a mountain somewhere in the Lake District, looking up at the sky and listening to the sound of silence.

Reading Literature 1

You must be able to:

- Read and understand a range of literature
- Critically evaluate literature texts.

Story Structure

- Most novels and stories begin by 'setting the scene', introducing characters or places and giving us a sense of the world we are entering.
- That world might be very like our own world but it could be unfamiliar, perhaps because the story is set in a different country or a different time.
- The writer might even, like Tolkien, have invented a complete fantasy world.
- This part of a story is called **exposition** and can take a chapter or more, or maybe just a few lines.
- The event that really gets the story going is sometimes called the **inciting incident**. This can be dramatic and shocking, like the Martians landing at the beginning of *War of the Worlds*, or it can be a seemingly ordinary event, like Darcy coming to stay with Bingley in *Pride and Prejudice*.
- Inciting incidents change the lives of the protagonists (the main characters) for ever.

Key Point

Every story has a beginning, a middle and an end. The extracts you will be given in Component 1 might come from any part of the story.

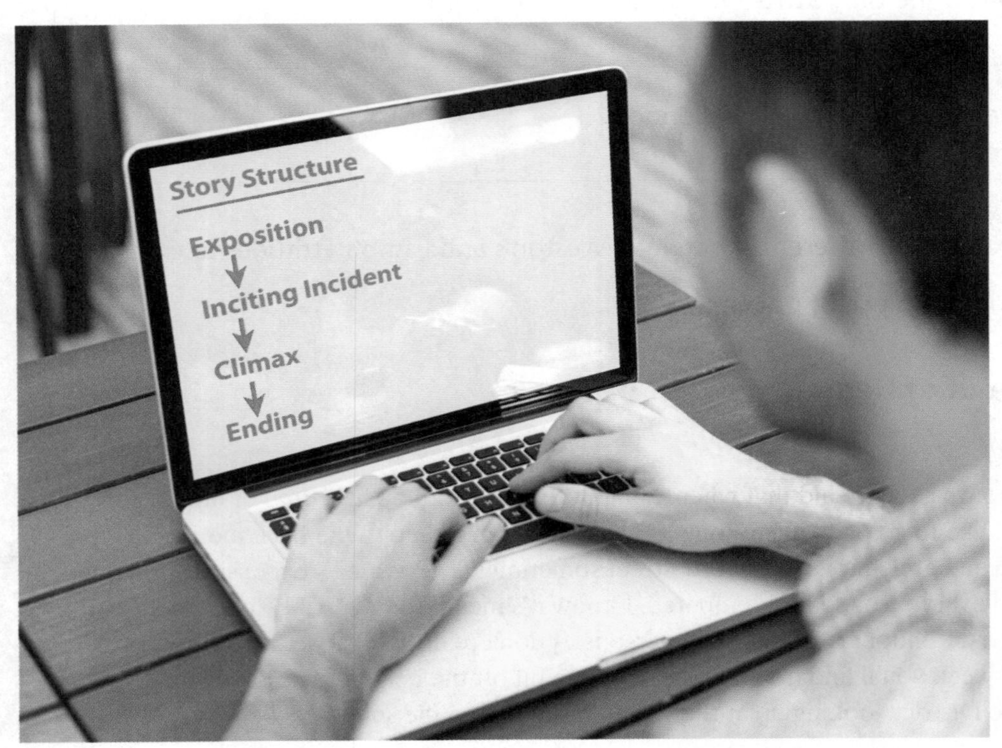

- During the course of a story there are usually several **turning points**. Turning points are events that change the direction of the story for good or ill. Sometimes we can see them coming; sometimes they are unexpected and surprising 'twists' in the plot.
- Towards the end, most stories reach a **climax**, or denouement, when things come to a conclusion, sometimes happily as in a fairy tale, sometimes not. This is the event the whole story has been building up to.
- The climax is not always at the end of the story. Most writers take some time to reflect on how things have turned out.
- Endings quite often refer back to openings, giving a sense of how things have changed.

Key Point

When analysing a literary text, always consider the 'narrative voice' and your reaction to it.

Narrative Perspectives

- Many stories are told in the first person singular ('I'), so that we see the story through the eyes of one of the characters, usually the **protagonist**, for example, Jane in *Jane Eyre* or Meena in *Anita and Me*. This encourages us to empathise with them.
- Sometimes the **narrator** is another character, acting more as an observer and putting some distance between the reader and the protagonist. Dr Watson in the Sherlock Holmes stories is an example of this.
- Each narrator has his or her own 'voice'. In *War of the Worlds*, for example, the kind of language the narrator uses tells us about his background and culture.
- A writer might use several different narrators so that we get different characters' experiences and points of view: Robert Louis Stevenson does this in *The Strange Case of Doctor Jekyll and Mr Hyde*.
- In a 'third-person **narrative**' the narrator is not involved in the story at all. If there is a sense of the narrator's 'voice', it is the voice of the author. This gives the writer the opportunity of sharing with us the thoughts, feelings and experiences of many characters.
- A narrator who can see everything in this way is called an **omniscient narrator**.
- Sometimes omniscient narrators comment on characters and action using the first person. If so they are called **intrusive**. Dickens uses this technique in *A Christmas Carol.*

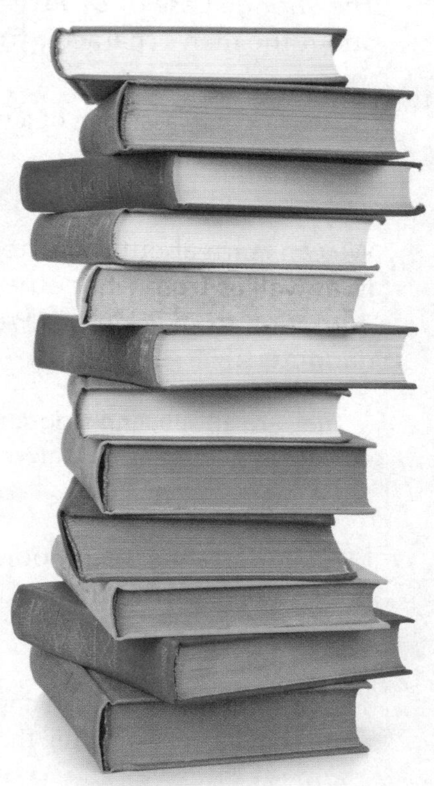

Quick Test

1. Does the exposition come at the beginning or end?
2. When the narrator is part of the action is it a first-person or third-person narrative?
3. Which comes first: the climax or the inciting incident?
4. What is an omniscient narrator?

Key Words

exposition
inciting incident
turning point
climax
protagonist
narrator
narrative
omniscient narrator
intrusive narrator

Reading Literature 2

You must be able to:

- Read and understand a range of literature
- Critically evaluate texts.

Character

- We learn about **characters** in different ways.
- The narrator can directly describe a character. In this example (from *The Strange Case of Dr Jekyll and Mr Hyde*) we can infer something about the man's character from his appearance.

> …the lawyer was a man of a rugged countenance, that was never lighted by a smile.

Key Point

Descriptions of people make the characters seem more real and can tell us a lot about them.

- We can learn about characters from what they say and how they say it, as well as from what other characters say about and to them. In this quotation from *Pride and Prejudice* Mr Bennet gives his opinion of his daughters:

> 'They are all silly and ignorant like other girls; but Lizzy has something more of quickness than her sisters.'

We can infer from this that Lizzy is the only daughter that Mr Bennet is interested in and that he can be quite blunt and dismissive. However, we might get a slightly different impression if we know that he is talking to his wife. It could be that he is trying to provoke her and/or that his remark about the girls being 'silly and ignorant' is intended as a joke.

- Most importantly, you should consider how characters behave and how others react to them. Dickens leaves us in no doubt about Scrooge's character:

> Even the blindmen's dogs appeared to know him; and when they saw him coming on, would tug their owners into doorways and up courts.

This comes at the beginning of *A Christmas Carol* and gives us a strong first impression, which is built on by descriptions of his treatment of his clerk, his nephew and the men who come collecting for charity.

Description

- This description (from *The Withered Arm* by Thomas Hardy) is fairly simple:

> …it was not a main road; and the long white riband of gravel that stretched before them was empty, save for one moving speck.

This tells us that the story is set in a remote place and sets up the encounter between the people in the carriage and the boy, whom they first see as a 'moving speck'.

- In the first chapter of *Great Expectations*, Dickens describes the **setting** in a way that gives us information about the landscape while creating an **atmosphere** that prepares us for the frightening event that is about to happen:

> …and that the dark flat wilderness beyond the churchyard, intersected with dykes and mounds and gates, with scattered cattle feeding on it, was the marshes; and that the low leaden line beyond, was the river; and that the distant savage lair from which the wind was rushing, was the sea…

Dickens uses adjectives like 'dark', 'low' and 'leaden' to give us a sense of an unattractive, featureless landscape, but adds words like 'wilderness' and 'savage' to make it seem dangerous and threatening.

- The description above uses **literal imagery** to create **mood** and atmosphere, the lonely, rather frightening place reflecting the feelings of the protagonist Pip.
- **Figurative imagery**, too, is often used in descriptive writing. In *The Withered Arm* Hardy uses a simile to describe one of his characters:

> Her face too was fresh in colour, but it was of a totally different quality – soft and evanescent, like the light under a heap of rose-petals.

The imagery helps us to picture her complexion and gives us a sense of her beauty and fragility.

Key Point

Writers describe places to root their stories in a time and place, and to create mood and atmosphere.

Quick Test

Identify what kind of imagery is being used in these sentences:

1. The lake shone like a silver mirror.
2. Angry crags surrounded us.
3. A veil of snow hid it from view.
4. There was a cluster of jagged black rocks.

Key Words

character
setting
atmosphere
literal imagery
mood
figurative imagery

Creative Writing 1

You must be able to:

- Write clear and imaginative narratives.

Narrative

- A narrative is an account of events – a story, whether real or imagined.
- The writing task in Component 1 (Section B) will ask you to write a story. Your story can be real or imagined.
- This gives you the opportunity to demonstrate creativity as well as accuracy in your use of the English language.
- You will be given a choice of four tasks. They will include a simple title, for example: 'A Terrible Event'.
- There could be an invitation to write about a personal experience, such as:
  - Write about a time when you were very happy.
- You might be provided with the opening words:
  - Write a story which begins: 'Stop that now or I'll go to the police', she shouted.
- You might get the closing words:
  - Write a story which ends: 'I left and did not look back.'.
- The tasks are varied and can be interpreted in many ways, allowing you to develop your own ideas in your own style.
- Do not, however, think that you can simply re-write a story you have previously written and try to fit it to one of the titles. The examiners are aware that some candidates do this and will mark you down if your story has little or no relevance to the title.

Key Point

You can tell a story in your own voice or you can invent a character (persona) to tell the story.

Planning

- Before you start to write, spend a few minutes planning, making decisions about the main elements of your story.

Character and Voice

- Decide whether you are going to write in the first or third person. If you opt for the first person, is the narrator the protagonist or an observer?
- The protagonist could be you or a version of you, but it can be much more interesting to write about someone who is completely different.
- There may also be an antagonist, someone who stands in the way of or opposes the protagonist.
- Think about other, minor characters – but beware of introducing too many. You don't want to make things too complicated.

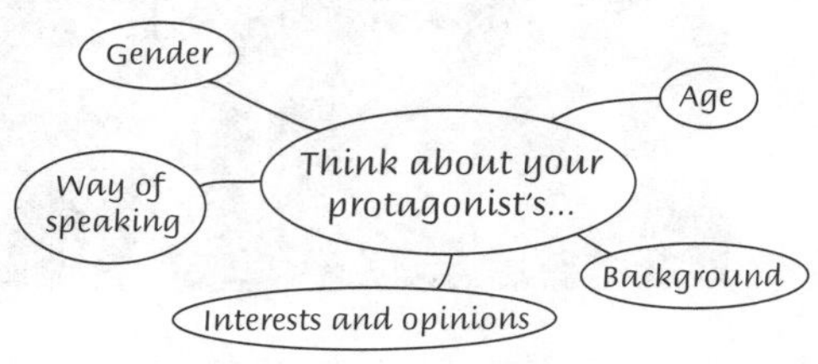

Structure

- The same applies to the plot. Because your story will not be very long, it is best to keep it fairly simple.
  - You need an inciting incident, a climax and at least one turning point.
  - Establish your 'world,' but don't spend too much time on exposition.

- You might end with a shock or surprise. It has been said that writers should give readers what they want but not in the way they expect.

- Stories are normally written mainly in chronological order but you might want to use 'flashbacks'.

Description

- Descriptive writing is an important part of creative writing. In the exam, you will not be asked directly to write a description. However, whichever task you choose to do, you will be expected to demonstrate your ability to write descriptively.
- During the course of your story you will need to describe people, places and feelings. To do this, depending on what you have chosen to write about, you might draw on your own memories, your reading and/or your imagination.
- Think about different aspects of the thing or person you are describing – and not just positive ones. This is especially important when describing a person – there is only so much you can write about how lovely someone is.
- Think about all five senses: sight, hearing, smell, taste and touch. When you have decided what you want to describe, it is a good idea to jot down what you experience through each sense. If you were describing a beach you might put:

Key Point

When you describe something, remember that you can use all five senses.

Taste	Touch	Hearing	Smell	Sight
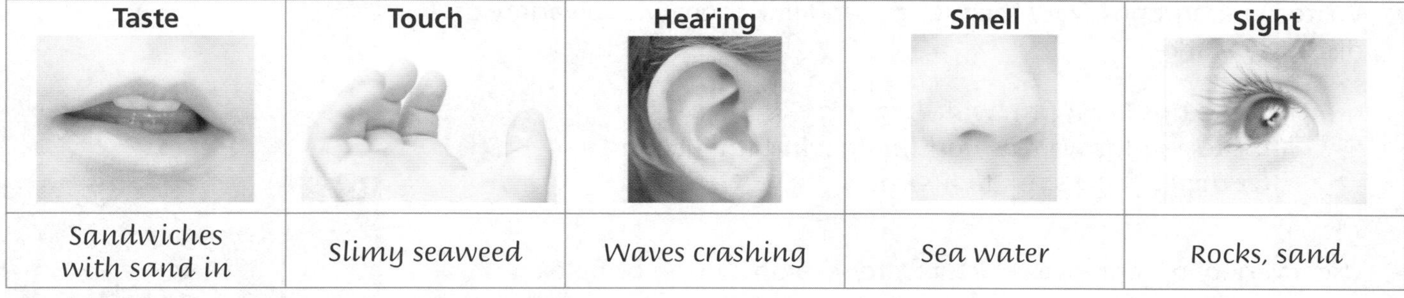				
Sandwiches with sand in	*Slimy seaweed*	*Waves crashing*	*Sea water*	*Rocks, sand*

- Another way of approaching description, which can be incorporated into the structure of your story, is 'big to small', starting with what something is like from a distance and moving in like a camera:

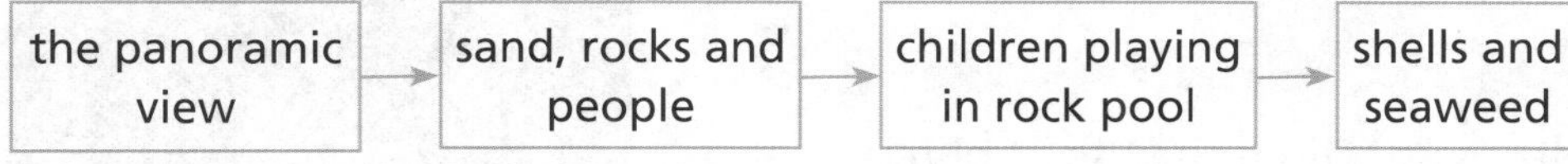

Key Point

Be careful not to just tell the 'bare bones' of the story. You also need to describe people and places.

Quick Test

What is meant by the following?

1. The protagonist.
2. The antagonist.
3. The inciting incident.
4. A turning point.

Key Words

narrative
protagonist
antagonist

Creative Writing 2

You must be able to:

- Write clear and imaginative narratives.

Language and Style

- Normally you would write in Standard English but if you use a first-person narrator, you should write in that person's **voice**. Think about its tone – formal or chatty? – as well as whether to use dialect or slang.
- Stories are usually written in the past tense. Using the present tense can make the action seem more immediate and vivid, though. You can use either, but stick to one.
- **Direct speech** can help to move on the story and tell us about character, but use it sparingly. Think about whether it adds anything – and make sure you set it out properly. Sometimes **indirect** (or **reported**) speech can be more effective.
- Write in paragraphs. Vary their length and link them with a variety of discourse markers:

  - *Beyond this lies a flat, wide bog.*
  - *But these sights were as nothing to what lay beyond.*
  - *After they left, he sank to his knees*

- Use a variety of sentence structures, for example using complex sentences for descriptions and simple or even minor sentences for dramatic impact:

  - *It was her.*
  - *A gun beneath the leaves.*

- Use techniques such as **parallel phrasing**. This is the use of phrases constructed in the same way and arranged in pairs or sequences:

  - *Tiny rivulets run down the lane; a massive lake covers the fields.*

- Use a range of punctuation but avoid using a lot of exclamation marks.
- Use **imagery** and figurative language, including metaphors and similes:

  The train roared like an angry lion.

- Use adjectives and adverbs:

  - *The deep mysterious sea*
  - *The engine spluttered fitfully.*

Key Point

Remember that when you describe something, you are not limited to describing what you can see.

- Be adventurous in your choice of vocabulary. Use words that have precise, rather than general, meanings. Does the man walk across the road? Or does he amble, trot, stride or even swagger?
- Use techniques such as alliteration, assonance and onomatopoeia:

  – *sparkling, shining sea*
  – *gloomy blue rooms*
  – *the fizz and pop of the fireworks*

- Use both active and passive voices:

  – *A dark forest surrounded the cottage.*
  – *The cottage was surrounded by a dark forest.*

Example

- This description of a person, the beginning of a short story, uses some of the techniques described above.

George lived alone. Gnarled and weather-beaten, he looked older than his sixty years: his skin was sun-baked and blemished; his forehead grooved with deep furrows; his few remaining teeth black and crooked, like ancient gravestones. His teeth were rarely seen, for he had few reasons to smile. His one companion was his terrier Barney, whom he loved. In return Barney offered unquestioning love, loyalty and apparent affection.

It is written in the past tense and the third person.
It describes George's appearance but also gives us some background.
The imagery is mainly literal but figurative imagery is also used.
Both active and passive voices are used.
There is a variety of sentence structures.

Quick Test

Look at the example above. Find examples of:

1. A simple sentence.
2. A simile.
3. Alliteration.
4. The passive voice.

Key Words

voice
direct speech
indirect speech
reported speech
parallel phrasing
imagery

Review Questions

1 Read the extract below by Charlotte Brontë, in which she describes how she and her sisters, Anne and Emily, went about publishing their poems, and answer the questions that follow.

From Charlotte Brontë's *Biographical Notice of Ellis and Acton Bell*

We agreed to arrange a small selection of our poems, and, if possible, get them printed. Averse to personal publicity, we veiled our own names under those of Currer, Ellis, and Acton Bell; the ambiguous choice being dictated by a sort of conscientious scruple at assuming Christian names positively masculine, while we did not like to declare ourselves women, because – without at that time suspecting that our mode of writing and thinking was not what is called 'feminine' – we had a vague impression that authoresses are liable to be looked on with prejudice […]

The bringing out of our little book was hard work. As was to be expected, neither we nor our poems were at all wanted; but for this we had been prepared at the outset; though inexperienced ourselves, we had read the experience of others. The great puzzle lay in the difficulty of getting answers of any kind from the publishers to whom we applied. Being greatly harassed by this obstacle I ventured to apply to the Messrs. Chambers, of Edinburgh, for a word of advice; they may have forgotten the circumstance, but I have not, for from them I received a brief and business-like, but civil and sensible reply, on which we acted, and at last made a way.

The book was printed; it is scarcely known, and all of it that merits to be known are the poems of Ellis Bell. The fixed conviction I held, and hold of the worth of these poems has not indeed received the confirmation of much favourable criticism; but I must retain it notwithstanding.

a) What were the Brontës' pseudonyms? [1]

____

b) What attitude did they expect publishers to have towards female authors? [1]

____

____

c) Why does Charlotte particularly remember the response of Messrs Chambers of Edinburgh? [1]

____

____

2 Read the extract below and answer the questions that follow.

How I Made My Own Luck

by Lily Fordyce

People often ask me for advice about writing, which really means they want me to give them the magic key that opens the door to publication, fame and fortune. I can't promise any of that. All I can do is say how it was for me, and that what worked for me won't work for everyone. There are two essential ingredients: hard work and luck. Some people say you make your own luck. If that's true, this is the luck I made:

1. I started reading out my poetry in public, travelling to Glasgow, Newcastle and Liverpool. It wasn't that hard for me. I'm one of life's show-offs. I was welcomed with enthusiasm, especially because I'm a woman. 'We don't get enough women' was a cry I heard again and again.
2. I sent my poems to every poetry magazine going, whether they pay or not (mostly they don't) and very soon I was seeing my work in print.
3. I entered almost every competition I could find.

And finally, I won a competition, which led to my first book, which did very well – and here I am: a hardworking and very lucky poet.

a) What does Fordyce say are the two essential ingredients for success? [1]

____

b) Name one city where she read her poetry. [1]

____

c) What does Fordyce think led to her having a book published? [1]

____

3 Using information from both texts explain the differences between Brontë and Fordyce's experiences of getting their poems published. [4]

____

____

____

____

____

____

____

Reading Literature

Read the passage below, which is the opening of *The Withered Arm* by Thomas Hardy, and then answer the questions.

It was an eighty-cow dairy, and the troop of milkers, regular and supernumerary, were all at work; [...] The hour was about six in the evening, and three-fourths of the large, red, rectangular animals having been finished off, there was opportunity for a little conversation.

'He do bring home his bride tomorrow, I hear. They've come as far as Anglebury today.'

The voice seemed to proceed from the belly of the cow called Cherry, but the speaker was a milking-woman, whose face was buried in the flank of that motionless beast.

'Hav' anybody seen her?' said another.

There was a negative response from the first. 'Though they say she's a rosy-cheeked, tisty-tosty little body enough,' she added; and as the milkmaid spoke she turned her face so that she could glance past her cow's tail to the other side of the barton,[1] where a thin fading woman of thirty milked somewhat apart from the rest.

'Years younger than he, they say,' continued the second, with also a glance of reflectiveness in the same direction.

'How old do you call him, then?'

'Thirty or so.'

'More like forty,' broke in an old milkman [...]

The discussion waxed so warm that the purr of the milk streams became jerky, till a voice from another cow's belly cried with authority, 'Now then, what the Turk do it matter to us about Farmer Lodge's age, or Farmer Lodge's new mis'ess? [...] Get on with your work, or 'twill be dark afore we have done. The evening is pinking in a'ready.' This speaker was the dairyman himself, by whom the milkmaids and men were employed.

Nothing more was said publicly about Farmer Lodge's wedding, but the first woman murmured under her cow to her next neighbour. ''Tis hard for she,' signifying the thin worn milkmaid aforesaid.

'O no,' said the second. 'He ha'n't spoke to Rhoda Brook for years.'

When the milking was done they washed their pails and hung them on a many-forked stand made as usual of the peeled limb of an oak-tree, set upright in the earth, and resembling a colossal antlered horn. The majority then dispersed in various directions homeward. The thin woman who had not spoken was joined by a boy of twelve or thereabout, and the twain[2] went away up the field also.

Their course lay apart from that of the others, to a lonely spot high above the water-meads, and not far from the border of Egdon Heath, whose dark countenance was visible in the distance as they drew nigh to their home.

'They've just been saying down in barton that your father brings his young wife home from Anglebury tomorrow,' the woman observed. 'I shall want to send you for a few things to market, and you'll be pretty sure to meet 'em.'

'Yes, Mother,' said the boy. 'Is Father married then?'

'Yes... You can give her a look, and tell me what she's like, if you do see her.'

[1] *barton* – cowshed
[2] *twain* – two

1. **Read lines 1–10.**

   How does the writer create a picture of life and work in the countryside in these lines?

   You must refer to the language used in the text to support your answer, using relevant subject terminology where appropriate. [10]

   Write your answer on a separate piece of paper.

2. **Read lines 9–22.**

   How does the writer interest the reader in 'the thin woman' (Rhoda Brook) in these lines?

   You should write about:
   - what happens in these lines to interest the reader in the thin woman
   - the writer's use of language and structure to create interest in her
   - the effects on the reader.

   You must refer to the text to support your answer, using relevant subject terminology where appropriate. [10]

   Write your answer on a separate piece of paper.

3. 'In the last 15 lines of this passage, the reader begins to feel sympathy for Rhoda Brook.' How far do you agree with this view?

   You should write about:
   - your own thoughts and feelings about how Rhoda Brook is presented here and in the passage as a whole
   - how the writer has created these thoughts and feelings.

   You must refer to the text to support your answer. [10]

   Write your answer on a separate piece of paper.

Creative Writing

4. Write about a time when you felt lonely or isolated.

   Write your answer on a separate piece of paper.

   [24 marks for content and organisation; 16 marks for technical accuracy; total 40]

Reading Non-fiction 1

You must be able to:

- Read and understand a range of non-fiction texts
- Compare writers' ideas and perspectives.

Viewpoints and Perspectives

- Component 2 of the English Language exam requires you to read, analyse and compare two non-fiction texts.
- One text will have been written in the 19th century and the other in the 21st century.
- You are expected to show that you can understand and respond to different **viewpoints** and **perspectives**, considering writers' opinions, ideas and feelings.

Key Point

Non-fiction is any writing that is not made up by the writer. It is not necessarily fact but it is what the writer believes to be true.

Form, Purpose and Audience

- Your texts could come from a number of **non-fiction forms** and **genres**. The most likely are discussed below.
- Think about the writer's purpose. It could be to describe, to inform and explain, to argue, to persuade or to advise. Remember that a text can have more than one purpose.
- Think about the intended audience. It might be aimed at people of a certain age (children, teenagers, older people). It could be intended for people in a particular job or with particular interests: for example, doctors, gardeners, cyclists. It might, however, be written for a general audience or with no audience in mind.

Diaries

- Diaries and **journals** are very personal. They are written by people who want to keep a record of what they have done and to express their opinions and feelings about what is happening around them.
- They can seem very immediate and spontaneous. We expect to get a genuine, uncensored and sincere point of view.
- They also give us an insight into what people really did and thought in the past.
- However, many diaries have been edited. We can still learn what the writer thought at the time of writing but it may not be exactly what he or she wrote.
- Some diaries may have been written with publication in mind by writers conscious of giving their 'version' of events.
- Diaries can vary a lot in style. Some use chatty, **informal language**. Others are quite formal.
- Some **diarists** jot down impressions and thoughts in a quite disorganised way. Other diaries are considered and crafted.
- Online **blogs** are similar to diaries. Like diaries, they can be about writers' everyday lives or focus on their opinions about current events.

Unlike most diaries, they are written to be read by others and are often used by writers to promote their ideas or products.

Letters

- Letters can give us an insight into people's everyday lives. Their style and tone depend a lot on their purpose.
- Letters give news and opinions, discuss ideas and express feelings. Letters might also be asking for something (like a job), complaining about something, or thanking someone for something.
- Unlike diarists, letter writers are always conscious of their audience. A letter to a close friend would be different in tone, style and content from a letter to a grandmother. It would be very different from a letter to a newspaper about current events, or to a prospective employer.
- The tone of a letter – friendly, angry, ironic, cold – will tell you a lot about the relationship between the writer and the **recipient** at the time of writing.

Autobiography and Biography

- **Biography** means writing about someone's life. **Autobiography** means writing about one's own life.
- An autobiography can be reflective, even 'confessional', as the writer considers his or her past actions. It may also be self-justifying, naive or untrue. Autobiographies written by current celebrities (or their 'ghostwriters') are often written with the purpose of promoting the subject's career.
- Biographies range from what are known as 'hatchet jobs', designed to ruin their subjects' reputations, to 'hagiographies' (originally written about saints), which have nothing but good to say. Most are something in between.
- A biographer's point of view may come from his or her own relationship with the subject. On the other hand, it might be based on a careful consideration of the evidence.

Key Point

An autobiography is written by someone looking on events, and so has the benefit of hindsight.

Key Words

viewpoint
perspective
non-fiction
form
genre
journal
informal language
diarist
blog
recipient
biography
autobiography

Quick Test

Where are you most likely to find the following?

1. An account of someone's whole life.
2. Thanks for a present.
3. The writer's secret feelings.
4. How the writer became a megastar.

Reading Non-fiction 2

You must be able to:

- Read and understand a range of non-fiction texts
- Compare writers' ideas and perspectives.

Travel Writing

- Travel writing includes newspaper and magazine **articles** about places to visit, which give readers opinions and advice about a place. These are similar to reviews.
- You are more likely to be given **autobiographical** accounts of more adventurous trips – a journey down the Amazon or climbing a mountain in the Himalayas. These contain information about the places described but are more concerned with the personal experience of challenge and adventure.
- Some writers might seem awestruck and/or delighted by everything they encounter. Others are more critical, especially when writing about people and their way of life. They might even give opinions on political or other controversial issues.
- Some writers use the techniques of fiction writers to build suspense and involve readers. Others go in for colourful, even poetic description. Some write wittily about their reactions to new experiences.
- Some writers are experts, perhaps using a lot of unfamiliar terminology, for example, about mountaineering. Others see themselves as naive travellers – 'innocents abroad' – who tell jokes at their own expense.

Key Point

Many non-fiction texts use 'literary' techniques associated with fiction.

Journalism

- **Journalism** is anything that is published in a newspaper or magazine.
- A lot of journalism is published on the internet, sometimes in online versions of 'hard copy' newspapers and magazines. There are also many publications that only exist online.
- Newspaper **reports** give the news and are mainly factual. **Features** – in both newspapers and magazines – look at issues in more depth. Sometimes they are balanced discussions. They can, however, strongly argue for a point of view.
- Articles can be serious or amusing. Most newspapers have regular feature writers. Some of them write about themselves and their families in a way that encourages readers to empathise with them. Others focus on more controversial issues.
- Most magazines are aimed at particular readerships – for example, women, men, teenagers, older people.
- Newspapers are aimed at a general, adult audience. However, different newspapers have different readerships, often associated with particular political views.

Reviews

- A **review** is an article that gives a point of view about, for example, a film, book, concert, game or restaurant.
- Reviews give information, such as venue, date, time and price. Their main purpose, however, is to give the writer's point of view.
- Some reviews are quite balanced, giving positive and negative views, though they usually do arrive at a judgement. Others express their views very strongly, sometimes in a witty way.

Comparing Points of View

- The two **sources** you are given will be about similar subjects but written from different points of view:
  - Both of these texts are about the environment. Compare:

  a) how the writers feel about the environment
  b) how they make their views clear to the reader.
- You should discuss what their feelings are:

Smith feels that we need to save rural areas, whereas Jones is happy for towns to expand.

- The attitudes or feelings shown in the sources might be directly stated or implied:

While Williams is shocked at the idea of women doing 'men's work', Roberts seems not to share the view as she does not comment on the fact that the engineer is a woman.

- Think about the impression you get of the writer:

Jones is clearly an expert on the subject, while Smith writes as a confused voter.

- Consider the general tone:

Williams uses humour to make his point, but Roberts writes seriously about her emotions.

- And remember to comment on structure and language:

Jones's use of subheadings breaks the article into clear 'points', making it more accessible.

Smith uses slang, trying to appeal to young readers, whereas Jones uses formal, quite technical language.

Quick Test

In which of the following are you least likely to find the writer's point of view?

1. A review.
2. A news report.
3. A feature.
4. Travel writing.

Key Point

Remember that you are being asked to compare the writers' views, not to give your own.

Key Words

article
autobiographical
journalism
report
feature
review
source

Transactional/Persuasive Writing 1

You must be able to:

- Communicate clearly, effectively and imaginatively
- Adapt your writing for different forms, purposes and audiences.

The Task

- Component 2 of the English Language exam includes **two compulsory** writing tasks. They give you the chance to express your views and ideas.
- For each task, you will be given a statement or scenario and instructions which include details of purpose, form and audience, e.g:

> Someone has written a letter to your local newspaper saying that school holidays should be shortened because they create problems for parents and damage children's education.
>
> Write a letter to the newspaper giving your response to this view.

> You have to give a talk to your school assembly about a charity that you would like the school to support.
>
> Write down what you would say.

Key Point

You will be expected to spend the same amount of time on each of the two compulsory writing tasks. Your answers should be roughly 300–400 words long.

Audience

- Sometimes the task specifies an **audience**:

> Write a letter to your head teacher.

- Sometimes the audience is implied by the form:

> Write an article for your school website.

- Your intended audience determines what sort of language you use. Think about whether a formal or informal tone is called for.
- You would write informally for people you know well, using the sort of language that you use when chatting with them. However, you should avoid using 'text language' (**abbreviations**, emoticons, etc.) in the exam.
- It can be appropriate to write informally for people you don't know, as if you were their friend, for example, in a magazine article aimed at teenagers.
- For almost everything else use a formal tone and Standard English.
- Whether you are writing formally or informally, be aware of your audience's interests and points of view. For example, if you were writing for a local audience you would focus on known local concerns:

> *Here in Bingley, we have always been proud of our green spaces.*

Key Point

If you are given a point of view in your stimulus, you are free to agree or disagree with it. The important thing is to try to convince the reader of your view.

- You would expect school governors to be concerned about the school's reputation:

I know that you are just as concerned as I am about recent complaints of unsocial behaviour.

- And a little flattery can go a long way:

I have always been impressed by your commitment to our community.

Purpose

- The purpose of your writing is to express your point of view and persuade your readers to come round to it. The wording of the task might give a slightly different emphasis. For example, 'argue' sounds more passionate than 'explain'. 'Encourage' is gentler than 'persuade' and both suggest more emphasis on the audience.

Constructing Your Argument

- In constructing your **argument**, start with a powerful opening paragraph, which grabs your audience and makes your point clear.
- Make sure you offer a number of points in support of your argument, starting a new paragraph for each.
- Acknowledge other points of view but then give your **counter-arguments**, pointing out why you think they are wrong:

Some people argue that school uniforms stifle individuality. However,...

- Structure your argument in a logical order, using **discourse markers** to 'signpost' the development of your argument:

Another point I would like to make is...

- Back up your points with evidence if you can.
- Give appropriate examples, including **anecdotes**:

Only last week, I encountered such behaviour...

- Address your audience directly (**direct address**), using 'you', and show your own involvement by using 'I' and 'we'.
- Use a full range of **rhetorical devices**, including lists of three, repetition and **hyperbole** (see pages 28–29).
- Use humour if you think it is appropriate.
- Use a variety of sentence structures, and the passive as well as the active.
- Finish with a strong conclusion, summing up the main points and strongly stating your opinion.

Key Point

Spend a few minutes (but only a few!) planning your answer, using whatever method works best for you.

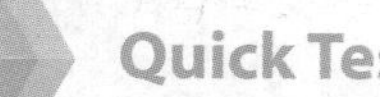

Quick Test

Your head teacher has banned packed lunches. You want to write to the governors giving your reaction. What would be your:

1. purpose? 2. audience? 3. form?

Key Words

audience
abbreviation
argument
counter-argument
discourse marker
anecdote
direct address
rhetorical device
hyperbole

Transactional/Persuasive Writing 2

You must be able to:
- Communicate clearly, effectively and imaginatively
- Adapt your writing for different forms, purposes and audiences.

Form: Articles

- You could be asked to write an article for a newspaper, magazine or website.
- **Broadsheets** are 'serious' newspapers, which look at news in more detail and depth, such as the *Daily Telegraph* and *The Guardian*.
- **Tabloids**, like *The Sun* and the *Daily Mirror*, cover news in less depth and devote more space to things like celebrity gossip.
- Do not try to make your answer look like a newspaper or magazine. There are no marks for design. Do not include:
  - a masthead (the newspaper's title)
  - columns
  - illustrations
  - any articles apart from the one you have been asked to write.
- You can, however, include organisational devices such as:
  - a **headline** – perhaps using alliteration ('Ban this Beastly Business'), a **pun** or a play on words ('A Tale of Two Kitties'). But don't put it in huge coloured letters!
  - a **strapline**, under the headline, expanding on or explaining the headline ('Why We Should Boycott Cosmetics')
  - **subheadings** – to guide the reader through the text.
- You must write in paragraphs.
- Magazine and website articles are similar to newspaper articles in form.

Key Point

You are not likely to be asked to write a tabloid article: it would not give you enough scope to demonstrate your skills.

Form: Speeches

- One of your tasks could be to write a speech.
- The audience is most likely to be people of your own age, perhaps in class or at a school assembly, but it could be a group of adults (for example, school governors or older people).
- Make sure that your tone and style suit both the audience and the subject matter.
- Use a variety of rhetorical devices.
- Use the second person (you) to engage the audience as well as the first person (I/we).
- Even though in reality a speech is meant to be heard and not read, remember that in the exam this is a writing exercise. Write in full sentences and paragraphs. Do not use abbreviations or bullet points.

Form: Letters

- There are a number of 'rules' or conventions that are used in letter-writing. These are often not used in informal letters.

- If you are asked to write a letter in the exam, it will probably be quite formal.

Example of How to Open a Letter

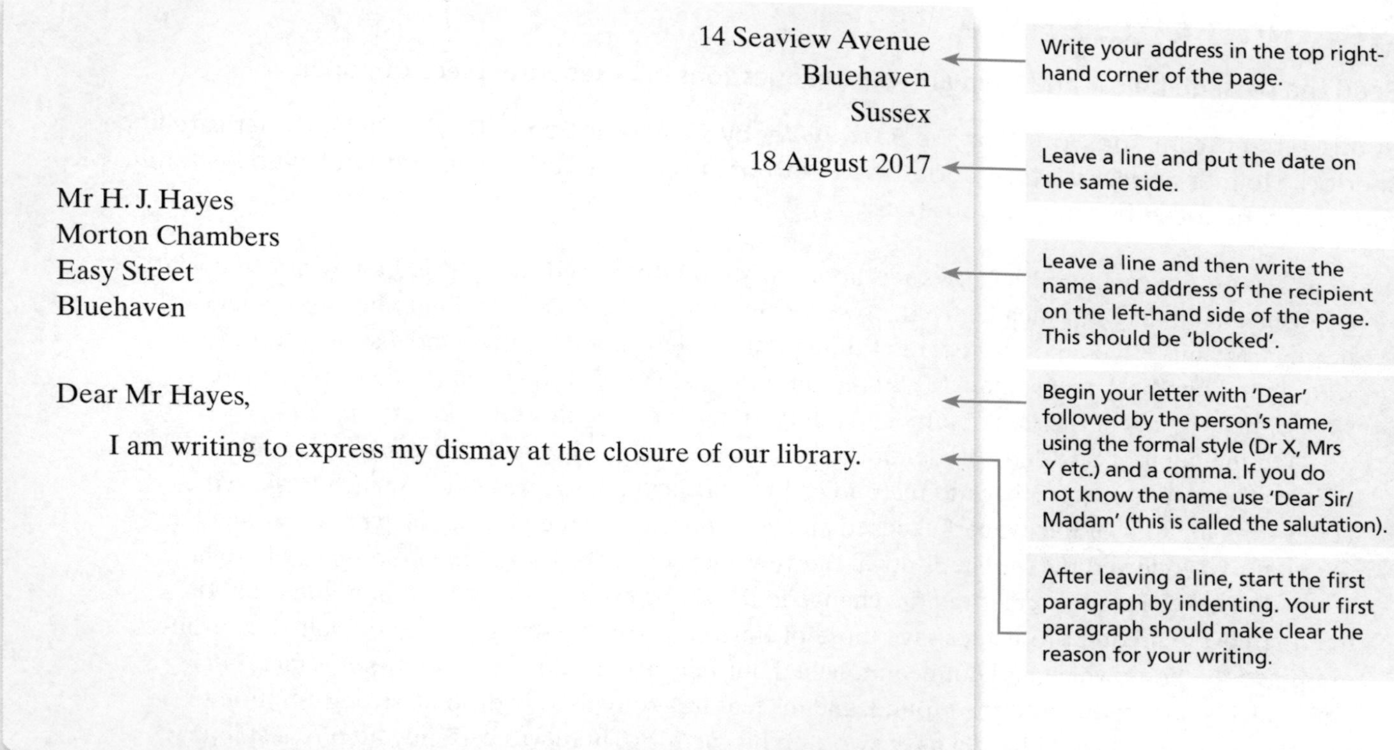
14 Seaview Avenue
Bluehaven
Sussex

18 August 2017

Mr H. J. Hayes
Morton Chambers
Easy Street
Bluehaven

Dear Mr Hayes,

I am writing to express my dismay at the closure of our library.

Write your address in the top right-hand corner of the page.
Leave a line and put the date on the same side.
Leave a line and then write the name and address of the recipient on the left-hand side of the page. This should be 'blocked'.
Begin your letter with 'Dear' followed by the person's name, using the formal style (Dr X, Mrs Y etc.) and a comma. If you do not know the name use 'Dear Sir/Madam' (this is called the salutation).
After leaving a line, start the first paragraph by indenting. Your first paragraph should make clear the reason for your writing.

- Continue with paragraphs that make further relevant points before ending with one that tells the reader what you would like to happen next.
- Connect your paragraphs with discourse markers.
- If you have addressed the reader by name, sign off with 'Yours sincerely'. If you haven't, use 'Yours faithfully'.
- Remember the 'five Cs':
  - **Clear** – Say what you mean in good English.
  - **Complete** – Include everything necessary, giving enough detail and explaining your points properly.
  - **Concise** – Don't 'ramble'. Do not include irrelevant information or ideas.
  - **Correct** – Say what you believe to be true.
  - **Courteous** – Be polite. Consider the recipient and his or her possible reaction to your letter.

Key Point

Unless you are writing informally for young people, avoid slang or dialect words, contractions and abbreviations.

Quick Test

How should you end a letter beginning with the following salutations?

1. Dear Mr Blenkinsop
2. Dear Principal
3. Dear Madam
4. Dear Sir Arthur

Key Words

broadsheet
tabloid
headline
pun
strapline
subheading

Reading Literature

Read the passage below and then answer the questions on a separate piece of paper.

In this extract from *The Hound of the Baskervilles* by Sir Arthur Conan Doyle, Dr Mortimer is telling Sherlock Holmes and Dr Watson about the death of Sir Charles Baskerville, who believed his family was cursed and haunted by a mysterious beast.

'It was at my advice that Sir Charles was about to go to London. His heart was, I knew, affected, and the constant anxiety in which he lived, however chimerical[1] the cause of it might be, was evidently having a serious effect upon his health. I thought that a few months among the distractions of town would send him back a new man. Mr Stapleton, a mutual friend who was much concerned at his state of health, was of the same opinion. At the last instant came this terrible catastrophe.

'On the night of Sir Charles's death Barrymore, the butler who made the discovery, sent Perkins the groom on horseback to me, and as I was sitting up late I was able to reach Baskerville Hall within an hour of the event. I checked and corroborated all the facts which were mentioned at the inquest. I followed the footsteps down the yew alley, I saw the spot at the moor-gate where he seemed to have waited, I remarked the change in the shape of the prints after that point, I noted that there were no other footsteps save those of Barrymore on the soft gravel, and finally I carefully examined the body, which had not been touched until my arrival. Sir Charles lay on his face, his arms out, his fingers dug into the ground, and his features convulsed with some strong emotion to such an extent that I could hardly have sworn to his identity. There was certainly no physical injury of any kind. But one false statement was made by Barrymore at the inquest. He said that there were no traces upon the ground round the body. He did not observe any. But I did – some little distance off, but fresh and clear.'

'Footprints?'

'Footprints.'

'A man's or a woman's?'

Dr Mortimer looked strangely at us for an instant, and his voice sank almost to a whisper as he answered:

'Mr Holmes, they were the footprints of a gigantic hound!'

---

[1] *chimerical* – fanciful or imagined

1 **Read lines 6–12.**

How does the writer build up to the discovery of the body in these lines?

You must refer to the language used in the text to support your answer. [10]

2 **Read lines 13–23.**

How does the writer create a sense of mystery and excitement in these lines?

You should write about:

- what happens in these lines to build mystery and excitement
- the writer's use of language and structure to create mystery and excitement
- the effects on the reader.

You must refer to the text to support your answer. [10]

3 'In this passage, Dr Mortimer is a convincing and reliable witness.' How far do you agree with this view?

You should write about:

- your own thoughts and feelings about how Dr Mortimer tells his story to Holmes and Watson
- how the writer has created these thoughts and feelings.

You must refer to the text to support your answer. [10]

Creative Writing

4 **Either**

Write a story entitled 'The Return'.

Or

Write about an occasion when you felt misunderstood.

Or

Write a story that begins: I recognised him immediately.

Or

Write a story that ends: I threw it in the river and walked away.

Write on a separate piece of paper.

[24 marks for content and organisation; 16 marks for technical accuracy; total 40]

Reading Non-fiction

Read the following letter to a newspaper and answer the question below.

14 Raglan Terrace
Tillingbourne

12 March 2018

Dear Editor,

I was saddened to read yet more negative coverage of so-called 'purse pets' in your paper. What is it about celebrities who own small dogs that inspires such vitriol?

I know some people think celebrities use their pets as fashion accessories – and this is questionable. But it is not, as you suggest, cruel. We like to think of our four-legged friends as free and independent spirits – equal companions on life's journey – but they're not. Dogs depend on us for food, shelter and love.

This is the case whether they are tiny little chihuahuas that can fit in a Versace handbag or massive Afghans – or even breeds like pit bulls. Now, I don't want to be accused of the kind of prejudice I'm criticising others for, but let's just reflect for a moment. Which is crueller? Pampering your pet with little treats or training her to fight and kill other dogs?

Of course, I'm not saying that all Staffie owners do this. But you should not imply that everyone who owns a little dog is cruel. Taking dogs shopping for little doggy clothes is a bit silly, but it does not damage their health or well-being. On the contrary, it shows that the owners care about their pets. In fact, many celebrity dog owners go further to show they care. Actress Kristin Chenoweth has even founded a charity, named after her tiny Maltese, to help homeless pets.

These dogs are beautiful, loyal and lovable. I know. I've got one. I don't keep her in my handbag or take her to canine boutiques, but I love and cherish her – and I wouldn't be without her. I don't think you'd write an article castigating me for those feelings, so why aim your vitriol at Paris Hilton and Mariah Carey, whose only crime is to love their pets?

Yours faithfully

Joanna P. Hanlon

1 How does the writer express her feelings about small dogs?

You should comment on:

- what she says
- her use of language and tone.

____

____

____ [10]

To answer the following questions, you will need to read the extract below from an article from *The Times* newspaper, 1914. Write your answers on a separate piece of paper.

The Cult of Little Dogs: An Irresistible Appeal by Our Correspondent

There is a certain melancholy attaching to shows of toy dogs. Not that toy dogs are themselves melancholy – indeed it is their sprightly unconsciousness of their degeneracy that most confounds the moralist – but that they suggest melancholy reflections. The Englishman, perhaps alone among the peoples of the world, understands fully the great soul of the dog; he feels his own kinship with it – as he did in former days with that of the fighting cock; and he has accepted with pride the bull-dog as the type of his national qualities. It is not, then, without misgiving that he watches the process of minimizing the dog, or a large proportion of him, in an eager competition to crib, cabin, and confine the great soul in the smallest possible body, until, in place of the dignified friend and ally of man, there will be left nothing but, at worst, a pampered toy; at best, a pathetic creature, all eyes and nerves, whose insurgent soul frets the puny body to decay.

Where will the process end? Already we have held up to the admiration of the world a Pomeranian puppy which, at the age of three months, can be comfortably bestowed in a tumbler, over the edge of which his picture shows him looking, with shy eyes and apprehensively, at the disproportionate scheme of things. Presently, maybe, we shall have a childhood's dream realized and really see the little dog of the fairy-story who was hidden in a walnut and, when the shell was cracked, leapt forth barking and wagging his tail to the delight of all the noble company.

2 What do you think about the writer's attitude to small dogs? [10]

You should comment on:

- what he says about the fashion for small dogs
- how he expresses his opinions on the subject of small dogs
- You must refer to the text to support your comments.

3 Both of these texts are about small dogs.

Compare:

a) how the writers feel about small dogs

b) how they make their views clear to the reader. [10]

You must use the text to support your comments and make it clear which text you are referring to.

Transactional/Persuasive Writing

4 Write an article for a magazine aimed at people of your age with the title, 'A dog is for life, not just for Christmas.'.

Write your answer on a separate piece of paper.

[12 marks for content and organisation, 8 marks for accuracy; total 20]

Context

You must be able to:

- Understand the social, historical and cultural context of a Shakespeare play
- Use this understanding to evaluate the play.

History

- The historical context in which Shakespeare lived was very different from ours.
- He lived from 1564 to 1616 and started writing during the reign of Queen Elizabeth I, a time of great prosperity for England, when explorers were discovering and colonising new lands across the world.
- There was also a great flowering of literature and theatre, inspired by the Renaissance in Italy.
- In 1603 Elizabeth I was succeeded by King James I, who was already King of Scotland. He became patron of Shakespeare's theatre company and *Macbeth* was written in his honour.

Religion

- England was an overwhelmingly Christian country. The official church was the Church of England, but many people were still Roman Catholics, while others (like Puritans) had stricter Protestant beliefs.
- Most people believed that after death God would judge them and decide whether they should spend eternity in Heaven or Hell. The idea of Hell is ever-present in *Macbeth*.
- The general attitude to non-Christians is reflected in the way other characters treat Shylock in *The Merchant of Venice*, although some would say that Shakespeare's writing causes the audience to question their assumptions.
- Many people also believed in astrology. The tension between the popular belief that everything is mapped out in the stars and the Christian belief in free will is present in many plays. We see this in *Romeo and Juliet*.

Key Point

Elizabethans and Jacobeans would have recognised the many biblical references found in Shakespeare.

Morality

- Society's moral and ethical standards were rooted in Christian teaching and the Ten Commandments.
- Most people shared similar ideas about sexual **morality**. Chastity, especially among women, was much more highly prized than in today's society and marriage was for life. This idea is central to *Much Ado About Nothing* and *Romeo and Juliet.*

Social Order

- Many people believed that the **social order**, with the King or Queen at the top, was derived from God and should not be tampered with.
- King James believed in 'the **divine right** of kings'.
  - This is a major theme in *Macbeth.*
  - The rights and responsibilities of rulers are also a theme of *Henry V.*
- The **authority** of parents over children might also be seen as sacred, although this authority is challenged in *Romeo and Juliet* and *Othello*.

Society

- Although there was a parliament, England was not democratic in the modern sense.
- Political power centred on the **court**, around the Queen or King. Here, aristocrats competed for the monarch's favour.
- There was a growing middle class. Shakespeare was the son of a well-off glover from Stratford-upon-Avon. He benefited from a good education at the local grammar school. In these schools boys studied ancient history and Latin literature, his knowledge of which is shown in many of his plays.
- Most people, however, were illiterate. Many worked on the land, although cities were expanding. London's thriving port attracted merchants and travellers from all over the world.
- Women were usually dependent on their husbands or fathers, so making the right marriage was important. However, there were examples of rich and powerful women.
  - Portia in *The Merchant of Venice* has inherited her wealth from her father but she still cannot choose her own husband.
- Many of Shakespeare's female characters, like Beatrice in *Much Ado About Nothing*, show themselves to be equal to men. However, both Portia, in disguising herself as a man, and Lady Macbeth, in her desire to be 'unsexed', are conscious of taking on a 'man's role'.

Key Point

It is important to understand the differences between Shakespeare's society and ours.

Quick Test

True or False?

1. *Macbeth* was written for Queen Elizabeth.
2. Astrology is a Christian belief.
3. Divorce was common in Shakespeare's time.
4. James I believed that his authority came from God.

Key Words

context
morality
social order
divine right
authority
court

Themes

You must be able to:

- Identify themes in a Shakespeare play
- Write about how Shakespeare presents themes.

Themes and Ideas

- A **theme** is part of the subject matter of a text – a concern that runs through the play.
- Shakespeare's plays are full of ideas about relationships, morality and society.
- Your exam question could focus on themes and ideas, for example:
  - Write about how Shakespeare presents ideas about kingship in *Macbeth.*
  - Write about how Shakespeare explores ideas about love in *Romeo and Juliet*.

Identifying Themes

- Throughout his career, Shakespeare would return to the same themes. Here are some themes that occur frequently in his plays:

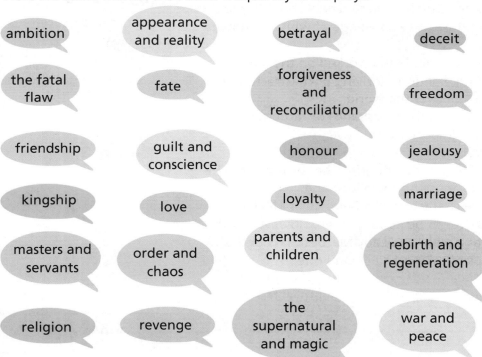

ambition
appearance and reality
betrayal
deceit
the fatal flaw
fate
forgiveness and reconciliation
freedom
friendship
guilt and conscience
honour
jealousy
kingship
love
loyalty
marriage
masters and servants
order and chaos
parents and children
rebirth and regeneration
religion
revenge
the supernatural and magic
war and peace

- You may think of more themes. In over 30 plays Shakespeare looked at almost every aspect of human life.
- Write down some themes that occur in the play you have studied. Try to find at least five. Here are some to get you started:
  - *Macbeth* – marriage…
  - *Much Ado About Nothing* – misunderstandings…

Key Point

Shakespeare uses his characters and plots to explore issues that mattered to people at the time he wrote. Most of them still matter.

- *The Merchant of Venice* – the outsider…
- *Othello* – jealousy…
- *Romeo and Juliet* – betrayal…
- *Henry V* – patriotism…

- Now write a sentence or two about each theme, for example:

> *Patriotism is an important theme in 'Henry V' because the king identifies himself with England. Characters from different classes and regions are shown to be united in fighting for him and their country.*
>
> *Othello's jealous nature is his 'fatal flaw', the cause of his downfall and tragedy. This human weakness is ruthlessly exploited by Iago, who is himself jealous of his master.*

How Themes are Presented

- Shakespeare's plays have been interpreted in many different ways over the past 400 years. You must come to your own conclusions about his themes by considering the evidence.
- Think about the **plot** – what happens in the play:
  - Macbeth's murder of Duncan brings together the themes of ambition and kingship.
  - The theme of friendship comes to the fore in *Much Ado About Nothing* when Beatrice asks Benedick to kill his friend Claudio because of how he has treated Hero.
- Theatre is a visual medium. Shakespeare presents powerful **images**:
  - The appearance of Banquo's ghost in *Macbeth* speaks volumes about betrayal and guilt.
  - Juliet's appearance on a balcony above Romeo demonstrates the kind of love that he has for her.
- **Dialogue** can give us insight into themes by presenting more than one point of view:
  - The trial scene in *The Merchant of Venice* gives us both Shylock's and Antonio's views about business ethics.
  - In *Much Ado About Nothing*, Benedick challenges Claudio's behaviour towards Hero.
- Characters can raise themes and **issues** when they speak directly to the audience in a soliloquy or aside. When they do this they reveal what they really think:
  - Macbeth shares his doubts about killing Duncan. His soliloquies draw us into a consideration of the themes of kingship, loyalty and ambition.
  - In *Romeo and Juliet*, Romeo expresses his love in soliloquies, making the audience consider the nature and depth of his feelings, as well as their consequences.

Key Point

Shakespeare does not tell us what he thinks or what we should think. There are more questions than answers.

Quick Test

Give a single word defined by the following:

1. A speech made to the audience.
2. Speech between two or more people.
3. What happens in the play.
4. A concern that runs through the play.

Key Words

theme
plot
image
dialogue
issue

Characters

You must be able to:

- Write about how Shakespeare presents characters.

Characters

- Shakespeare is known for his huge range of characters and his understanding of human psychology.
- Your question will be in two parts. One part or both parts could focus on character.
- You will get an extract from the play as a starting point for the first part. You should analyse what this reveals about the character at this point in the play.
  - Look at how Othello speaks and behaves here. What do we learn about his character?
- The second part will have a different focus and will ask you to write about the play as a whole. If it is about a character, consider how s/he develops throughout the play.
  - Write about Beatrice and the way she is presented at different points in *Much Ado About Nothing.*
- When revising, think about each character's:
  - background
  - personality
  - relationships
  - **motivation**
  - function in the plot.
- Identify the main characters in your play and draw up a chart like the (partially completed) one below:

Character	Background	Personality	Relationships	Motivation	Function
Romeo	The son of the Montagues			Wants to be with Juliet whatever the cost	
Juliet		Innocent but very determined			
Capulet			Loves his family but expects obedience		
Nurse		Chatty, bawdy, devoted, pragmatic			Juliet's confidante – but advises her to forget Romeo

- The main characters all find themselves in different situations by the end of the play. How did they get there and how did their experiences change them?
- Try tracing your characters' development through events that have influenced them. Here is an example for Macbeth.

Key Point

When looking at characters, consider their historical and social context.

What happens?	What effect does it have?
He meets the witches.	Starts to think about his future and becoming king.
He kills Duncan.	Becomes king. He has power but fears losing it and turns against Banquo.
He sees Banquo's ghost.	Feels guilty and acts strangely.
He visits the witches.	Fears losing his crown, which makes him more ruthless.
Malcolm invades Scotland.	Thinking he is invincible, becomes defiant and brave.

How Characters are Presented

What They Say

- A soliloquy is a speech to the audience, usually with no other characters on stage. Soliloquies let us into characters' thought processes, revealing a lot about their character and motivation:
  - Juliet shows her excitement and impatience when waiting for the Nurse to return from seeing Romeo.
- Sometimes characters comment briefly on what others are saying and doing in an aside. We can assume they mean what they say.
- Characters do not always tell the truth. All Shakespeare plays include people who lie to others. But we do not have to guess who is lying. It is clear when someone cannot be trusted:
  - Lady Macbeth tells Macbeth to 'look like the innocent flower / But be the serpent under't'.

What Others Say

- We learn about characters through what others say to/about them.
- Sometimes we get a consensus of opinion:
  - Macbeth changes from being universally praised for his bravery and loyalty to being hated and feared as a 'devil' and 'fiend'.
- A difference of opinion can give us something to think about:
  - The violent Tybalt in *Romeo and Juliet* is a favourite of both Lady Capulet and the Nurse. This tells us about both his character and theirs.
- Always be aware of who the speaker is:
  - In *The Merchant of Venice*, Bassanio's assessment of Antonio's character is very different from Shylock's.

How They Act and React

- We learn about characters by their actions:
  - When Bassanio chooses the lead casket in *The Merchant of Venice* we know he is genuine.
- Their reactions also reveal a lot:
  - Benedick's reaction to Beatrice's command to 'kill Claudio' reveals his growing feelings for her, and tells us about his sense of honour.

Key Point

When Shakespeare wants us to know what characters are really thinking and feeling, they speak to the audience.

Quick Test

True or False?

1. Everyone tells the truth.
2. Characters never address the audience.
3. Characters can change.
4. We can get differing views of a character.

Key Words

motivation
soliloquy
aside

Language and Structure

You must be able to:

- Analyse Shakespeare's use of language and structure
- Use relevant terminology.

Verse and Prose

- Shakespeare wrote in a mixture of verse and prose. Most of his verse is in iambic pentameter. 'Pentameter' means there are five stressed syllables on every line. 'Iambic' refers to the stress falling on every second syllable:

> O, **she** doth **teach** the **torch**es **to** shine **bright**.

- It is often said that the iambic pentameter follows the natural rhythms of speech and that it resembles a heartbeat.
- Sometimes Shakespeare varies the metre to emphasise certain words: for example, stressing the first syllable in a line or adding an extra syllable. He might create a pause (known as a caesura) in the middle of the line.
- Rhyming couplets might end a scene or emphasise an important thought.
- Other metres are occasionally used in Shakespeare, for example in songs.
- Verse tends to be used for higher-status characters when discussing serious things. However, much of the banter in *Much Ado About Nothing* is in prose. Characters such as servants usually speak in prose, but there are exceptions.

Structure

- Shakespeare's plays are divided into five acts. The first introduces the characters and their concerns. Then something happens that changes the characters' lives. In the third act things become more complicated. The fourth act tends to be about the complications being sorted out. The final act brings a resolution and the play ends with the restoration of order.
- Think about how Shakespeare uses contrasting scenes. He sometimes uses comic scenes to release tension before building to a tragic climax: for example, the 'porter scene' in *Macbeth*.

Key Point

You can tell verse from prose just by looking at it. Verse has definite line endings and a rhythm, often in a regular pattern or metre.

Imagery

- Shakespeare's imagery tells us about characters, creates mood and underlines key themes. His techniques include simile, metaphor and personification.
- Sometimes characters use extended metaphors or conceits. Romeo and Juliet use the sonnet form to develop the idea of Romeo being a pilgrim and Juliet a saint.

- Look for patterns of imagery in your play. Animal imagery, much of it connected to the Bible, runs through *The Merchant of Venice*:

> Why he hath made the ewe bleat for the lamb.

Rhetorical Language

- Rhetorical questions are common when characters are wondering what to do:

> I have railed so long against marriage, but doth not the appetite alter?

- Repetition emphasises important ideas or feelings:

> Tomorrow and tomorrow and tomorrow.

- The 'rule of three' is used by characters trying to convince others:

> Why he cannot abide a gaping pig,
> Why he a harmless necessary cat,
> Why he a woollen bagpipe,

- Shakespeare uses rhetorical techniques in situations where they might be used in life, for example in the trial scene in *The Merchant of Venice.*

Playing with Words

- Elizabethans loved experimenting with words. Shakespeare shows this in characters like Romeo, who uses **oxymoron** to express his confusion:

> Feather of lead, bright smoke, cold fire, sick health.

- Romeo also uses puns (double meanings), as do Beatrice and Benedick when they pit their wits against each other.
- Double meanings are often used to make sexual innuendoes.
- Shakespeare also uses techniques such as alliteration and assonance to create feelings and mood:

> I would be trebled twenty times myself.

Key Point

Whatever the focus of the question, you must write about Shakespeare's language in your answer.

Key Words

verse
prose
iambic pentameter
metre
caesura
rhyming couplet
extended metaphor
conceit
sonnet
oxymoron

Quick Test

Of what are the following examples?

1. What, must I hold a candle to my shames?
2. Pure impiety and impious purity.
3. O mighty Caesar! Dost thou lie so low?
4. Hence will I to my ghostly sire's close cell,
   His help to crave and my dear hap to tell.

Reading Non-fiction

Read the following extract from the Journal of Dorothy Wordsworth, and answer the question on a separate piece of paper.

Thursday 15 April 1802

It was a threatening, misty morning, but mild. We set off after dinner from Eusemere. Mrs Clarkson went a short way with us, but turned back. The wind was furious and we thought we must have returned. We first rested in the large boat-house, then under a furze bush opposite Mr Clarkson's. Saw the plough going into the field. The wind seized our breath. The lake was rough. There was a boat by itself floating in the middle of the bay below Water Millock. We rested again in the Water Millock Lane. The hawthornes are black and green, the birches here and there greenish, but there is yet more of purple to be seen on the twigs. We got over into a field to avoid some cows – people working. A few primroses by the roadside – woodsorrel flower, the anemone, scentless violets, strawberries, and that starry yellow flower which Mrs C. calls pile wort. When we were in the woods beyond Gowbarrow Park we saw a few daffodils close to the water-side. We fancied that the lake had floated the seeds ashore, and that the little colony had so sprung up. But as we went along there were more and yet more; and at last, under the boughs of the trees, we saw that there was a long belt of them along the shore, about the breadth of a country turnpike road. I never saw daffodils so beautiful. They grew among the mossy stones about and about them; some rested their heads upon those stones as on a pillow for weariness; and the rest tossed and reeled and danced, and seemed as if they verily laughed with the wind that blew upon them over the lake; they looked so gay, ever glancing, ever changing.

1 How does Dorothy Wordsworth show her enjoyment of a walk in the countryside?

You should comment on:

- What she says;
- Her use of language and tone. [10]

Now read the following extract and answer the question that follows.

Betsy's Blog, 2nd June

Yesterday was a complete washout. First, it was a two-hour trip in the rickety school minibus squashed in with rucksacks, suitcases and sweaty bodies.

We made it – just – and were decanted from ancient minibus into even more ancient, more rickety and smellier youth hostel. Six in a room! It's like the workhouse in Dickens. We were barely given time to unpack – although time enough to notice that Anoushka O'Reilly had brought six pairs of high-heeled shoes and eight towels – before the Camp Commandant, alias Miss Frobisher, marched in with her whistle round her neck.

'Right, girls! Gentle walk round the lake before lunch!' Gentle! It was like one of those forced marches they do in boot camps. Hours of wading through mud and getting soaked to our skin. As for the wonderful scenery we were promised. What scenery? We could barely see six inches in front of our faces through the driving rain.

Thankfully, today's been a huge improvement – they took us to an assault course thing, swinging on ropes and stuff, which is a lot better than boring walking. And there was actually a shop and a café – so I was able to replace my lost energy with a massive dose of CAKE. So now I'm feeling maybe the country's not so bad – as long as we don't have to stay much longer.

2 To answer the following question you will need to refer to both texts.

Both texts are about the countryside.

Compare:

a) how the writers feel about the countryside.

b) how they make their views clear to the reader. [10]

Transactional/Persuasive Writing

3 A proposal has been made by your school governors that there should be no more school trips because they are a waste of time and money.

Write an article for your school magazine or paper giving your views on this statement.

Write your answer on a separate piece of paper.

[12 marks for communication and organisation, 8 marks for accuracy; total 20]

Answer the question on the play you have studied. Write your answer on a separate piece of paper.

1. *Romeo and Juliet.*

Read the extract and answer the question below. You are advised to spend about 20 minutes on your answer.

JULIET The clock struck one when I did send the nurse;
In half an hour she promised to return.
Perchance she cannot meet him. That's not so.
O she is lame! Love's heralds should be thoughts,
Which ten times faster glide than the sun's beams
Driving back shadows over louring hills;
Therefore do nimble-pinioned doves draw Love,
And therefore hath the wind-swift Cupid wings.
Now is the sun upon the highmost hill
Of this day's journey; and from nine till twelve
Is three long hours, yet she is not come.
Had she affections and warm youthful blood,
She would be as swift in motion as a ball.

How does Shakespeare present Romeo and Juliet's love in this speech?
Refer closely to details from the extract to support your answer. [15]

2. *Macbeth*

Read the extract and answer the question below. You are advised to spend about 20 minutes on your answer.

MACBETH Two truths are told
As happy prologues to the swelling act
Of the imperial theme. I thank you, gentlemen.
(*Aside*) This supernatural soliciting
Cannot be ill, cannot be good. If ill,
Why hath it given me earnest of success
Commencing in a truth? I am Thane of Cawdor.
If good, why do I yield to that suggestion
Whose horrid image doth unfix my hair
And make my seated heart knock at my ribs
Against the use of nature? Present fears
Are less than horrible imaginings.
My thought, whose murder yet is but fantastical,
Shakes so my single state of man that function
Is smothered in surmise, and nothing is
But what is not.

What does this extract tell the audience about Macbeth's feelings about power and ambition at this point in the play? Refer closely to details from the extract to support your answer. [15]

3 *Henry V*

Read the extract and answer the question below. You are advised to spend about 20 minutes on your answer.

KING We are glad the Dauphin is so pleasant with us.
His present and your pains we thank you for.
When we have matched our rackets to these balls,
We will in France, by God's grace, play a set
Shall strike his father's crown into the hazard.
Tell him he hath made a match with such a wrangler
That all the courts of France shall be disturbed
With chases. And we understand him well,
How he comes o'er us with our wilder days,
Not measuring what use we made of them.
We never valued this poor seat of England,
And therefore, living hence, did give ourself
To barbarous licence – as 'tis ever common
That men are merriest when they are from home.
But tell the Dauphin I will keep my state
Be like a king, and show my sail of greatness
When I do rouse me in my throne of France.
For that have I laid by my majesty
And plodded like a man for working days,
But I will rise there with so full a glory
That I will dazzle all the eyes of France,
Yea strike the Dauphin blind to look on us

Look at how King Henry speaks and behaves here. What do we learn about Henry as a leader at this point in the play? Refer closely to details from the extract in your answer. [15]

4 *The Merchant of Venice*

How does Shakespeare present Shylock's relationship with Jessica in *The Merchant of Venice?* You are advised to spend about 40 minutes on your answer. [25]

5 *Othello*

Write about how Shakespeare presents the relationship between Othello and Desdemona at different points in the play. You are advised to spend about 40 minutes on your answer. [25]

6 *Much Ado About Nothing*

To what extent does Shakespeare present Beatrice as an independent woman *in Much Ado About Nothing*? Refer to the whole of the play. You are advised to spend about 40 minutes on your answer. [25]

Context

You must be able to:

- Understand the social, historical and cultural context of poetry
- Use this understanding in your evaluation of texts.

Time and Place

- Many poems focus on personal memories, and the poets evoke a sense of the time and place they are remembering:
  - Seamus Heaney's memories of his childhood in 'Death of a Naturalist' include references to the 'townland' where he grew up, to his school and his teacher.
  - Wordsworth in 'The Prelude' uses a specific incident from his childhood to describe the influence of nature on his growth as a poet.
- Some poems are about historical events, and some knowledge and understanding of these events can be helpful:
  - 'Dulce et Decorum Est' is both personal and historical as it is based around Owen's own experiences in the First World War. His reactions are personal and immediate.
  - Simon Armitage's 'The Manhunt' is inspired by the memories of a soldier who fought in the recent war in Iraq.
- The attitudes of the poets to their subjects should be seen in the context of their own time:
  - Rupert Brooke's 'The Soldier' reflects the patriotism felt by many during the First World War, when it was written. Hardy's 'A Wife in London' reflects the feeling of waste and pointlessness many at the time felt about the Boer War.
- When a poet writes about something in the past, consider both the time when it was written and the time it was written about.
  - In 'Mametz Wood', Owen Sheers looks at the First World War from a modern perspective.

Key Point

When comparing poems from the anthology, you must think about similarities and differences between their contexts.

The Romantic Movement

- Blake, Byron, Shelley, Keats and Wordsworth were all part of the Romantic movement in literature. An understanding of Romanticism will inform your reading of their poetry.
- In the eighteenth century most English poets admired and imitated Greek and Latin poetry. Intellectuals valued logic and reason above feelings.
- The Romantics rebelled against this. They used more traditional forms of poetry, such as the ballad, using simpler rhythms and rhyme schemes and more everyday language. They sometimes wrote about ordinary people.

- Most of their poetry, whether **lyric** poetry (short poems about feelings) like 'She Walks in Beauty' or the lengthy autobiographical 'Prelude', focuses on emotions, which they often associated with nature.
- They could also be political, inspired by events like the French Revolution to write anti-establishment poems like 'London'.
- Later poets continued to be influenced by the Romantics. You can see this in Hardy and Barrett Browning, and modern poets like Sheers and Hughes.

Social Issues

- Gender is important in several of the poems:
  - Both 'A Wife in London' and 'The Manhunt' look at the experience of war through the eyes of women whose husbands are killed or injured.
  - Relationships between men and women, and the roles they play in those relationships, are looked at in different ways in Sonnet 43, 'She Walks in Beauty', 'Afternoons' and 'Cozy Apologia'.
- 'London' is concerned with the poverty, disease and inequality of its time; Imitaz Dharker's 'Living Space' looks at similar issues in India today.

Key Point

'Context' refers to literary traditions and movements as well as to social and historical influences.

Quick Test

True or False?

1. Romantic poets were not political.
2. When a poem is set does not matter.
3. Wordsworth is a Romantic poet.
4. Lyric poetry is about feelings.

Key Words

movement
ballad
lyric

Poetry

Themes

You must be able to:

- Identify themes in poetry
- Compare how themes are presented.

Themes and Ideas in the Anthology

- Think about what the main theme or idea of each poem is.
- Look for other themes, ideas and issues that might be present.
- Consider the poet's **attitudes** to these themes.
- Connect the poems through their treatment of themes, looking for both similarities and differences.

How Themes are Presented in Poetry

- Because most poems are quite short, they tend not to explore themes and ideas in great depth or detail.
- Poems often focus on an incident or moment in life, perhaps an anecdote or a snapshot of someone's feelings at a certain time.
- Poems that tell a story include 'A Wife in London', 'Death of a Naturalist' and 'Dulce et Decorum Est'.
- Some poems, like 'Dulce et Decorum Est', tell a story and then reflect on its meaning. Others, like 'Death of a Naturalist', do not include the poet's thoughts, leaving readers to infer meaning.
- Many poems have no story but tell us directly about the poet's thoughts and feelings. Some poets express strong views and feelings, as in Carol Ann Duffy's 'Valentine' and Barrett Browning's Sonnet 43.
- Others, like 'As Imperceptibly as Grief' by Emily Dickinson, present us with images and experiences, leaving us to infer the poet's attitudes and feelings.
- At times it is impossible to 'work out' what the poet's feelings are, as the poem is **ambiguous**. The poet might not have the answer or might want readers to come up with their own answers.

Key Point

The same poem can mean different things to different people. Your response and interpretation is as valid as anyone else's – and it is your response that the examiner wants to read.

Connections

- In the exam you are required to compare two poems (one named) from the cluster you have studied. Here are some questions you could ask when comparing poems during revision.
- Is the poem about a personal relationship? If so, what sort of relationship is it?

Lovers | Husband and wife | Parents and children | Other family relationships | Friends or comrades

Revise

- Is the poem about war or conflict? If so, what kind of conflict is it?

A battle

An argument

A war

A psychological conflict

- Is it about power? If so, what kind of power?

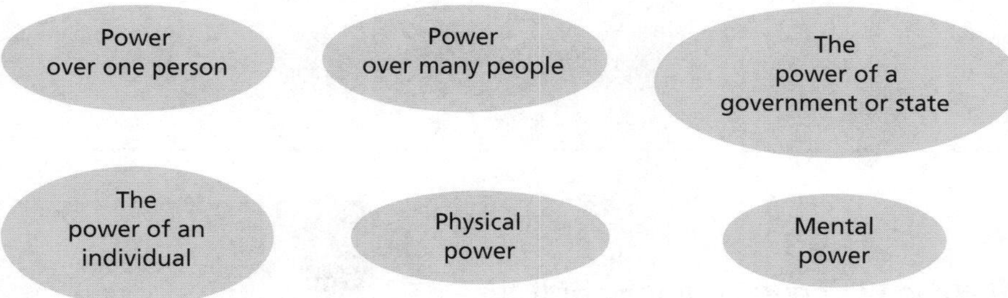

- Or is it about lack of power?
- Is the poem about nature? If so, what aspect of nature?

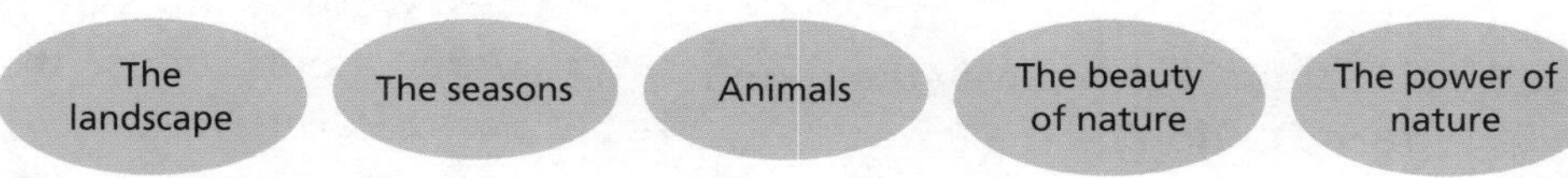

- What else is the poem about?

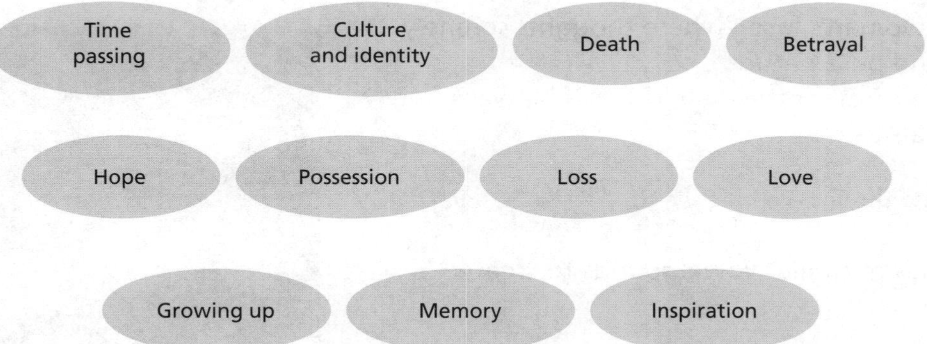

- What feelings does the **voice** or **persona** in the poem have about the subject of the poem?

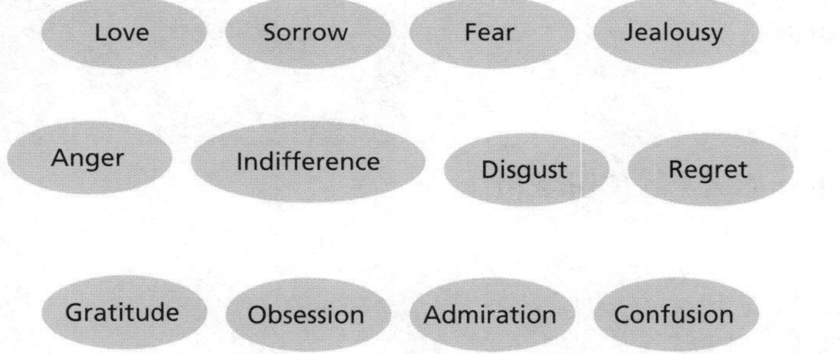

- How does the poem make you feel?
- What is the attitude of the subject to the **voice** / **persona**?

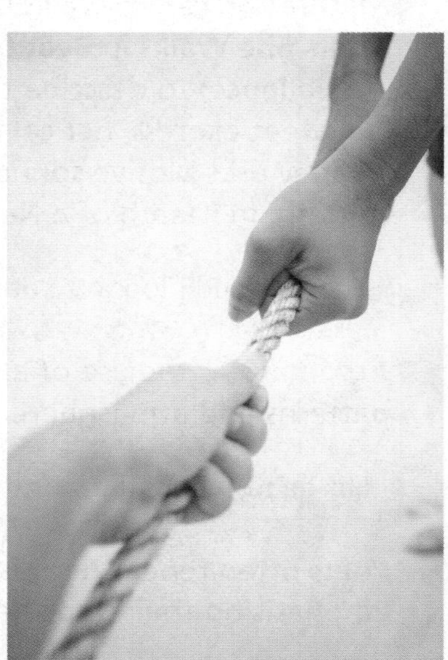

Key Point

You will also need to think about and comment on themes and ideas when writing about unseen poetry.

Quick Test

1. Can a poem have more than one theme?
2. How many poems from the Anthology will you have to write about in the exam?
3. Should you write about your response to the poems?
4. Will you always know what the poet's feelings are?

Key Words

attitude
ambiguous
voice
persona

Language

You must be able to:

- Analyse poets' use of language, using appropriate terminology
- Compare how poets use language.

Sound

- Look at the ways poets use sound. Read the poems out loud or listen to someone else reading them.
- The most obvious way in which sound reflects meaning is through **onomatopoeia**:
  - Hardy uses the phrase 'knock cracks smartly' to convey the sound made by the messenger in 'A Wife in London'.
- **Alliteration** can convey different moods, according to the sound used:
  - In 'She Walks in Beauty' Byron uses 's' sounds (also known as sibilance) to describe the woman's face, 'where thoughts serenely sweet express' her calm and pure nature.
- Heaney uses plosive sounds to sinister effect, almost as if he were spitting, in 'Death of a Naturalist':

> The slap and plop were obscene threats.

- **Assonance** is the use of a series of similar vowel sounds to create patterns and atmosphere:

> His hand, whom the worm now knows ('A Wife in London')

- Poets often repeat not just sounds, but whole words and phrases, emphasising their importance, as in Blake's 'London':

> In every cry of every Man

  Or reflecting the repetition of an action and its impact, as in 'Dulce et Decorum Est':

> Gas! GAS! Quick, boys!

- A phrase that is repeated at the end of each stanza is often called a **refrain**.

Key Point

The poet Coleridge defined poetry as 'the best words in the best order'. Poets choose their words carefully.

Diction

- When poets use a **persona**, their choice of words helps to create the character.
- Armitage in 'Manhunt' uses a mixture of words related to war and the army ('parachute'; 'mine') and parts of the body ('collar-bone'; 'ribs') to give a sense of the persona's concerns as the wife of an injured serviceman.

- In 'Hawk Roosting' the speaker is a hawk whose subject is himself, his language reflecting his megalomania and violence:

> I kill where I please because it is all mine.

- In 'Death of a Naturalist', Heaney uses a combination of scientific and baby-ish language to convey how the teacher speaks to her class:

> Miss Walls would tell us how
> The daddy frog was called a bullfrog
> And how he croaked and how the mammy frog
> Laid hundreds of little eggs and this was
> Frogspawn.

- You might see self-consciously 'poetic' or even **archaic** (outdated) words used for effect, as in Barrett Browning's use of 'thee' rather than 'you'.

Imagery

- Imagery is central to our understanding of how poets create meaning. When a poet compares something to something else, think about why that comparison has been made.
- In 'The Prelude' Wordsworth uses a **simile** to describe his journey:

> And, as I rose upon the stroke, my boat
> Went heaving through the water like a swan;

By doing so he makes the boat and himself part of nature.
- In 'Mametz Wood' Owen Sheers uses the **metaphor** of a 'broken bird's egg' to convey the fragility of the dead soldiers.
- In 'To Autumn' Keats personifies autumn:

> Who has not seen thee oft amid thy store?

- In 'Ozymandias' Shelley's description of the statue can be read as a **symbol** of the futility of power and the passing of time.

Key Point

Think about the 'voice' in the poem. Is the poet writing as him/herself or as a character – a 'persona'?

Quick Test

Give the correct term for:
1. The use of a word that sounds like what it describes.
2. Writing about a thing or idea as if it were a person.
3. Starting a series of words with the same sound.
4. A character in a poem who speaks in the first person.

Key Words

onomatopoeia
alliteration
assonance
refrain
persona
archaic
simile
metaphor
symbol

Form and Structure

You must be able to:

- Analyse poets' use of form and structure, using appropriate terminology
- Compare how poets use form and structure.

Stanzas

- Look at how many **stanzas** there are and whether they are equal in length.
- Blake's 'London' is divided into four stanzas of four lines each. This is the traditional form of the ballad, a poem that tells a story. It is about strong feelings, so you might expect the poet to lose control. Instead he imposes order on his emotions. What effect does the tension between form and content have on the reader?
- Other poets, like Duffy in 'Valentine', vary the length of their stanzas. If this is the case, think about what is happening in the poem when a poet adds an extra line or includes a very short stanza.
- Think about when the poet starts a new stanza. Is there a new idea being introduced? Or is there a change in place or time?
- Where a poem is not divided into stanzas, think about why this might be. The lack of divisions in Dharker's 'Living Space' might reflect the lack of space in the environment she describes.
- Single-stanza poems can have their own internal structure. Sonnets, such as Sonnet 29, follow strict rules, in this case those of the **Petrarchan sonnet**. These consist of an **octave** (8 lines) followed by a **sestet** (6 lines). Traditionally the change from the octave to the sestet reflects a turn (called the **volta**) or change in the argument or mood. You may also come across **Shakespearean sonnets**, which consist of three **quatrains** followed by a rhyming couplet.
- If a line ends with a punctuation mark, it is called **end-stopping**. If a poet continues across lines or even stanzas without a pause, it is called **enjambment**. Think about why the poet would choose one or the other.

Key Point

'Stanza' is Italian for 'room', so if a poem is a house the stanzas are its rooms.

Rhyme

- **Rhyme** is easy to spot but can be difficult to comment on. It can be used to make us laugh, to emphasise something, or to give a sense of order.
- The simplest form of rhyme is the **rhyming couplet**, rhyming one line with the next. This is an almost childish use of rhyme, so it can be used to tell us something about the persona or subject matter. Rita Dove uses rhyming couplets in 'Cozy Apologia', perhaps reflecting the simplicity of her love.
- Rhyming couplets are also used to underline important points.

- The traditional rhyme scheme of the ballad is *abab.* This is used in 'London'.
- Some poets use more complex rhyme schemes, while others use rhyme occasionally for effect, sometimes within lines (internal rhyme).
- You might come across sight or eye rhymes, where the words look as if they should rhyme but do not, for example, 'rough' and 'bough'.
- Many poets use 'half rhyme' (also known as 'slant rhyme' and 'pararhyme'), where the final consonants agree but the vowel sounds do not match, softening the effect of the rhyme. In 'As Imperceptibly as Grief', Dickinson rhymes 'began' with 'afternoon' and 'keel' with 'beautiful'.

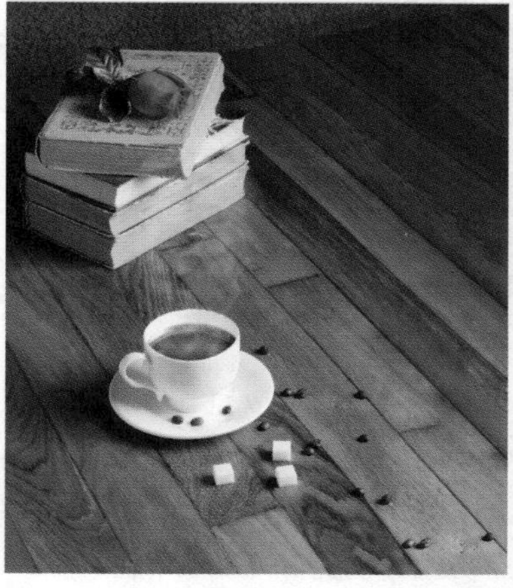

Rhythm

- A poem's rhythm comes from its pattern of stressed and unstressed syllables. You can get a sense of this by reading a poem aloud.
- Some poems have a very strong rhythm. 'The Charge of the Light Brigade' is written in **dactyls** (a stressed syllable followed by two unstressed syllables), giving a sense of the pounding of horses' hooves and cannons:

> **Half** a league **half** a league

- One of the most commonly used metres is the iambic pentameter. This is quite a gentle rhythm, often compared to a heartbeat. Wordsworth uses it in 'The Prelude':

> And **as** I **rose** up**on** the **stroke**, my **boat**

- Some poems have a very strong rhythm. 'London' is written partly in pentameter and partly in **trochees** (a stressed syllable followed by an unstressed syllable), giving a sense of urgency and power in the third stanza:

> How the chimney sweeper's cry
>
> Every black'ning church appals

- Contemporary poets are less likely to use strong rhythmical patterns, though there are exceptions. However, if you listen carefully you should still hear a rhythm.
- If you hear a rhythm, think about how the poet uses it to create the mood and tone of the poem.
- Poetry that has a regular metre but no rhyme is called blank verse.
- Poetry that has no regular pattern, either of rhyme or metre, is called free verse.

Quick Test

Give the correct term for:

1. A set of two lines that rhyme.
2. A rhyme within a line.
3. A poem that tells a story in four-line stanzas.
4. Poetry that has no regular pattern.

Key Point

When looking at rhyme and metre, look for patterns and variations in patterns.

Key Words

stanza
Petrarchan sonnet
octave
sestet
volta
Shakespearean sonnet
quatrain
end-stopping
enjambment
rhyme
rhyming couplet
rhythm
stress
syllable
metre
blank verse
free verse

Unseen Poetry

You must be able to:

- Respond to and analyse a poem you have not seen before
- Compare two unseen poems.

Approaching an Unseen Poem

- In Section C of Component 2 you will be given two poems you have never seen before. You will have to answer a question about one of them, before comparing them.
- Start by reading the poem to gain a general sense of its themes, mood and atmosphere. Then use your knowledge of poetry to 'interrogate' the text. Here are some questions you could ask yourself when reading an unseen poem.

Title	What does it make you think about? Does it tell you what the poem is about or is it ambiguous?
Speaker	Is the voice in the poem that of the poet or a persona? Who, if anyone, is being addressed?
Setting	Where and when is it set? Does the place change? Does the time change?
Form and structure	How is it arranged? When and why does the poet start a new stanza? Is there a strong regular rhythm? If so, what effect does it have? Does it rhyme? If so, is there a regular rhyme scheme? What is the effect of the rhyme?
Language	How does the poet use sound? What kind of vocabulary/register does the poet use? What sort of imagery does the poet use? Is there anything else interesting about the language?
Themes and ideas	Is there a story? If so, what is it? What do you think the poem is really about? Is more than one theme touched on? What do you think is the poet's attitude / point of view?
Personal response	What does the poem make you think about? How does it make you feel?

Key Point

To answer the questions, you will need all the skills you have learned studying poems from the anthology.

Comparing Unseen Poems

Revise

- You will be asked to compare a poem that you have already written about with another poem on a similar theme.
- Be careful not to repeat everything you have already said about the first poem. Focus on the second poem but make sure that every point you make refers back to the first one.
- You could go through the new poem line by line, linking it to the first poem as you go.
- Or you could take different aspects of the poem in turn, starting a new paragraph for each.
- Whichever way you approach the comparison, consider:

Structure and form	*Brown's structure is regular, the four stanzas of four lines giving a sense of order and logic, whereas Smith's stanzas vary in length, as if her memories are random and disordered.*
Language	*Brown's use of harsh-sounding words such as 'rough' and 'dour' contrast with the softness of Smith's 'silken voice' and 'shuffling step'.*
Imagery	*Both poets use imagery connected with nature but in very different ways...*
How the poets approach the theme	*Both poems focus on the child's relationship with her father.*
The poets' feelings and attitudes	*Unlike Brown, Smith remembers her father with affection.*
Your response to the poems	*Brown conveys a sense of regret and anger, whereas the way Smith describes her feelings, although sad, is somehow comforting.*

- Back up every point you make with short quotations from both poems.
- Try to use correct **terminology** but remember that you do not get marks just for 'spotting' things like alliteration and metaphors. You must show that you understand how they are used and their effect on the reader.

Key Point

Remember to comment on both similarities and differences.

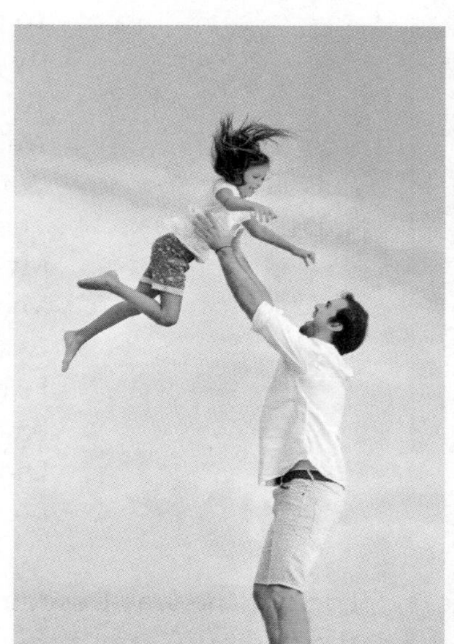

Quick Test

Would you use the following connectives to express a similarity or a difference?

1. Both...and
2. whereas...
3. On the other hand...
4. Neither...nor

Key Word

terminology

Answer the question on the play you have studied.

Write your answer on a separate piece of paper.

1 *Othello*

Read the extract and answer the question below. You are advised to spend about 20 minutes on your answer.

OTHELLO	Most humbly, therefore, bending to your state, I crave fit disposition for my wife, Due reverence of place, and exhibition, With such accommodation and besort As levels with her breeding.
DUKE	If you please, Be't at her father's.
BRABANTIO	I'll not have it so.
OTHELLO	Nor I.
DESDEMONA	Nor I, I would not there reside To put my father in impatient thoughts, By being in his eye: most gracious duke, To my unfolding lend a gracious ear, And let me find a charter in your voice,
DUKE	What would you…speak.
DESDEMONA	That I did love the Moor, to live with him, My downright violence, and scorn of fortunes, May trumpet to the world: my heart's subdued Even to the utmost pleasure of my lord: I saw Othello's visage in his mind, And to his honours, and his valiant parts Did I my soul and fortunes consecrate;

Look at the way Desdemona and Othello speak and behave here. What does it reveal to the audience about their relationship at this point in the play? Refer closely to the extract to support your answer. [15]

2 *Much Ado About Nothing*

Read the extract and answer the question below. You are advised to spend about 20 minutes on your answer.

BEATRICE	Good Lord, for alliance! Thus goes everyone to the world but I, and I am sunburnt. I may sit in a corner and cry, 'Heigh-ho for a husband!'
DON PEDRO	Lady Beatrice, I will get you one.
BEATRICE	I would rather have one of your father's getting. Hath your grace ne'er a brother like you? Your father got excellent husbands if a maid could come by them.
DON PEDRO	Will you have me, lady?
BEATRICE	No, my lord, unless I might have another for working days. Your grace is too costly to wear everyday. But I beseech your grace, pardon me. I was born to speak all mirth and no matter.
DON PEDRO	Your silence most offends me, and to be merry best becomes you; for out o'question, you were born in a merry hour.
BEATRICE	No, sure, my lord, my mother cried. But then there was a star danced, and under that was I born.

Look at how Beatrice and Don Pedro speak and behave here. What does it show the audience about Beatrice's character? Refer closely to the extract to support your answer. [15]

3 *The Merchant of Venice*

Read the extract and answer the question below. You are advised to spend about 20 minutes on your answer.

TUBAL	Your daughter spent in Genoa, as I heard, one night fourscore ducats.
SHYLOCK	Thou stick'st a dagger in me. I shall never see my gold again. Fourscore ducats at a sitting, fourscore ducats!
TUBAL	There came divers of Antonio's creditors in my company to Venice that swear he cannot choose but break.
SHYLOCK	I am very glad of it. I'll plague him; I'll torture him. I am glad of it.
TUBAL	One of them showed me a ring that he had of your daughter for a monkey.
SHYLOCK	Out upon her! Thou torturest me, Tubal. It was my turquoise; I had it of Leah when I was a bachelor. I would not have given it for a wilderness of monkeys.

What does the extract show the audience about Shylock's relationship with Jessica? Refer closely to the extract to support your answer. [15]

4 *Romeo and Juliet*

Explore how Shakespeare presents the growing love of Romeo and Juliet throughout the whole of the play. You are advised to spend about 40 minutes on your answer. [25]

5 *Macbeth*

Write about how Shakespeare present Macbeth's feelings about power and ambition at different points in the play. You are advised to spend about 40 minutes on your answer. [25]

6 *Henry V*

Write about how Shakespeare uses the character of Henry V to present ideas about kingship at different points in the play. You are advised to spend about 40 minutes on your answer. [25]

Practice Questions

You will need your copy of the Anthology to answer questions 1 and 2. Write your answer on a separate piece of paper.

1 Read 'Hawk Roosting' by Ted Hughes and answer the following questions.

a) What person is the poem written in?

b) What tense is used?

c) What effect do the person and tense have?

d) Briefly describe where and when it is set.

e) How is it organised?

f) What is the effect of this?

g) Briefly describe the character of the persona (the hawk).

h) What does the poem have to say about power?

i) Find an example of repetition and explain its effect.

j) The last stanza consists of four short statements, each a separate sentence. What is the effect of this? [20]

Or

2 Read 'Sonnet 43' by Elizabeth Barrett Browning and answer the following questions.

a) What person(s) is the poem written in?

b) What tense is used?

c) What effect do the person and tense have?

d) The poem is a sonnet. What is the normal purpose of a sonnet?

e) How is it organised?

f) What is the effect of the repetition of 'I love thee'?

g) What is the significance of the phrase 'by sun and by candlelight'?

h) What do you think the poet means by her 'lost Saints'?

i) What does the poem tell us about the poet's beliefs?

j) What is your impression of the poet's feelings for the person to whom the poem is addressed (thee)? [20]

3 Read the poem below and answer the questions that follow.

The Song of the Old Mother by W. B. Yeats

I rise in the dawn, and I kneel and blow
Till the seed of the fire flicker and glow;
And then I must scrub and bake and sweep
Till stars are beginning to blink and peep;
And the young lie long and dream in their bed
Of the matching ribbons for bosom and head,
And their day goes over in idleness,
And they sing if the wind but lift a tress:
While I must work because I am old,
And the seed of the fire gets feeble and cold.

a) Is the voice in the poem that of the poet or a persona? What sort of person is speaking?

b) Where and when is it set?

c) Is there a strong, regular rhythm? If so, what effect does it have?

d) Does it rhyme? If so, is there a regular rhyme scheme? What is the effect of the rhyme?

e) What sort of imagery does the poet use?

f) Is there a story? If so, what is it?

g) What is the significance of the line 'And the seed of the fire gets feeble and cold'?

h) What do you think the poem is really about?

i) What do you think is the poet's attitude / point of view?

j) How does the poem make you feel?

[20]

Context

You must be able to:

- Understand the social, historical and cultural context of a modern text
- Use this understanding to evaluate the text.

Context

- You need to consider the social and historical context of your text. Think about the kind of society presented in the text.
- Think about 'cultural context', including genre and intended audience.

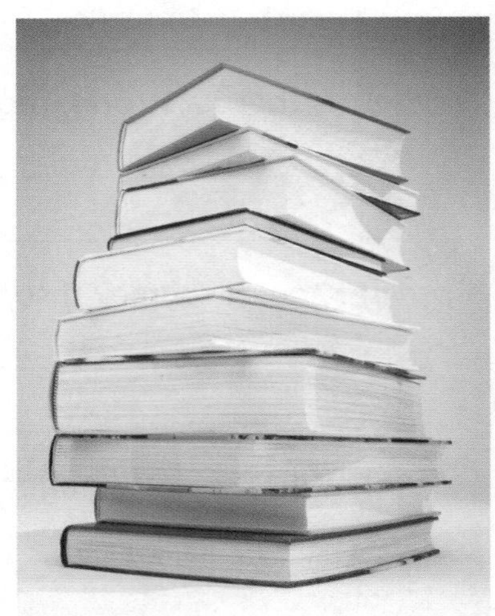

Time

- British society has changed a lot over the last 100 years. The set texts were written over a period of more than 60 years.
- The Britain portrayed in them ranges from the hypocritical, class-conscious world of 1912 shown in *An Inspector Calls* to the confusing, twenty-first-century world shown in *The Curious Incident of the Dog in the Night-Time*.
- *An Inspector Calls*, written in 1945, looks back on an earlier **period**. This is 1912 seen from the perspective of a country that had experienced two world wars and in which many were looking forward to a new, fairer society. Someone writing in 1912 would have seen things differently.
- Other texts set in earlier periods include:
  - *Blood Brothers* (written 1983, set 1950s–1970s)
  - *The History Boys* (written 2004, set 1980s)
  - *Anita and Me* (written 1996, set 1960/1970s).
  - *The Woman in Black* (written 1983, set early 20th century).
- If you have studied one of these texts, think about why the writer has chosen the period and how his or her view of it is coloured by the events, ideas and attitudes of later years.
- *Lord of the Flies* (1954) is not set at a particular time but is a product of its time. It picks up on post-war concerns about what is meant by civilisation.
- *A Taste of Honey* (1956) and *The Curious Incident of the Dog in the Night-Time* (2011) reflect the world at the time they were written.

Key Point

Think about how your text reflects the concerns, attitudes and assumptions of the time and how these might differ from those of today.

Place

- The place where a text is set can help to give it a distinctive tone and atmosphere.
- Regional differences come out most strongly in the way characters speak:
  - Meera Syal presents the way people from a Black Country village speak by writing their speech phonetically, imitating the way they pronounce words.

- Helen in *A Taste of Honey* uses dialect expressions, such as 'I'd sooner be put on't street', reflecting the play's Lancashire setting.
- Some texts establish a sense of place by referring to specific **locations**:
  - *Blood Brothers* references places in and around Liverpool. The family's move from the city to a 'new town' marks the end of Act 1.
- Factors such as whether the setting is urban or rural, in the inner city or the suburbs, can be more important than the exact location:
  - *An Inspector Calls* takes place in a 'large suburban house' in a fictional industrial city.
- Some texts are set within a particular community or communities:
  - *Anita and Me* is about two very different communities co-existing: the village of Tollington and Meena's 'family' of Indians, who visit her house.

Cultural Context

- If you are studying a play, think about where and for whom it was/is performed.
  - *Blood Brothers* is a musical. In **musical theatre** characters use songs to express emotion and to move the story on.
  - *The Curious Incident of the Dog in the Night-Time* was adapted from a successful novel. You might want to read the novel and explore how and why it has been changed.
- With prose, too, genre can be important:
  - *Never Let Me Go* is sometimes categorised as science fiction. It is about what could happen as a result of science.
  - Golding has called *Lord of the Flies* a **fable**. *The Woman in Black* is a ghost story and has been described as '**Gothic**'. What are the implications of these descriptions?

Key Point

Think about whether the place where your text is set makes a difference and, if so, how.

Quick Test

True or False?

1. A text's setting can determine how characters speak.
2. Characters in musicals express emotion by singing.
3. Science fiction is about things that have really happened.
4. Some texts are set in imaginary places.

Key Words

period
location
musical theatre
fable
Gothic

Themes

You must be able to:
- Identify themes in a modern text
- Write about how themes are presented.

Identifying Themes

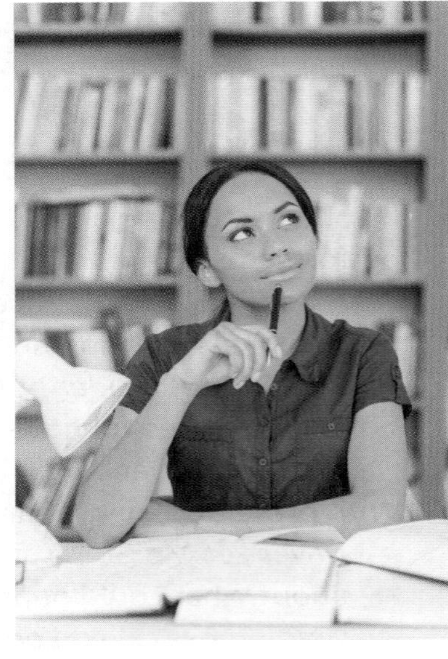

- Think about:
  - what the writer is saying
  - what the text makes you think about.
- Try answering, in one sentence, the question, 'What is the text about?'

> *Lord of the Flies* is about a group of boys stranded on an island.

- Ask yourself why the writer might want us to read about this situation and what it makes us think about. You are now moving from the situation to the themes.
- Try to come up with some new answers to the question, 'What is the text about?' You could make a spider **diagram** or a list:

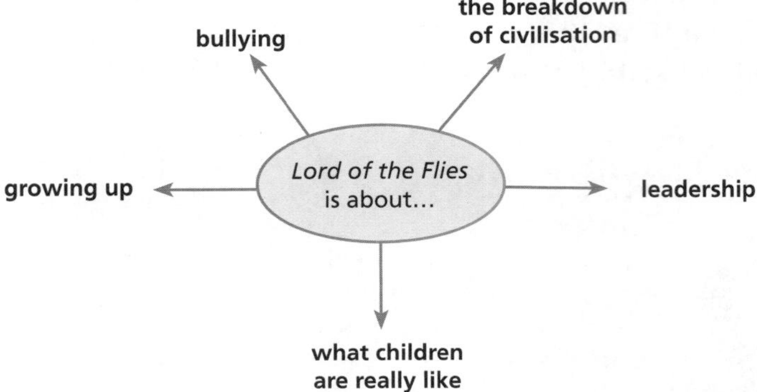

- Some themes crop up again and again in the set texts. Here are some questions that might get you thinking about themes and ideas in your text:

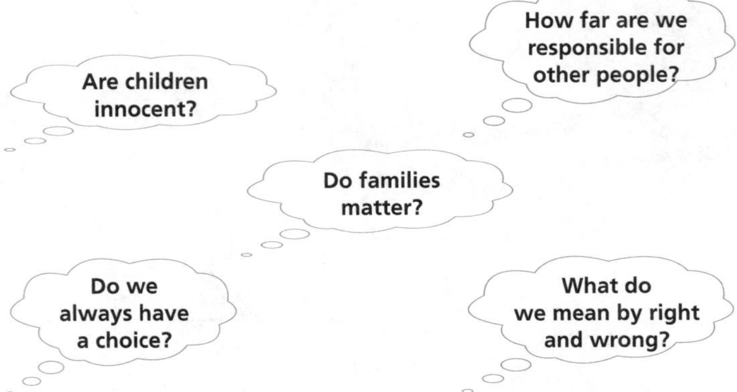

- Write down as many questions as you can that might come out of your text. Then try to find more than one answer to each, backing up your answer with evidence from the text.

Key Point

Themes in modern texts reflect current concerns, as well as issues that have always interested writers.

How Themes are Presented in Novels and Short Stories

Modern **prose** presents themes:

- through events:
  - In *Never Let Me Go* the trip to Norfolk makes Kathy think about issues of identity and humanity.
- through the narrator:
  - In *Anita and Me*, Meena draws lessons from her experiences about culture, friendship and growing up.
- through characters:
  - The woman in black in the novel of the same name, makes us think not only about the supernatural but also about grief and vengeance.
- through what characters say:
  - In *Lord of the Flies*, the boys discuss issues like responsibility and survival.
- through motifs and symbols:
  - In *Oranges are not the Only Fruit*, oranges symbolise lack of choice and freedom.

How Themes are Presented in Plays

- The stage is a visual **medium**. It is about showing, not telling. Look in the stage directions for striking **images** which encapsulate themes:
  - The image of Mickey and Edward lying dead at the end of *Blood Brothers* brings together many of the play's themes.
- Remember, though, that play **scripts** can be interpreted differently by different **directors**, designers and actors. The images of one production may not be the same as those of another.
- Characters sometimes speak directly to the audience, bringing our attention to themes and issues:
  - In *The History Boys*, Scripps occasionally steps out of the action to reflect on the meaning of the boys' experiences.
- Mostly, we encounter themes and ideas through dialogue. There can be as many different points of view about an issue as there are characters on stage:
  - In *A Taste of Honey,* we encounter different ideas about love and responsibility through Jo's conversations with Helen and Geof.
- Some writers present us with several viewpoints and leave us to make up our own minds. Others give their preferred point of view to a character who is presented as being wiser or more trustworthy than others:
  - Inspector Goole in *An Inspector Calls* stands apart from the action, and his **interpretation** of what has happened can be seen as that of the writer.

Key Point

Our interpretation of themes and ideas can depend as much on our background and opinions as on those of the writer.

Key Words

diagram
prose
medium
image
script
director
interpretation

Quick Test

In the theatre, which of the following influence how themes are presented?

1. The writer.
2. The director.
3. The actors.
4. The designer.

Characters

You must be able to:

- Write about how characters are presented in a modern text.

Prose: First-Person Narratives

- *Never Let Me Go*, *Anita and Me*, *The Woman in Black* and *Oranges are not the Only Fruit* are first-person narratives.
- Kathy in *Never Let Me Go,* Jeanette in *Oranges are not the Only Fruit* and Meena in *Anita and Me* write as adults looking back on events from childhood and early adulthood. Arthur Kipps in *The Woman in Black* looks back on events that happened when he was a younger man.
- We might expect the adult narrators to have a greater understanding of their stories. Kathy, like Arthur Kipps, seems quite detached and thoughtful. She writes as if she is trying to work out the meaning of the things she remembers.
- We can get an idea of what other characters think of the narrators, but this is always filtered through the narrator's perspective:
  - In *Never Let Me Go* Kathy does not always understand how others are responding to her, but the reader can make inferences from what she reports.
- Readers might draw conclusions about narrators which the narrators (and possibly writers) do not foresee:
  - Some readers might think Meena in *Anita and Me* comes across as a snob who looks down on her old friends. The narrator's attitude to, and treatment of, others in *Oranges are not the Only Fruit* might disturb some readers.
- We might draw our own conclusions, different from those of the narrator, about other characters:
  - Meena could be seen as a **naive** and perhaps **unreliable narrator**: she refers to herself as a 'liar' early in the novel.
  - Arthur Kipps might also be seen as a naïve narrator, though he is dealing with events that no-one could be expected to understand. He thinks he has successfully dealt with the woman in black until the cruel twist of the final chapter.
- In *Oranges are not the Only Fruit*, the writer occasionally switches from first person narrative to tell the fairy-tale like stories of the prince and Winnet. At other times she comes out of the narrative to address the reader directly, in the manner of an **intrusive narrator**.

Prose: Third-Person Narratives

- Golding is an **omniscient** narrator in *Lord of the Flies*. The character we are given most insight into is the protagonist, Ralph, but he also takes us into the minds of other characters.

Key Point

Modern novelists tell us about characters in the same ways as nineteenth-century novelists did.

- In *Lord of the Flies* there is a strong antagonist in Jack. Other characters, like Piggy and Simon, are important because of what they do in the story and because of what they represent.

Drama

- Sometimes **playwrights** tell us about characters in stage directions:
  - Arthur Birling in *An Inspector Calls* is described as 'a heavy-looking, rather portentous man in his middle fifties, with fairly easy manners but rather provincial in his speech'.
- Characters can reveal themselves, either directly to the audience or to other characters. Judy in *The Curious Incident of the Dog in the Night-Time* gives her side of things through letters:

> And your father is really patient, but I'm not. I get cross, even though I don't mean to […] and I felt really lonely.

- We learn about characters through dialogue. When Dakin and Scripps converse in *The History Boys* we hear their differing points of view, and we see that they are both intellectually, if not emotionally, mature as they can express themselves well, using sophisticated diction:

> No more the bike's melancholy long withdrawing roar as he dropped you off at the corner, your honour still intact.

- What really matters is what characters do:
  - Mrs Johnstone in *Blood Brothers* gives away one of her children. Why? And what are the consequences?

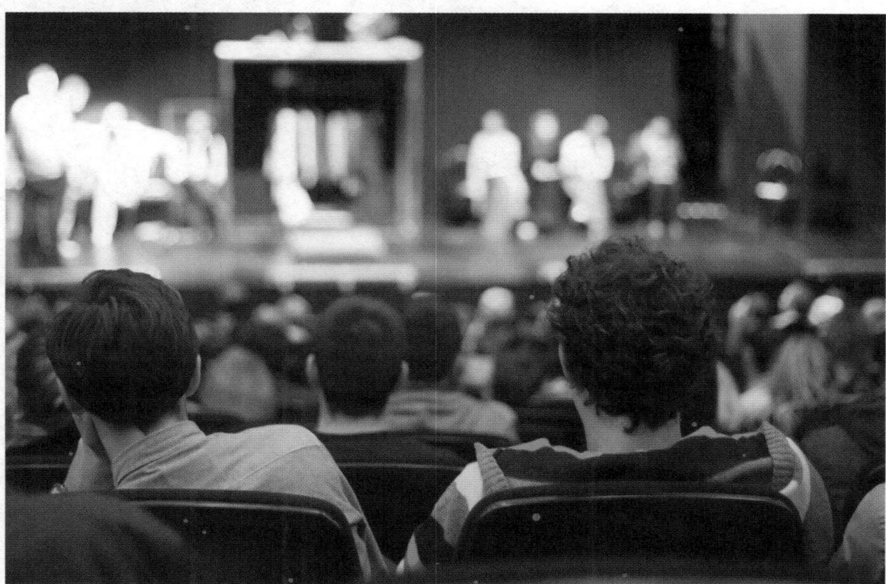

Key Point

Always remember when writing about a play, that it is a script to be performed. Actors can interpret characters in different ways.

Quick Test

Rearrange the letters to find a useful term:

1. TSGNROAPTOI
2. RRRTNAOA
3. GIDOULEA
4. GATES TIRODENIC

Key Words

naive narrator
unreliable narrator
intrusive narrator
omniscient narrator
playwright

Language and Structure

You must be able to:
- Analyse the use of language and structure in a modern text
- Use relevant terminology.

Prose

The Narrative Voice

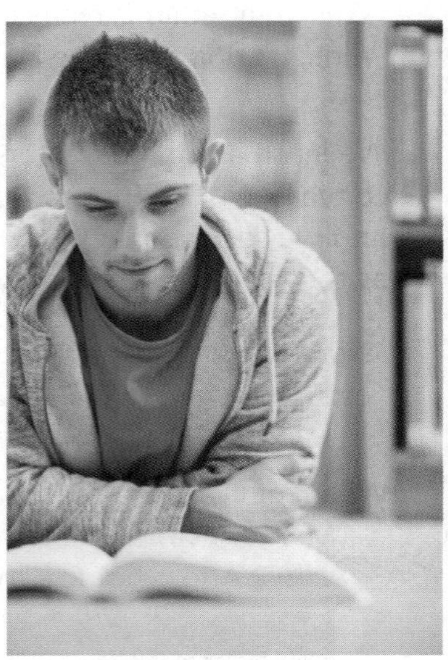

- In *The Woman in Black*, the narrator uses Standard English of a rather old-fashioned, formal type. This reflects both his character and the time when the novel is set.
- In *Oranges are not the Only Fruit*, the writer also uses Standard English, her diction reflecting both her religious background and her literary education.
- Some narrators, like Kathy in *Never Let Me Go*, adopt a colloquial tone while using Standard English, as if explaining things to a friend:

  I suppose that might sound odd.

Speech

- The language characters use adds to our understanding of them and the world they inhabit.
- Most of the boys in *Lord of the Flies* speak in Standard English, but in the rather clipped manner of public schoolboys in the 1950s:

  'Give him a fourpenny one!'

  Piggy is shown to be from a different class:

  'I got the conch, ain't I Ralph?'

- In *Anita and Me*, the local people use dialect and their **accent** is shown phonetically:

  'Ay up, Mr K! Havin a bit of a do then?'

  The Indian characters use Standard English except when speaking Punjabi.

Structure

- Most of the set texts are written in chronological order, although some of them (*Anita and Me, Never Let Me Go, Oranges are not the Only Fruit*) jump backwards and forwards as one event reminds the narrator of another.
- Think about how the text is divided. Why does the writer decide to start a new chapter at a certain point?

Key Point

In first-person narratives, the language of the narration can reflect the background of the narrator.

- Look for anything different or odd about your text's structure:
  - Chapter titles in *Oranges are not the Only Fruit* are also the titles of books in the Old Testament.

Drama

Language

- Dialogue can reflect where the play is set and also tell us about the characters.
- The class divisions of *Blood Brothers* are shown in the contrast between the way the Johnstone and Lyons families speak:

> EDWARD: Do you…Do you really? Goodness, that's fantastic.

> MICKEY: Come on, bunk under y'fence, y'Ma won't see y'.

- Christopher in *The Curious Incident of the Dog in the Night-Time* speaks in a deliberate, rather impersonal way:

> I remember 20 July 2006. I was 9 years old. It was a Saturday.

Key Point

When we discuss language in a play we are discussing the language the characters use.

Structure

- Most plays are in two acts, with an interval between them. Because of this, writers usually build up to a turning point at the end of Act 1, leaving the audience wanting to know what happens next.
- When *An Inspector Calls* was written, most plays had a three-act structure, so both Act 1 and Act 2 end with turning points.
- *An Inspector Calls* and *A Taste of Honey* have clear act and scene divisions. Within each section, action is continuous and happens in one place.
- In other, more recent plays the action flows from one short scene to another, time and place changing frequently.
- Look for anything unusual about your play's structure, for example:
  - At the end of *An Inspector Calls*, it looks as though the play is about to start all over again.
  - In *The History Boys* characters seem to jump out of the 'past' to speak to us and then return seamlessly.

Key Words

accent
dialogue
act
interval
turning point
scene

Quick Test

1. Can a narrator use a colloquial tone and Standard English?
2. In the same play, which is longer, a scene or an act?
3. What would the use of dialect tell us about a character?
4. Are the events in a play or novel always in chronological order?

Review Questions

1 **Answer part (a) and part (b) and write your answers on a separate piece of paper.**

Spend about 20 minutes on part (a) and 40 minutes on part (b).

a) Read the poem below, 'The Soldier' by Rupert Brooke. In this poem Brooke explores ideas about death in war. Write about the ways in which he presents war and death in this poem. [15]

b) Choose one other poem from the anthology in which the poet writes about war.

Compare the presentation of war in your chosen poem to the presentation of war in 'The Soldier'. [25]

In your answer to part (b) you should compare:

- the content and structure of the poems – what they are about and how they are organised;
- how the writers create effects, using appropriate terminology where relevant; the context of the poems, and how these may have influenced them.

The Soldier

by Rupert Brooke

If I should die, think only this of me:
That there's some corner of a foreign field
That is for ever England. There shall be
In that rich earth a richer dust concealed;
A dust whom England bore, shaped, made aware,
Gave, once, her flowers to love, her ways to roam,
A body of England's, breathing English air,
Washed by the rivers, blest by suns of home.

And think, this heart, all evil shed away,
A pulse the eternal mind, no less
Gives somewhere back the thoughts by England given;
Her sights and sounds; dreams happy as her day;
And laughter, learnt of friends; and gentleness,
In hearts at peace, under an English heaven.

2 **Read the two poems below and answer both part (a) and part (b) on a separate piece of paper.**

Spend about 20 minutes on part (a) and 40 minutes on part (b).

a) Write about the poem 'Sonnet' by John Clare, and its effect on you. [15]

You may wish to consider:

- what the poem is about and how it is organised;
- the ideas the poet may have wanted us to think about;
- the poet's choice of words, phrases and images and the effects they create;
- how you respond to the poem.

Sonnet

by John Clare

I love to see the summer beaming forth
And white wool sack clouds sailing to the north
I love to see the wild flowers come again
And Mare drops stain with gold the meadow drain
And water lilies whiten on the floods
Where reed clumps rustle like a wind shook wood
Where from her hiding place the Moor Hen pushes
And seeks her flag nest floating in bull rushes
I like the willow leaning half way o'er
The clear deep lake to stand upon its shore
I love the hay grass when the flower head swings
To summer winds and insects happy wings
That sport about the meadow the bright day
And see bright beetles in the clear lake play.

The Eagle

by Alfred Tennyson

He clasps the crag with crooked hands;
Close to the sun in lonely lands,
Ring'd with the azure world he stands.

The wrinkled sea beneath him crawls;
He watches from his mountain walls,
And like a thunderbolt he falls.

b) Now compare 'The Eagle' to 'Sonnet'. [25]

You should compare:

- what the poems are about and how they are organised;
- the ideas the poets may have wanted us to think about;
- the poets' choice of words, phrases and images and the effects they create;
- how you respond to the poems.

Practice Questions

Answer the question on the text you have studied.

Write your answer on a separate piece of paper.

Your answer should be in note form, using bullet points.

1. J. B. Priestley: *An Inspector Calls*

   Make notes on the character and significance of Inspector Goole in *An Inspector Calls*.

   Write down five statements about the character and give evidence from the text in support of each one. [10]

2. Willy Russell: *Blood Brothers*

   Make notes on the character and significance of Mrs Lyons in *Blood Brothers*.

   Write down five statements about the character and give evidence from the text in support of each one. [10]

3. Alan Bennett: *The History Boys*

   Make notes on the character and significance of Dakin in *The History Boys*.

   Write down five statements about the character and give evidence from the text in support of each one. [10]

4. Simon Stephens: *The Curious Incident of the Dog in the Night-Time*

   Make notes on the character and significance of Christopher in *The Curious Incident of the Dog in the Night-Time*.

   Write down five statements about the character and give evidence from the text in support of each one. [10]

5. Shelagh Delaney: *A Taste of Honey*

   Make notes on the character and significance of Jo in *A Taste of Honey*.

   Write down five statements about the character and give evidence from the text in support of each one. [10]

6. William Golding: *Lord of the Flies*

   Make notes on the character and significance of Simon in *Lord of the Flies*.

   Write down five statements about the character and give evidence from the text in support of each one. [10]

7 Kazuo Ishiguro: *Never Let Me Go*

Make notes on the character and significance of Tommy in *Never Let Me Go.*

Write down five statements about the character and give evidence from the text in support of each one. [10]

8 Meera Syal: *Anita and Me*

Make notes on the character and significance of Anita in *Anita and Me.*

Write down five statements about the character and give evidence from the text in support of each one. [10]

9 Susan Hill: *The Woman in Black*

Make notes on the character and significance of Arthur Kipps in *The Woman in Black*.

Write down five statements about the character and give evidence from the text in support of each one. [10]

10 Jeanette Winterson: *Oranges are not the Only Fruit*

Make notes on the character and significance of Jeanette's mother in *Oranges are not the Only Fruit.*

Write down five statements about the character and give evidence from the text in support of each one. [10]

Context

You must be able to:

- Understand the social, historical and cultural context of a nineteenth-century novel
- Use this understanding to evaluate the text.

Religion and Morality

- In the nineteenth century, Britain was a Christian country, with many more churchgoers than now; religion was part of the fabric of most people's lives. Ministers of religion feature in *Jane Eyre* and *Pride and Prejudice.* The churches at Lantern Yard and Raveloe are of great importance to their communities in *Silas Marner*.
- People tended to share similar ideas about what was acceptable, particularly sexually. Deviations from the norm, like Lydia eloping with Wickham in *Pride and Prejudice*, are shocking.
- Many novels are concerned with right and wrong. Dr Jekyll wants to separate his 'evil' and 'good' sides. In *A Christmas Carol*, Dickens asks his readers to think about what Christmas and Christianity really mean.

Society

- Britain was a very wealthy country with a worldwide empire. Some people made huge fortunes, giving them as much power as the old aristocrats.
- There was a growing middle class of people who had comfortable homes and money to spend – including on novels.
- However, there was also great poverty, especially in towns and cities. With no welfare state and low wages, many people lived in terrible conditions.
- Social reformers fought against inequality. Dickens's work made people think about social issues.

Gender

- Women did not have a vote (although neither did most men) and their career options were limited. *Pride and Prejudice* is based on the need of middle-class women to find husbands. Jane Eyre has to earn her living as a governess.
- Many writers and thinkers, including George Eliot, supported women's rights, although Charlotte Brontë did not always agree with feminist ideas.

Race

- It is unusual to find characters who are not white. Some modern readers are shocked by the attitudes shown to ethnic minorities. They are often seen as wild and savage or exotic and mysterious, like the 'Creole' Bertha in Jane Eyre. Some critics think reactions to the aliens in *War of the Worlds* reflect attitudes to foreigners and non-white people.

Key Point

The nineteenth century was a time of great change in Britain. Literature reflected this.

Science

- There were many scientific discoveries and advances. In *The Strange Case of Dr Jekyll and Mr Hyde, Stevenson* uses science as a starting point to consider 'what if', as science fiction writers do today. Jekyll mixes chemicals to find his formula.
- In *War of the Worlds*, Wells imagines what would happen if there were life forms elsewhere in the universe. This reflects a growing interest in astronomy and the possibility of space travel.
- Many writers took an interest in new ideas about **psychology**. *Silas Marner* reflects discussion of 'nature and nurture' and the importance of childhood experiences, as do *Jane Eyre* and *A Christmas Carol.* Stevenson explores ideas about behaviour and responsibility.

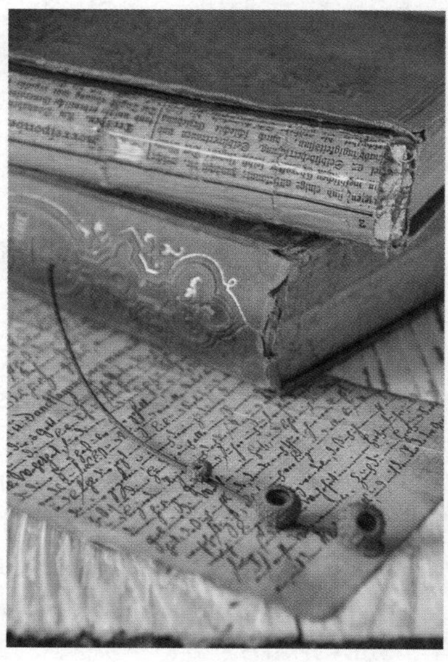

Literature: Movements and Genre

- Novelists were influenced by the Romantic movement, led by poets like Wordsworth. This movement rejected the eighteenth-century taste for order and rationality in favour of an emphasis on personal feelings and nature.
- While Jane Austen belongs more to the eighteenth-century tradition, her characters do reflect the fashion for **sentiment** and poetry.
- Many popular novels and stories of the period are often described as Gothic, a genre related to Romanticism but more sensational, thrilling its readers with horror and the **supernatural**.
- Brontë, Dickens and Stevenson use elements of the Gothic. *A Christmas Carol* and *The Strange Case of Dr Jekyll and Mr Hyde* both cashed in on the popular taste for ghost stories. *The Strange Case of Dr Jekyll and Mr Hyde* also owes something to the increasingly popular detective story.
- H.G. Wells, author of *War of the Worlds*, was one of the first science fiction writers.

Key Point

Whatever aspect of a text you are looking at, consider its context.

Quick Test

True or False?

1. All men had the vote.
2. Nobody cared about social injustice.
3. Romantic poets thought feelings mattered.
4. Britain changed a lot during the nineteenth century.

Key Words

psychology
sentiment
supernatural

Themes

You must be able to:

- Identify themes in a nineteenth-century novel
- Write about how themes are presented.

Identifying Themes

- Here are some themes you will find in the set books.
- Look at the themes of the books you have not studied and think about whether they are also present in your novel.
- *Pride and Prejudice*
  - Marriage: marrying well is vital for the women. They want to marry for love but they also think in practical terms.
  - Class: the class system seems rigid and there is a lot of snobbery but Elizabeth breaks through it.
- *Silas Marner*
  - The outsider and the community: Silas is an outsider in Raveloe.
  - Religious faith: Silas has lost his faith.
- *A Christmas Carol*
  - The spirit of Christmas: the 'spirit of Christmas' is the true message of Christianity.
  - Ignorance and want: the monstrous children are a warning of what will happen if society does not tackle poverty and improve education.
- *Jane Eyre*
  - Women's roles: Jane does not accept an inferior role. She is independent, determined and outspoken.
  - Integrity: Jane remains honest and true to herself, and is rewarded by true love.
- *War of the Worlds*
  - Science and technology: technology gives power to those who control it.
  - 'The other': do reactions to the Martians represent how we sometimes see other humans?
- *The Strange Case of Dr Jekyll and Mr Hyde*
  - Good and evil: Jekyll's attempts to separate the good and evil parts of himself are doomed to failure.
  - Secrets: Victorian London is not as respectable as it seems, but is full of dark secrets.

Key Point

Novels often focus on issues of personal morality, but they are also concerned with society as a whole.

How Themes are Presented

- Consider events in the novel:
  - In *Silas Marner* Silas loses his money but finds Eppie. The rest of the novel is about how these events change him.
  - The arrival of the Martians in *War of the Worlds* changes how people behave and how they look at the world.
- Narrators might discuss themes:
  - In *A Christmas Carol* Dickens uses his **authorial voice** to give us his views on social problems.
  - The opening lines of *Pride and Prejudice* tell us straightaway that the novel will be about courtship and marriage.
- Characters can embody themes:
  - Edward Hyde is evil personified.
  - The character of Bertha Rochester in *Jane Eyre* brings together themes of madness and duty.
- Characters discuss themes and **issues**:
  - Elizabeth in *Pride and Prejudice* discusses money, class, love and marriage with her sister Jane, and with Darcy, who has a quite different **perspective** on life.
  - Jane Eyre has lengthy discussions with other characters about emotions and morality.
- It can be helpful to look for **motifs** in a novel. A motif is an image, idea or situation that recurs through a work, suggesting a theme:
  - Silas Marner's gold represents everything that is wrong with his attitude to life.
  - Fire is a recurring motif in *Jane Eyre*, symbolising passion as well as moving on the story.
- **Settings** can encapsulate themes:
  - Scrooge's lodgings in *A Christmas Carol* reflect his solitary and mean nature, drawing our attention to themes of avarice and loneliness.
  - The London of *The Strange Case of Dr Jekyll and Mr Hyde* gives us a sense of the dark side of life.

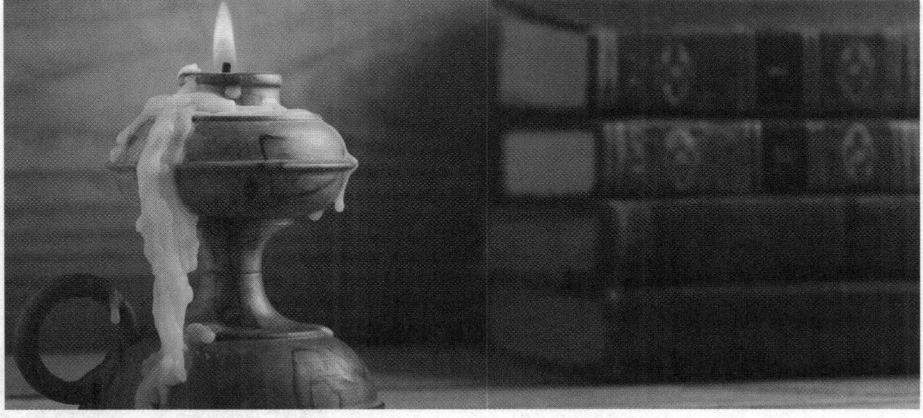

Key Point

A novel's themes emerge in many ways. Think about the themes of your novel. How do you know they are there?

Quick Test

1. Can a novel have more than one theme?
2. What is a motif?
3. Can a narrator discuss themes and ideas?
4. Can a writer give us differing perspectives on a theme?

Key Words

authorial voice
issue
perspective
motif
setting

Characters

You must be able to:

- Write about how characters are presented in a nineteenth-century novel.

Characters

- Your exam question might focus on a character.
- It could be about a character's personality:
  - Write about how Elizabeth Bennet changes during the novel.
- Or attitudes and feelings:
  - Write about how Stevenson conveys Jekyll's feelings about good and evil at different points in the novel.
- Or relationships:
  - Write about how Eliot presents Silas and Eppie's relationship at different points in the novel.

Protagonists

- When the protagonist is also the narrator, we are invited to share the character's thoughts and feelings.
- Jane Eyre and the narrator in *War of the Worlds* speak to the reader as if they are looking back over their past, sharing feelings and thoughts as well as experiences.
- The narrator in *War of the Worlds* could be seen as a **naive narrator**, as he does not understand what is going on. Jane Eyre is more perceptive, even though she does not fully understand everything she experiences.
- *Jane Eyre* is an account of growing up. This sort of novel is known by the German word **Bildungsroman**.
- Part of *The Strange Case of Dr Jekyll and Mr Hyde* is narrated by Jekyll, giving us some insight into his mind and a degree of empathy for him. In *War of the Worlds*, the main narrator passes on narratives by other characters about events that he himself has not witnessed.
- Although Elizabeth in *Pride and Prejudice* and Scrooge in *A Christmas Carol* do not tell their own stories, the writers give us access to their thoughts and feelings. However, the third-person narrative allows authors to stand aside and comment on their characters.

Key Point

Questions on character are most likely to be about the protagonists, but you should not neglect other characters.

Other Characters

- You could be asked to focus on other characters as individuals or as a group.
- Look at these in terms of:
  - their relationship to the protagonist: for example, Elizabeth Bennet's relationship with her sisters
  - their **function** in the novel, perhaps as a way of looking at themes: for example, Eliot's use of Eppie to present ideas about redemption.

– their significance in terms of plot: for example, Miss Havisham's influence on Pip's life.

How Characters are Presented

What They Say

- Characters who are also narrators have plenty to say about their ideas and feelings.
- Those who are not main narrators sometimes express themselves in letters.
- Characters reveal themselves in conversation with other characters. Sometimes this is by giving an opinion or expressing their feelings. Sometimes it is by the way they talk. Mr Collins, in *Pride and Prejudice*, reveals his snobbery by constantly referring to Lady Catherine de Burgh.

What the Narrator Says

- Narrators describe characters' personalities as well as their appearance. Jane Eyre describes Blanche Ingram as 'remarkably self-conscious'. We see her through Jane's eyes.
- In a third-person narrative, however, we can take comments on characters as being trustworthy and neutral, as when Stevenson describes Mr Utterson as having 'an approved tolerance for others'.
- A narrator might go further and describe a character's thoughts and feelings. Jane Austen often takes us into her characters' heads.

Key Point

Look for what one character says about another and think about what this tells you about both.

How They Act and React

- As in life, character is best seen through actions. In *Pride and Prejudice* Wickham charms everyone, including Elizabeth and the reader, but when he runs away with Lydia, we can all see him for what he is.
- Reactions are just as important. Darcy's reaction to the elopement of Lydia and Wickham makes Elizabeth and the reader see his true character.

Quick Test

1. Without looking at your novel or your notes, write down the names of as many characters as you can in 10 minutes.

Key Words

naive narrator
Bildungsroman
function
significance

Language and Structure

You must be able to:

- Analyse the use of language and structure in a nineteenth-century novel
- Use relevant terminology.

Structure

- *Jane Eyre* starts near the beginning of the protagonist's life and tells her story in chronological order. The novel starts at Gateshead (her aunt's house), moves to Lowood school, then Thornfield Hall, on to Moor House and back again to Thornfield. These places represent five stages in Jane's development.
- In *A Christmas Carol* each chapter (Stave) is devoted to a different spirit. Dickens uses the power of his spirits to introduce 'flashbacks' to Scrooge's past life and 'flash forwards' to show how things might turn out.
- In *Silas Marner* George Eliot uses a flashback to tell us about Silas's history, before jumping another 15 years to the point at which she started. She then jumps another 16 years between Part One and Part Two.
- *Pride and Prejudice* is written in chronological order but uses letters as a form of flashback, filling in details about events in London, for example, which have previously been kept from the reader.
- Stevenson uses multiple narratives in *The Strange Case of Dr Jekyll and Mr Hyde*. The third-person narrative focuses on Mr Utterson, the reader knowing only what he knows, until the events leading up to Jekyll's death are revealed in his own and Dr Lanyon's narratives.
- *War of the Worlds* is told in chronological order and divided into two distinct 'books'. The narrator uses his brother's experiences, told in the third person, to report things he could not have seen. He also reports the artilleryman's experience at some length, using direct speech.

Key Point

Although all stories follow more or less the same structure (see page 36), novelists arrange their narratives in very different ways.

The Narrative Voice

- Narrators in nineteenth-century novels always use Standard English. However, narratives can be very different in **tone**. In a first-person narrative this can reflect the character of the protagonist. In other novels, we can detect a distinctive authorial voice.
- Is your narrator's tone:
  - friendly?
  - **colloquial**?
  - **formal**?
  - **ironic**?
  - **authoritative**?

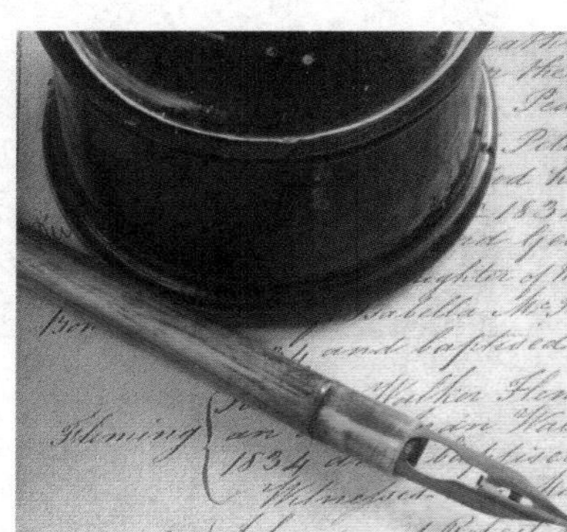

- As you are reading, do you feel the narrator is talking to you personally?
- In *A Christmas Carol* Dickens tells the story as if we were in a room with him.
- George Eliot frequently intervenes in the narrative. Some readers find her intrusions 'preachy'.
- Jane Austen's authorial voice is more detached – amused and ironic.

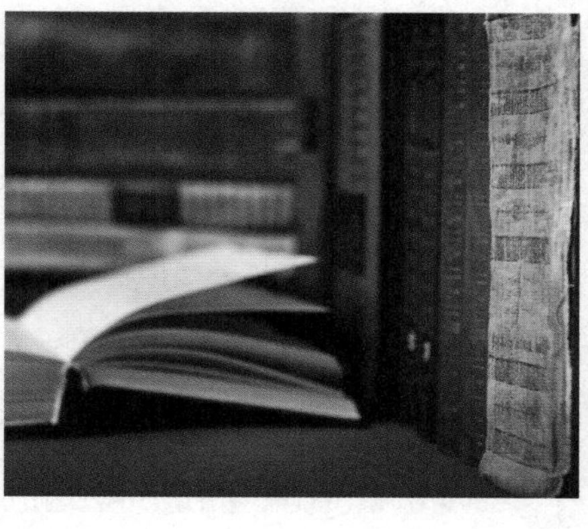

Speech

- Different characters can use language in different ways, adding to our understanding of them.
- They might:
  - use dialect or slang
  - use language in a comic way
  - have oddities or peculiarities of speech
  - use over-formal language
  - use language others might not understand.
- Dolly's language, in *Silas Marner*, tells us a lot about her. Her use of abbreviation ('Could it ha' been') and her pronunciation ('carril', 'erol') 'place' her in terms of social class and region, while her references to religion and her politeness help to build a picture of a kind-hearted, honest woman.
- In *War of the Worlds* the narrator is clearly at home using scientific and technological terms, helping to establish him as a knowledgeable and reliable witness.

Descriptive Language

- Novelists use techniques in the same way as poets do to create mood and atmosphere. You might find that your novelist uses:
  - detail
  - varied sentence structures
  - alliteration, assonance and onomatopoeia
  - imagery
  - symbolism.
- Stevenson uses detail to build a vivid picture of Soho, where Hyde lives.
- In *Jane Eyre*, Brontë's description of the chestnut tree is hugely **symbolic**.

Key Point

The question in the exam will include a short extract from your novel. You should analyse the language used in it in detail.

Quick Test

What is meant by the following terms?

1. Dialect
2. Colloquial
3. Symbol
4. Flashback

Key Words

tone
colloquial
formal
ironic
authoritative
symbolic

Review Questions

Answer the question on the text you have studied.

Write your answer on a separate piece of paper.

Your answer should be in note form, using bullet points.

1 J. B. Priestley: *An Inspector Calls*

How does Priestley write about attitudes to women in *An Inspector Calls*?

Write down five statements and give evidence from the text to support each statement. [10]

2 Willy Russell: *Blood Brothers*

How does Russell write about fate in *Blood Brothers*?

Write down five statements and give evidence from the text to support each statement. [10]

3 Alan Bennett: *The History Boys*

How does Bennett write about history in *The History Boys*?

Write down five statements and give evidence from the text to support each statement. [10]

4 Simon Stephens: *The Curious Incident of the Dog in the Night-Time*

How does Stephens explore ideas about families in *The Curious Incident of the Dog in the Night-Time*?

Write down five statements and give evidence from the text to support each statement. [10]

5 Shelagh Delaney: *A Taste of Honey*

How does Delaney present ideas about love in *A Taste of Honey*?

Write down five statements and give evidence from the text to support each statement. [10]

6 William Golding: *Lord of the Flies*

How does Golding explore ideas about civilisation in *Lord of the Flies*?

Write down five statements and give evidence from the text to support each statement. [10]

7 Kazuo Ishiguro: *Never Let Me Go*

How does Ishiguro write about friendship in *Never Let Me Go*?

Write down five statements and give evidence from the text to support each statement. [10]

8 Meera Syal: *Anita and Me*

How does Syal write about living in two cultures in *Anita and Me*?

Write down five statements and give evidence from the text to support each statement. [10]

9 Susan Hill: *The Woman in Black*

How does Hill write about the supernatural in *The Woman in Black*?

Write down five statements and give evidence from the text to support each statement. [10]

10 Jeanette Winterson: *Oranges are not the Only Fruit*

How does Winterson explore ideas about belonging in *Oranges are not the Only Fruit*?

Write down five statements and give evidence from the text to support each statement. [10]

Practice Questions

Answer the question on the novel you have studied.

Write your answer on a separate piece of paper.

1 Robert Louis Stevenson: *The Strange Case of Dr Jekyll and Mr Hyde*

In this extract, the murder of Sir Danvers Carew has been witnessed by a maid.

Read Chapter 4

From

When they had come within speech (which was just under the maid's eyes) the older man bowed and accosted the other with a very pretty manner of politeness.

To

And next moment, with ape-like fury, he was trampling his victim under foot and hailing down a storm of blows, under which the bones were audibly shattered and the body jumped upon the roadway.

Write about how Stevenson conveys a sense of horror in this extract, referring closely to the extract. [20]

2 Charles Dickens: *A Christmas Carol*

In this extract, two gentlemen have just asked Scrooge to make a contribution to charity to help the poor.

Read Stave (Chapter) 1

From

'Are there no prisons?' asked Scrooge.

To

'It's not my business', Scrooge returned. 'It's enough for a man to understand his own business, and not to interfere with other people's. Mine occupies me constantly. Good afternoon, gentlemen!'

Write about how Dickens presents Scrooge's attitude to other people in this extract, referring closely to the extract. [20]

3 Jane Austen: *Pride and Prejudice*

In this extract, Mr Darcy and his friend Mr Bingley are attending a ball at Meryton, where they meet the Bennet family.

Read Chapter 3

From

Elizabeth Bennet had been obliged, by the scarcity of gentlemen, to sit down for two dances; and during part of that time, Mr Darcy had been standing near enough for her to overhear a conversation between him and Mr Bingley, who came from the dance for a few minutes to press his friend to join it.

To

'You had better return to your partner and enjoy her smiles, for you are wasting your time with me'.

Write about how Mr Darcy is portrayed in this extract, referring closely to the extract. [20]

4 H.G. Wells: *War of the Worlds*

Write about how Wells presents ideas about how fear affects human beings at different points in the novel. [20]

In your answer you should:

- refer to the novel as a whole;
- show your understanding of characters and events in the novel;
- refer to the contexts of the novel.

5 George Eliot: *Silas Marner*

Write about the character and significance of Godfrey Cass in *Silas Marner*. [20]

In your answer you should:

- refer to the novel as a whole;
- show your understanding of characters and events in the novel;
- refer to the contexts of the novel.

6 Charlotte Brontë: *Jane Eyre*

Write about how Brontë presents Jane's feelings for Mr Rochester at different points in the novel. [20]

In your answer you should:

- refer to the novel as a whole;
- show your understanding of characters and events in the novel;
- refer to the contexts of the novel.

Review Questions

Answer the question on the novel you have studied.

Write your answer on a separate piece of paper.

1 George Eliot: *Silas Marner*

In this extract, Duncan Cass threatens to tell his father about his brother's secret marriage.

Read Chapter 3

From

The door opened, and a thick-set, heavy-looing young man entered, with the flushed face and the gratuitously elated bearing which mark the first stage of intoxication.

To

'You'll get a hundred pounds for me – I know you will.'

Write about how Eliot presents the Cass family in this extract, referring closely to the extract. [20]

2 H.G.Wells: *War of the Worlds*

In this extract the narrator sees the Martians' 'cylinder' for the first time.

Read Chapter 3

From

I found a little crowd of perhaps twenty people surrounding the huge hole in which the cylinder lay.

To

'Extra-terrestrial' had no meaning for most of the onlookers.

Write about the reactions of humans to the arrival of the Martians and how Wells presents them in this extract, referring closely to the extract. [20]

3 Charlotte Brontë: *Jane Eyre*

In this extract, Jane meets Mr Rochester for the first time.

Read Chapter 12

From

I was in the mood for being useful, or at least officious, I think, for I now drew near him again.

To

He looked at me when I said this; he had hardly turned his eyes in my direction before.

Write about Jane's feelings about Mr Rochester and how Brontë presents them in this extract, referring closely to the extract. [20]

4 Robert Louis Stevenson: *The Strange Case of Dr Jekyll and Mr Hyde*

Write about how Stevenson conveys an atmosphere of mystery and horror at different points in the novel.

In your answer you should:

- refer to the novel as a whole;
- show your understanding of characters and events in the novel;
- refer to the contexts of the novel. [20]

5 Charles Dickens: *A Christmas Carol*

Write about Scrooge's attitude to other people and how it is presented at different points in the novel.

In your answer you should:

- refer to the novel as a whole;
- show your understanding of characters and events in the novel;
- refer to the contexts of the novel. [20]

6 Jane Austen: *Pride and Prejudice*

Write about how Austen presents Mr Darcy and his 'pride' at different points in the novel.

In your answer you should:

- refer to the novel as a whole;
- show your understanding of characters and events in the novel;
- refer to the contexts of the novel. [20]

Mixed Exam-Style Questions

Write your answers on separate pieces of paper.

English Language

Reading

The following exam-style questions will help you to revise for Component 1: 20th Century Literature Reading and Creative Prose Writing.

Read carefully the passage below. Answer the five questions that follow it.

In this extract from 'Tickets, Please', D. H. Lawrence describes the trams of an English mining area, and the people who work on them, during the First World War.

There is in the Midlands a single-line tramway system which boldly leaves the county town and plunges off into the black, industrial countryside, up hill and down dale, through the long ugly villages of workmen's houses, over canals and railways, past churches perched high and nobly over the smoke and shadows, through stark, grimy cold little market-places, tilting away in a rush past cinemas and shops down to the hollow where the collieries are, then up again, past a little rural church, under the ash trees, on in a rush to the terminus, the last little ugly place of industry, the cold little town that shivers on the edge of the wild, gloomy country beyond. There the green and creamy coloured tram-car seems to pause and purr with curious satisfaction. But in a few minutes-the clock on the turret of the Co-operative Wholesale Society's Shops gives the time-away it starts once more on the adventure. Again there are the reckless swoops downhill, bouncing the loops: again the chilly wait in the hill-top market-place: again the breathless slithering round the precipitous drop under the church: again the patient halts at the loops, waiting for the outcoming car: so on and on, for two long hours, till at last the city looms beyond the fat gas-works, the narrow factories draw near, we are in the sordid streets of the great town, once more we sidle to a standstill at our terminus, abashed by the great crimson and cream-coloured city cars, but still perky, jaunty, somewhat dare-devil, green as a jaunty sprig of parsley out of a black colliery garden.

To ride on these cars is always an adventure. Since we are in war-time, the drivers are men unfit for active service: cripples and hunchbacks. So they have the spirit of the devil in them. The ride becomes a steeple-chase.[1] Hurray! We have leapt in a clear jump over the canal bridges – now for the four-lane corner. With a shriek and a trail of sparks we are clear again. To be sure, a tram often leaps the rails – but what matter! It sits in a ditch till other trams come to haul it out. It is quite common for a car, packed with one solid mass of living people, to come to a dead halt in the midst of unbroken blackness, the heart of nowhere on a dark night, and for the driver and the girl conductor[2] to call, 'All get off – car's on fire!' Instead, however, of rushing out in a panic, the passengers stolidly reply: 'Get on – get on! We're not coming out. We're stopping where we are. Push on, George.' So till flames actually appear.

The reason for this reluctance to dismount is that the nights are howlingly cold, black, and windswept, and a car is a haven of refuge. From village to village the miners travel, for a change of cinema, of girl, of pub. The trams are desperately packed. Who is going to risk himself in the black gulf outside, to wait perhaps an hour for another tram, then to see the forlorn notice 'Depot Only', because there is something wrong! Or to greet a unit of three bright cars all so tight with people that they sail past with a howl of derision. Trams that pass in the night.

This, the most dangerous tram-service in England, as the authorities themselves declare, with pride, is entirely conducted by girls, and driven by rash young men, a little crippled, or by delicate young men, who creep forward in terror. The girls are fearless young hussies.[3] In their ugly blue uniform, skirts up to their knees, shapeless old peaked caps on their heads, they have all the *sang-froid*[4] of an old non-commissioned officer. With a tram packed with howling colliers, roaring hymns downstairs and a sort of antiphony[5] of obscenities upstairs, the lasses are perfectly at their ease. They pounce on the youths who try to evade their ticket-machine. They push off the men at the end of their distance. They are not going to be done in the eye – not they. They fear nobody – and everybody fears them.

'Hello, Annie!'

'Hello, Ted!'

'Oh, mind my corn, Miss Stone. It's my belief you've got a heart of stone, for you've trod on it again.'

'You should keep it in your pocket,' replies Miss Stone, and she goes sturdily upstairs in her high boots.

'Tickets, please.'

---

[1] *steeple-chase* – a horse race over fences
[2] *conductor* – someone who sells tickets on a tram, bus or train
[3] *hussies* – cheeky or immoral girls
[4] *sang-froid* – coolness
[5] *antiphony* – singing in responses (usually in hymns)

1 **Read lines 1–7.**

List five things that the tram passes in these lines. [5 marks]

2 **Read lines 8–14.**

What impressions does the writer create of a journey on the trams in these lines? [5 marks]
You must refer to the language used in the text to support your answer.

3 **Read lines 15–23.**

How does the writer make these lines exciting and dramatic? [10 marks]

You should write about:

- what happens in these lines to build excitement and drama
- the writer's use of language and structure to create excitement and drama
- the effect on the reader.

You must refer to the text to support your answer.

4 **Read lines 24–31.**

How does the writer show the problems of travelling by tram in these lines? [10 marks]
You must refer to the language used in the text to support your answer.

5 **Read lines 29–41.**

'Towards the end of this passage, Lawrence writes about Annie and the other girl conductors as independent, tough and even heroic young women.'
How far do you agree with this view? [10 marks]

You should write about:

- your own thoughts and feelings about how Annie and the other conductors are presented here and in the passage as a whole
- how the writer has created these thoughts and feelings.

You must refer to the text to support your answer.

Writing

 **Either**

a) Write a story entitled 'The Journey'.

Or

b) Write about a time when you were alone in a strange place.

Or

c) Write a story that begins: 'As I turned the corner, I knew I would never return.'

Or

d) Write a story that ends 'I could see her waving, but I could not tell what she was thinking.'

[24 marks for content and organisation, 16 marks for technical accuracy; total 40]

Reading

The following exam-style questions will help you prepare for Component 2: 19th and 21st Century Non-fiction reading and Transactional/Persuasive Writing.

In this article for *The Times* (13 October 1982) Joyce Rackham discusses the problems caused by tourism in the Italian city of Florence.

FLORENCE: A city of dilemma

by Joyce Rackham

The bust of Benvenuto Cellini looks down sternly on the tourists littering the Ponte Vecchio. The younger ones loll – even sleep beneath him. Graffiti, although rarer than in the past, still scar some walls, and there is a very ugly souvenir stall. Yet the bridge is lined with fine shops, including jewellers whose best work follows Cellini's tradition of superb craftsmanship.

This scene reflects the dilemma of contemporary Florence – a matchless medieval city which has to stand up to the pressures, dirt and overcrowding of life in the 1980s.

Dr Silvio Abboni, a heart specialist who is also cultural assessor of the municipality, told me: 'We are victims of our big tourist boom. Florence was built as a fortress to withstand invaders. Now we must defend ourselves against too much mass tourism and potential speculators.'

Among his solutions are promoting itineraries off the beaten track, which will be published for visitors, as well as out of season attractions, both artistic and musical. He said that traffic jams could be intolerable in Florence and pointed to a new map showing plans to restrict car and bus parking and extend pedestrian precincts 'to allow city life to unfold in an orderly and pleasant manner'.

Dr Giorgio Chiarelli, Director of the Florence Tourist Board, said: 'We are a Renaissance city with about half a million inhabitants and an annual influx of around two million tourists.' He admitted that traffic pollution, litter and policing had been neglected, but said that this was changing.

Off-season tourism, with special art weekends from November to March, as well as extended shop and museum hours and more accommodation for young tourists, are intended to help ease pressures. The great Uffizi Gallery, the first public museum in the world, built by the Medici, celebrates its 400th anniversary this year. Professor Luciano Berti, its director since 1969, is also superintendent of the artistic and historic patrimony of Florence. 'Restoration is a continuous necessity and costs a great deal of money, and we don't have enough', he told me. 'We are most anxious that people see far more than the Uffizi. We cannot cope with a further growth of crowds. Since 1975 their volume has doubled.' He explained that dust from clothes and tramping feet, humidity from breath and wet clothes all have an adverse effect on paintings, many of which are now protected by glass. Crowd control measures are helping, as are the extended hours. Since August the Uffizi and most important museums, which used to close at 2pm, have been open until 7pm.

7 **a)** Name one sort of shop that can be found on the Ponte Vecchio. [1 mark]

b) Of what body is Dr Chiarelli the director? [1 mark]

c) Give one example of something which, according to Dr Chiarelli, has been neglected in Florence. [1 mark]

8 How does Joyce Rackham explain the 'dilemma' faced by the city of Florence? [10 marks]

You should comment on:

- what she says;
- her use of language and tone.

Mixed Exam-Style Questions

To answer the following questions, you will need to read the extract below, taken from *Pictures from Italy*, in which Charles Dickens describes his visit to Florence in the 1840s.

But, how much beauty of another kind is here, when, on a fair clear morning, we look, from the summit of a hill, on Florence! See where it lies before us in a sun-lighted valley, bright with the winding Arno, and shut in by swelling hills; its domes, and towers, and palaces, rising from the rich country in a glittering heap, and shining in the sun like gold!

Magnificently stern and sombre are the streets of beautiful Florence; and the strong old piles of building make such heaps of shadow, on the ground and in the river, that there is another and a different city of rich forms and fancies, always lying at our feet. Prodigious palaces, constructed for defence, with small distrustful windows heavily barred, and walls of great thickness formed of huge masses of rough stone, frown, in their old sulky state, on every street. In the midst of the city – in the Piazza of the Grand Duke, adorned with beautiful statues and the Fountain of Neptune – rises the Palazzo Vecchio, with its enormous overhanging battlements, and the Great Tower that watches over the whole town. In its courtyard – worthy of the Castle of Otranto[1] in its ponderous gloom – is a massive staircase that the heaviest waggon and the stoutest team of horses might be driven up. Within it, is a Great Saloon, faded and tarnished in its stately decorations, and mouldering by grains, but recording yet, in pictures on its walls, the triumphs of the Medici and the wars of the old Florentine people. The prison is hard by, in an adjacent court-yard of the building – a foul and dismal place, where some men are shut up close, in small cells like ovens; and where others look through bars and beg; where some are playing draughts, and some are talking to their friends, who smoke, the while, to purify the air; and some are buying wine and fruit of women-vendors; and all are squalid, dirty, and vile to look at. 'They are merry enough, Signore,' says the jailer. 'They are all blood-stained here,' he adds, indicating, with his hand, three-fourths of the whole building. Before the hour is out, an old man, eighty years of age, quarrelling over a bargain with a young girl of seventeen, stabs her dead, in the market-place full of bright flowers; and is brought in prisoner, to swell the number.

[1] *Castle of Otranto* – the setting of a popular Gothic horror story of the same name.

9 **a)** To what does Dickens compare the buildings as they shine in the sun? [1 mark]

b) According to Dickens, for what purpose were the palaces built? [1 mark]

c) Give an example of something the prisoners buy. [1 mark]

10 What do you think and feel about Dickens's experience of Florence? [10 marks]

You should comment on:

- what he tells the readers about what he saw in Florence;
- how he describes his reactions to what he saw.

You must refer to the text to support your comments.

To answer the following questions you will need to use both texts.

11 What are the main differences between the two descriptions of Florence? [4 marks]

12 Both texts are about Florence. Compare:

- how the writers feel about Florence;
- how they make their views clear to the reader. [10 marks]

You must use the text to support your comments and make it clear which text you are referring to.

Writing

13 'Travel might broaden the mind, but tourism is destroying some of the world's most beautiful places. It is time we put the good of the planet before our own pleasure.'

Write an article for a broadsheet newspaper in which you put your point of view on this statement.

[12 marks for content and organisation; 8 marks for technical accuracy; total 20 marks]

14 You have seen an advertisement in your local newspaper for a job as a travel guide. Write a letter applying for the job.

[12 marks for content and organisation; 8 marks for technical accuracy; total 20 marks]

Mixed Exam-Style Questions

English Literature

Shakespeare

The following exam-style questions will help you revise for English Literature Component 1.

Answer the question on the play you have studied.

15 ***Much Ado About Nothing***

Answer both parts a) and b).

Read the extract and answer the question below.

Here, Benedick approaches Beatrice after Hero has been rejected by Claudio.

Act 4 Scene 1

From

BENEDICK Lady Beatrice, have you wept all this while?

To

BEATRICE It is a man's office but not yours.

a) Look at how Benedick and Beatrice speak and behave here. How does Shakespeare present ideas about honour here? Refer closely to details from the extract to support your answer. [15 marks]

b) Write about how Shakespeare presents the relationship between Benedick and Beatrice at different points in the play. [20 + 5 marks for Spelling, Punctuation and Grammar]

16 ***Macbeth***

Answer both parts a) and b).

Read the extract and answer the question below.

Here, Macbeth has murdered Duncan, and has returned with the blood-stained daggers.

Act 2 Scene 2

From

LADY MACBETH Infirm of purpose!

To

LADY MACBETH I hear a knocking

At the south entry. Retire we to our chamber.

A little water clears us of this deed.

a) Look at how Macbeth and Lady Macbeth speak and behave here. What does this tell you about their relationship at this point in the play? Refer closely to details from the extract to support your answer. [15 marks]

b) Write about how Macbeth changes during the course of the play. [20 marks + 5 marks for SPG]

17 ***Romeo and Juliet***

Answer both parts a) and b).

Read the extract and answer the question below.

Here, Romeo has just seen Juliet for the first time.

Act 1 Scene 5

From

ROMEO O, she doth teach the torches to burn bright.

To

Did my heart love till now? Forswear it sight.

For I ne'er saw true beauty till this night.

a) How does this speech show an audience Romeo's love for Juliet at this point in the play? Refer closely to details from the extract to support your answer. [15 marks].

b) Write about how Shakespeare presents ideas about love and marriage in Romeo and Juliet. Write about the whole of the play. [20 marks + 5 marks for SPG]

Mixed Exam-Style Questions

18 ***The Merchant of Venice***

Answer both parts a) and b).

Read the extract and answer the question below.

Here, Portia, disguised as a man, pleads with Shylock to be merciful.

Act 4 Scene 1

From

PORTIA The quality of mercy is not strained.

To

And earthly power doth then show likest God's
When mercy seasons justice.

a) How does Shakespeare explore ideas about justice and mercy in this passage? Refer closely to details from the extract to support your answer. [15 marks]

b) Write about how Shakespeare presents Shylock as an outsider at different points in *The Merchant of Venice*. [20 marks + 5 marks for SPG]

19 ***Henry V***

Answer both parts a) and b).

a) Read the extract and answer the question below.

Act 2 Scene 2 *lines 162–178*

From

KING God quit you in his mercy! Hear your sentence.

To

Bear them hence.

a) Look at how King Henry speaks and behaves here. What does this reveal to an audience about his character? Refer closely to details from the extract to support your answer. [15 marks]

b) Write about how Shakespeare presents ordinary soldiers and their attitudes at different points in *Henry V*. [20 marks + 5 marks for SPG]

20 *Othello*

Answer both parts a) and b).

Read the extract and answer the question below.

Act 1 Scene 3 *lines 375-396, from*

From

IAGO Thus do I ever make my fool my purse:

To

I have't. It is engendered. Hell and night
Must bring this monstrous birth to the world's light.

a) Look at how Iago speaks and behaves here. What does this reveal to an audience about his character and motivation? Refer closely to details from the extract to support your answer. [15 marks]

b) Write about how Shakespeare presents Othello as a tragic hero at different points in the play. [20 marks + 5 marks for SPG]

Mixed Exam-Style Questions

Poetry

21 Answer part (a) and part (b)

a) Read the poem *Ozymandias* by Percy Bysshe Shelley. In this poem, Shelley explores idea about power and mortality. Write about the ways in which he presents these themes in this poem. [15 marks]

b) Choose **one** other poem from the anthology in which the poet writes about power.

Compare the presentation of power in your chosen poem to the presentation of power in *Ozymandias*. [25 marks]

In your answer to part (b) you should compare:

- the content and structure of the poems – what they are about and how they are organised;
- how the writers create effects, using appropriate terminology where relevant;
- the context of the poems, and how these may have influenced them.

Ozymandias by Percy Bysshe Shelley

I met a traveller from an antique land
Who said: Two vast and trunkless legs of stone
Stand in a desert. Near them on the sand,
Half sunk, a shatter'd visage lies, whose frown
And wrinkled lip and sneer of cold command
Tell that its sculptor well those passions read
Which yet survive, stamp'd on these lifeless things,
The hand that mock'd them and the heart that fed.
And on the pedestal these words appear:
'My name is Ozymandias, king of kings:
Look on my works, ye Mighty, and despair!'
Mothing beside remains. Round the decay
Of that colossal wreck, boundless and bare,
The lone and level sands stretch far away.

Post-1914 Prose/Drama

The following questions will help you prepare for English Literature Component 2.

Answer the question on the text you have studied.

22 J. B. Priestley: *An Inspector Calls*

Write about the character of Mr Birling and how he is presented in *An Inspector Calls*.

In your response you should:
- refer to the extract and the play as a whole
- show your understanding of the characters and events in the play. [35 marks + 5 marks for SPG]

Re-read Act 1 from

BIRLING: I'm delighted about this engagement and I hope it won't be too long before you're married.

to

MRS BIRLING: Arthur!

23 Willy Russell: *Blood Brothers*

Write how Russell uses the narrator in *Blood Brothers*.

In your response you should:
- refer to the extract and the play as a whole
- show your understanding of the characters and events in the play. [35 marks + 5 marks for SPG]

Re-read Act 1 from

NARRATOR: There's gypsies in the wood

to

NARRATOR: He's creeping down the hall.

24 Alan Bennett: *The History Boys*

Write about how Bennett presents Irwin as a teacher in *The History Boys*.

In your response you should:
- refer to the extract and the play as a whole
- show your understanding of the characters and events in the play. [35 marks + 5 marks for SPG]

Re-read Act 1 from

TIMMS: Where do you live, sir?

to

IRWIN: It's a performance. It's entertainment. And if it isn't, make it so.

Mixed Exam-Style Questions

25 Simon Stephens: *The Curious Incident of the Dog in the Night-Time*

Write about the character of Siobhan and how she is presented in *The Curious Incident of the Dog in the Night-Time*.

In your response you should:
- refer to the extract and the play as a whole
- show your understanding of the characters and events in the play. [35 marks + 5 marks for SPG]

Re-read Act 1 from

SIOBHAN: How are you today Christopher?

to

CHRISTOPHER: Will you help me with the spelling and the grammar and the footnotes?

26 Shelagh Delaney: *A Taste of Honey*

Write about how Delaney presents attitudes to sex in *A Taste of Honey*.

In your response you should:
- refer to the extract and the play as a whole
- show your understanding of the characters and events in the play. [35 marks + 5 marks for SPG]

Re-read Act 1 from

HELEN: You should have sewn some buttons on your pyjamas if you din't want me to see. Who give it to you?

to

JO: Where's your husband?

27 William Golding: *Lord of the Flies*

Write about how Golding uses symbols in *Lord of the Flies*.

In your response you should:
- refer to the extract and the novel as a whole
- show your understanding of the characters and events in the novel. [35 marks + 5 marks for SPG]

Re-read Chapter 2 from

He held the conch before his face and glanced round the mouth.

to

Ralph took the conch from his hands.

28 Kazuo Ishiguro: *Never Let Me Go*

Write about the character of Tommy and how he is presented in *Never Let Me Go*.

In your response you should:
- refer to the extract and the novel as a whole
- show your understanding of the characters and events in the novel. [35 marks + 5 marks for SPG]

Re-read Chapter 2 from

This was all a long time ago so I might have got some of it wrong;

to

...if it hadn't been for that encounter on the stairs, I probably wouldn't have taken the interest I did in Tommy's problems over the next several weeks.

29 Meera Syal: *Anita and Me*

Write about how Syal presents Meena's relationship with her parents in *Anita and Me*.

In your response you should:
- refer to the extract and the novel as a whole
- show your understanding of the characters and events in the novel. [35 marks + 5 marks for SPG]

Re-read Chapter 1 from

My humiliation had been compounded by the fact that Mama was an infants' teacher in the adjoining school;

to

He let go of my hand and walked back towards our house without looking back.

30 Susan Hill: *The Woman in Black*

Write about how Hill uses the character of Arthur Kipps in *The Woman in Black* to affect the reader's response to the story.

In your response you should:
- refer to the extract and the novel as a whole
- show your understanding of the characters and events in the novel. [35 marks + 5 marks for SPG]

Re-read the second chapter ('A London Particular') from

It was a Monday afternoon in November and already growing dark,

to

...I can feel the sensation in my ears, as though they had been stuffed with cotton.

Mixed Exam-Style Questions

31 Jeanette Winterson: *Oranges are not the Only Fruit*

Write about how Winterson presents the relationship between Jeanette and her mother in *Oranges are not the Only Fruit.*

In your response you should:

- refer to the extract and the novel as a whole
- show your understanding of the characters and events in the novel. [35 marks + 5 marks for SPG]

Re-read 'Exodus' from

'Why do you want me to go?' I asked her the night before.

to

And it was.

Nineteenth-Century Prose

Answer the question on the text you have studied. You should use the extract given and your knowledge of the whole novel to answer the question.

32 Charlotte Brontë: *Jane Eyre*

Write about how Brontë presents Jane as an outsider.

In your response you should:

- refer to the extract and the novel as a whole
- show your understanding of the characters and events in the novel
- refer to the contexts of the novel. [40 marks]

Re-read Chapter 2 from

'Unjust! – unjust!' said my reason, forced by the agonising stimulus into precocious though transitory power: and Resolve, equally wrought up, instigated some strange expedient to achieve escape from insupportable oppression – as running away, or, if that could not be effected, never eating or drinking more, and letting myself die.

to

It must have been most irksome to find herself bound by a hard-wrung pledge to stand in the stead of a parent to a strange child she could not love, and to see an uncongenial alien permanently intruded on her own family group.

33 Jane Austen: *Pride and Prejudice*

Write about how Austen presents Elizabeth's changing feelings towards Mr Darcy.

In your response you should:
- refer to the extract and the novel as a whole
- show your understanding of the characters and events in the novel
- refer to the contexts of the novel.

[40 marks]

Re-read Chapter 43 (Volume 3, Chapter 1) from

The housekeeper came; a respectable-looking, elderly woman, much less fine, and more civil, than she had any notion of finding her.

to

'Perhaps we might be deceived.'
'That is not very likely; our authority was too good.'

34 Robert Louis Stevenson: *The Strange Case of Dr Jekyll and Mr Hyde*

Write about how Stevenson uses Utterson to present 'the strange case'.

In your response you should:
- refer to the extract and the novel as a whole
- show your understanding of the characters and events in the novel
- refer to the contexts of the novel.

[40 marks]

Re-read Chapter 1 ('The Story of the Door') from

No doubt the feat was easy to Mr Utterson; for he was undemonstrative at the best, and even his friendship seemed to be founded in a similar catholicity of good-nature.

to

'Indeed?' said Mr Utterson, with a slight change of voice, 'and what was that?'

Mixed Exam-Style Questions

35 Charles Dickens: *A Christmas Carol*

Explore how Dickens writes about 'the spirit of Christmas'.

In your response you should:
- refer to the extract and the novel as a whole
- show your understanding of the characters and events in the novel
- refer to the contexts of the novel. [40 marks]

Re-read Chapter 3 ('The Second of the Three Spirits') from

'And how did little Tim behave?' asked Mrs Cratchit, when she had rallied Bob on his credulity and Bob had hugged his daughter to his heart's content.

to

'I see a vacant seat,' replied the Ghost, 'in the poor chimney-corner, and a crutch without an owner, carefully preserved. If these shadows remain unaltered by the Future, the child will die.'

36 H.G.Wells: *War of the Worlds*

Explore how Wells uses the Martian invasion to make readers think about how humans might react to oppressive power.

In your response you should:
- refer to the extract and the novel as a whole
- show your understanding of the characters and events in the novel
- refer to the contexts of the novel. [40 marks]

Re-read Book 2 Chapter 7 from

'Eh' he said with his eyes shining. 'I've thought it out, eh?

to

And I succumbed to his convictions.

37 George Eliot: *Silas Marner*

Write about how Eliot portrays faith and religion in *Silas Marner*.

In your response you should:
- refer to the extract and the novel as a whole
- show your understanding of the characters and events in the novel
- refer to the contexts of the novel. [40 marks]

Re-read Chapter 1 from

Silas was still looking at his friend.

to

In little more than a month from that time, Sarah was married to William Dane; and not long afterwards it was known to the brethren in Lantern Yard that Silas Marner had departed from the town.

Unseen Poetry

38 Read the two poems, 'The Man He Killed' by Thomas Hardy and 'The Next War' by Wilfred Owen. In both these poems the poets write about the experience of soldiers in war.

a) Write about 'The Man He Killed' and its effect on you. [15 marks]

You may wish to consider:

- what the poem is about and how it is organised
- the ideas the poet may have wanted us to think about
- the poet's choice of words, phrases and images and the effects they create
- how you respond to the poem.

The Man He Killed

by Thomas Hardy

'Had he and I but met
By some old ancient inn
We should have sat us down to wet
Right many a nipperkin!

'But ranged as infantry
And staring face to face,
I shot at him as he at me,
And killed him in his place.

'I shot him dead because –
Because he was my foe,
Just so: my foe of course he was;
That's clear enough; although

'He thought he'd 'list, perhaps,
Off-hand like – just as I –
Was out of work – had sold his traps –
No other reason why.

'Yes; quaint and curious war is!
You shoot a fellow down
You'd treat if met where any bar is,
Or help to half-a-crown.'

b) Now compare 'The Man He Killed' and 'The Next War'. [25 marks]

You should compare:

- what the poems are about and how they are organised
- the ideas the poets may have wanted us to think about
- the poets' choice of words, phrases and images and the effects they create
- how you respond to the poems.

The Next War

By Wilfred Owen

Out there, we've walked quite friendly up to Death,-
Sat down and eaten with him, cool and bland,-
Pardoned his spilling mess-tins in our hand.
We've sniffed the green thick odour of his breath,-
Our eyes wept, but our courage didn't writhe.
He's spat at us with bullets and he's coughed
Shrapnel. We chorussed when he sang aloft,
We whistled while he shaved us with his scythe.

Oh, Death was never enemy of ours!
We laughed at him, we leagued with him, old chum.
No soldier's paid to kick against His powers.
We laughed, -knowing that better men would come,
And greater wars: when each proud fighter brags
He wars on Death, for lives; not men, for flags.

Answers

Pages 6–15 Revise Questions

Page 7 Quick Test

1. no, where
2. It's
3. whether to
4. practice

Page 9 Quick Test

1. 'Where's my hamster?' Leo cried.
2. He had gone. There was no doubt about it.
3. Maureen, who lived next door, searched her bins.
4. Maureen's son found Hammy in the kitchen.

Page 11 Quick Test

1. d 2. a 3. b 4. c

Page 13 Quick Test

1. First – to give order.
2. On the other hand – to introduce a contrasting idea or point of view.
3. Before – to express passing time.
4. Therefore – to express cause and effect.

Page 15 Quick Test

1. Jay and I were put on detention.
2. I saw you on Saturday.
3. You were the best player we (ever) had.
4. After we had sung the first number, we did a dance.

Pages 16–17 Practice Questions

1. We **were** hoping for good **weather** for Sports Day. Unfortunately, on Friday morning it was **pouring** with rain. Luckily, by ten o'clock it was clear and sunny. I was very **excited** when I got to the stadium but I had a long **wait** for my race, the 200 **metres**. **There** were eight of us in the final. I was in the inside lane, **which** I don't usually like, but I ran well round the bend and was second **coming** into the straight. As I crossed the line I was neck and neck with Jo. It wasn't until the teacher congratulated me that I knew I had **definitely** won.
   [1 mark for each correct spelling – maximum 10]
2. **a)** Peter, who was the tallest boy in the class, easily won the high jump.
   b) 'What are you doing in the sand pit?' shouted Miss O'Connor. 'Get out of there at once!'
   c) Francesca won medals for the long jump, the high jump and the relay.
   d) I wasn't entered in any of the races because I'm hopeless at running.
   e) Jonathan finished last. However, he was pleased with his time.
   [1 mark for each sentence – maximum 5]
3. **a) i)** Julia stayed off school because she had a stomach ache.
   ii) He might be in the changing rooms or he might have already left.
   b) i) Michael, who has a really loud voice, announced the results.
   ii) The form with the best results won a cup, which was presented by Mr Cadogan.
   c) Maria, who had won the discus competition, went home early because she was feeling sick.
   [1 mark for each sentence – maximum 5]
4. **a)** Hayley and I are going to town tomorrow.
   b) You can come with us if you want to.
   c) We were very pleased with what we bought.
   d) I do not (don't) know anything about what they did at school.
   e) I am not truanting again because I want to get my GCSEs.
   [1 mark for each – maximum 5]
5. (1) As well as (2) As a result of (3) also (4) Consequently (5) However **[5]**
6. My first **experience [1]** of Bingley Park Library was when I was five. My grandmother, who **was [1]** an avid reader, **visited [1]** the library every week and always borrowed four books. She read more or less anything but she especially liked detective **stories [1]**, gardening books, and film **stars' [1] biographies [1]**. Naturally, she wanted the rest of her family to be as enthusiastic as she was about books. **[1]** Therefore, as soon as I could read, **she and I [1]** marched down to **B**ingley **P**ark **[1]**. It was an imposing and rather frightening edifice for a child of five. **[1]** The librarian, Miss Maloney, was just as imposing and twice as intimidating.
   [Maximum 10]

Pages 18–31 Revise Questions

Page 19 Quick Test

1. Openly stated.
2. Yes.
3. Yes.
4. No.

Page 21 Quick Test

1. The writer.
2. The reader.
3. No.
4. Yes.

Page 23 Quick Test

1. Yes.
2. Yes.
3. No.
4. No.

Page 25 Quick Test

1. Quotation and paraphrase.
2. Everything that is in the original text.
3. When it does not fit easily into the sentence.
4. Point Evidence Explanation (or exploration).

Page 27 Quick Test

1. Horse and oats.
2. Was munching.
3. Old.
4. On.
5. Thoughtfully.

Page 29 Quick Test

1. Personification.
2. Alliteration.
3. Simile.
4. Metaphor.

Page 31 Quick Test

1. b, c, d, a
2. a, d, c, b
3. c, a, b, d

Pages 32–33 Review Questions

1. **a)** except, accept
   b) effect, affect
   c) allowed, aloud
   d) right, write
   e) whose, who's
   [1 mark for each pair – maximum 5]
2. 'Don't you think we should wait for him?' asked Eve.
   'Not at all,' Henry replied. 'He never waits for us.'
   'Well, that's true,' Eve said, 'but he doesn't know the way.'
   [½ mark for each correct punctuation mark – maximum 10]
3. **This is a suggested answer only. There are other ways of doing it.**
   Henry and Eve waited for another ten minutes but Joel did not arrive, so they left without him and walked to the bus stop. There was no-one there, suggesting they had just missed the bus. Henry was very annoyed with Joel. However, Eve told him to calm down and forget about Joel. After an uneventful journey, they got off the bus by the lake, which looked eerie in the moonlight. Having sat down on a grassy bank, they took their sandwiches and drinks out of the bag. Henry felt a hand on his shoulder.
   [Maximum 10 marks]
4. b, d, f, h, i **[Maximum 5 marks]**
5. **a)** pizzas
   b) latches
   c) mosquitoes
   d) sheep
   e) donkeys
   f) stadia
   g) qualities
   h) churches
   i) women
   j) hypotheses
   [½ mark for each – maximum 5]
6. e, c, d, a, b **[Maximum 5 marks]**

Pages 34–35 Practice Questions

1.
   - He is old.
   - He is 'cold' within (unfeeling)
   - He has a pointed nose
   - His cheek is shrivelled
   - He walks stiffly ('his 'gait' is 'stiffened')
   - His eyes are red
   - His lips are thin and blue
   - He has a grating voice.
   - He has a wiry chin.

   [Maximum 5 marks]

2. **Look at the mark scheme below, decide which description is closest to your answer and then decide what mark to give it.**

Marks	Skills
5	• You have made accurate and perceptive comments about Scrooge. • You have analysed the effects of the choice of language. • You have used well-considered subject terminology accurately.
4	• You have given accurate impressions of Scrooge. • You have begun to analyse the choice of language. • You have used relevant subject terminology appropriately.

You might have commented on some or all of the following points:
- The first sentence starts with 'nobody' so we know Scrooge is not liked by others.
- His character stops people approaching him in the street.
- Even the dogs avoid him, showing an instinctive dislike/distrust.
- He is mean – the beggars assume he will not give to them.
- Children are wary/afraid of him.
- He does not socialise.
- He is associated with evil.
- Dickens uses a list of details to build up an unpleasant picture of Scrooge.

[Maximum 5 marks]

3. **a) One of:** Fleet Street; The Strand; Covent Garden **[1]**
   b) Wordsworth's company; Being with Wordsworth and his sister **[1]**
   a) Joy (happiness) **[1]**

4. **Look at the mark scheme below, decide which description is closest to your answer and then decide what mark to give it.**

Marks	Skills
4	• You have shown clear understanding of both texts. • You have synthesised evidence from texts. • You have used a range of relevant detail from both texts.
3	• You have shown some understanding of both texts. • You have shown clear connections between texts. • You have used relevant detail from both texts.

You might have included some or all of the following points:
- The writers have opposite views on the countryside.
- Weston is a 'city hater'.
- Lamb 'never wants to see a mountain' in his life.
- They are both careful not to insult people who disagree with them.
- Lamb likes things like 'crowded streets'.
- These are the things Weston hates, calling it 'dirty' and 'noisy'.
- Weston knows it is supposed to be exciting but does not find it so.

[Maximum 4 marks]

Pages 36–43 **Revise Questions**

Page 37 Quick Test
1. The beginning.
2. First.
3. The inciting incident.
4. One who knows everything.

Page 39 Quick Test
1. Simile.
2. Personification/pathetic fallacy.
3. Metaphor.
4. Literal imagery.

Page 41 Quick Test
1. The main character.
2. A character who opposes the protagonist.
3. Something that happens to get the story going.
4. An event that changes the direction of the story.

Page 43 Quick Test
1. George lived alone.
2. Like ancient gravestones.
3. skin was sun-baked/Love, loyalty/apparent affection.
4. His teeth were rarely seen.

Pages 44–45 **Review Questions**

1. **a)** Currer, Ellis and Acton Bell **[1]**
   b) They thought the publishers would be prejudiced against them **[1]**
   c) It was civil and sensible (polite)/they acted on the advice given. **[1]**
   [Maximum 3 marks]
2. **a)** Hard work and luck **[1]**
   b) One from Glasgow/Newcastle/Liverpool. **[1]**
   c) Winning a competition **[1]**
   [Maximum 3 marks]

3. **Look at the mark scheme below, decide which description is closest to your answer and then decide what mark to give it.**

Marks	Skills
4	• You have shown clear understanding of both texts. • You have synthesised evidence from texts. • You have used a range of relevant detail from both texts.
3	• You have shown some understanding of both texts. • You have shown clear connections between texts. • You have used relevant detail from both texts.

You might have included some or all of the following points:
- It took Brontë a long time to get published.
- She had to work out the 'puzzle' of why no-one was interested and seek advice.
- Fordyce was published quickly.
- Fordyce is often asked for advice by other poets.
- They had very different reactions to being female.
- Brontë had a 'vague impression' her sex would be a disadvantage, while Fordyce feels it is a positive thing.
- Fordyce performed her poetry and entered competitions, whereas Brontë just sent it off to publishers.

[Maximum 4 marks]

1. **Look at the mark scheme below, decide which description is closest to your answer and then decide which mark to give yourself.**

Marks	Skills
9-10	• You have made accurate and perceptive comments about the text. • You have given a detailed analysis of how the writer uses language to achieve effects. • You have chosen an appropriate range of examples. • You have used well-considered subject terminology accurately to support your comments.
7-8	• You have made accurate comments about the text. • You have begun to analyse how the writer uses language to achieve effects. • You have chosen appropriate examples. • You have used relevant subject terminology accurately to support your comments.

In your answer you might have made some of the following points:

- The setting is established immediately.
- The setting is rural but busy – the people are working hard.
- The 'barton' is a big building.
- It is early evening.
- The characters are able to talk while they work as the day comes to an end.
- They clearly are on friendly terms and know each other well.
- It seems to be a small community where people know each other's business.
- The cows are mentioned several times.
- Direct speech is used to give an impression of the people and their world as well as information.
- They talk in non-standard English, in a dialect that gives a sense of place and of their class.

[Maximum 10 marks]

2. **Look at the mark scheme below, decide which description is closest to your answer and then decide which mark to give yourself.**

Marks	Skills
9-10	• You have made accurate and perceptive comments about the text. • You have given a detailed analysis of how the writer uses language and the organisation of events (structure) to achieve effects. • You have chosen an appropriate range of examples. • You have used well-considered subject terminology accurately to support your comments.
7-8	• You have made accurate comments about how details are used. • You have begun to analyse how the writer uses language and the organisation of events (structure) to achieve effects. • You have chosen appropriate examples. • You have used relevant subject terminology accurately to support your comments.

In your answer you might have made some of the following points:

- Rhoda Brook is introduced as a 'thin fading woman'.
- She is a milkmaid, indicating her rural working-class background, but the writer's use of the phrase 'apart from the rest' suggests that she is somehow different.
- Perhaps she thinks she is better than the others or perhaps they look down on her.
- It may be a mixture of both, as the conversation between the milkers hints that she had a relationship with the farmer.
- The comment that the farmer's bride is 'years younger than she' is delivered as the speaker looks at Rhoda, suggesting contrast/connection.
- The reader is made to wonder why they should all look at Rhoda when talking about the bride.
- When the woman murmurs, 'Tis hard for she', it is clear that Rhoda's past must be connected to the farmer.
- Although they refer to her and look at her, the others do not include Rhoda in the conversation.
- Rhoda makes no attempt to join in so we do not know her feelings/ reaction.

3. **Look at the mark scheme below, decide which description is closest to your answer and then decide which mark to give yourself.**

Marks	Skills
9-10	• You have persuasively evaluated the text and its effects. • You have used convincing, well-selected examples from the text to explain your views. • Your response shows engagement and involvement, taking an overview and making comments on the text as a whole. • You have explored with insight how the writer has created thoughts and feelings.
7-8	• You have critically evaluated the text and its effects. • You have used well-selected examples from the text to explain your views. • Your response shows critical awareness and clear engagement with the text. • You have explored how the writer has created thoughts and feelings.

In your answer you may have made some of the following points:

- At first Rhoda Brook is seen as someone apart from the others.
- There is an air of mystery about her.
- We are not told her name for a while.
- She is obviously the subject of gossip and we might feel sympathy for her.
- Other characters acknowledge that the farmer's marriage must be difficult for her.
- She is introduced as a 'thin fading woman', contrasting with the young healthy bride.
- The writer tells us she also lives 'apart' from others, emphasising her solitary nature.
- The personification of the heath's 'dark countenance' suggests sadness and maybe mystery. This is reflected in Rhoda's nature and her situation.
- The revelation that she has a son by the farmer might increase sympathy.
- Her suggestion that he 'give her a look' suggests she is still interested in the farmer and what he does.
- However, we are given no indication of their feelings for each other, now or in the past.
- The contrast between Rhoda and the farmer's social class suggests this could be why he has not married her.

[Maximum 10 marks]

4. **Look at the mark scheme below, decide which description is closest to your answer and then decide which mark to give yourself. This task is marked for communication and organisation, and for technical accuracy.**

Communication and Organisation (maximum 24)

Marks	Skills
20-24	• Your writing is fully coherent and controlled. Plot and characterisation are developed with detail, originality and imagination. • Your writing is clearly and imaginatively organised. The narrative is sophisticated and fully engages the writer's interest. • You have used structure and grammatical features ambitiously to give the writing cohesion and coherence. • You have communicated ambitiously and consistently to convey precise meaning.
15-19	• Your writing is clear and controlled. Plot and characterisation show convincing detail, and some originality and imagination. • Your writing is clearly organised. The narrative is purposefully shaped and developed. • You have used structure and grammatical features to give the writing cohesion and coherence. • You have communicated with some ambition to convey precise meaning.

Vocabulary, sentence structure, spelling and punctuation (maximum 16)

Marks	Skills
14-16	• You have used appropriate and effective variations in sentence structure. • Virtually all your sentence construction is controlled and accurate. • You have used a range of punctuation confidently and accurately. • You have spelled almost all words, including complex and irregular words, correctly. • Your control of tense and agreement is totally secure. • You have used a wide range of appropriate, ambitious vocabulary to create precise meaning.
11-13	• You have used varied sentence structure. • Your sentence construction is secure. • You have used a range of punctuation accurately. • You have spelled most words, including irregular words, correctly. • Your control of tense and agreement is secure. • You have used a range of ambitious vocabulary with precision.

[Maximum 40 marks]

Pages 48–55 **Revise Questions**

Page 49 Quick Test

1. Biography.
2. Letter.
3. Diary.
4. Autobiography.

Page 51 Quick Test

2 (news report).

Page 53 Quick Test

1. To argue your point of view.
2. The governors.
3. Letter.

Page 55 Quick Test

1. Yours sincerely.
2. Yours faithfully.
3. Yours faithfully.
4. Yours sincerely.

Pages 56–57 **Review Questions**

1. **See table on p133 (for pp46-47 Practice Questions, Q1) for marks and skills.**
   You should have included some of the following points in your answer:
   - The writer wants to keep the reader curious about what has been discovered.
   - He 'distances' the death of Sir Charles by using Dr Mortimer to describe it.
   - The use of direct speech gives a sense of listening to an eye witness.
   - The sending of the servant to him creates a sense of urgency.
   - The discovery was made late at night.
   - The doctor speaks calmly and without excitement.
   - His position as a professional makes the evidence credible and, therefore, harder to explain.
   - The reference to 'no other footsteps' adds mystery.

   [Maximum 10 marks]
2. **See table on p.133 (for pp46-47 Practice Questions, Q2) for marks and skills.**
   You should have included some of the following points in your answer:
   - Until this point the doctor's description has been very calm.
   - He gives a detailed description of the body.
   - He describes its position without speculating on the reasons for it, leaving the reader to speculate.
   - The 'fingers dug into the ground' suggest violence and fear.
   - The face is 'convulsed with some strong emotion', again suggesting fear but the word 'some' keeps it vague.
   - He says he could barely recognise the body.
   - His position as a professional makes the evidence credible and, therefore, harder to explain.
   - The apparent absence of physical injury is mysterious.
   - Barrymore's 'false statement' about footprints raises the question of why he would lie.
   - Holmes's simple questions delay the revelation that they are the prints of a 'gigantic hound', something unexpected and unnatural.
3. **See table on p131 (for pp46-47 Practice Questions, Q3) for marks and skills.**
   You should have included some of the following points in your answer:
   - We are not told anything about the doctor's character, but the fact that he is a professional, scientific man implies he is a reliable witness.
   - This is confirmed by his suspicion that Sir Charles's illness was 'chimerical', suggesting he is not easily convinced of things.
   - He describes how he 'checked and corroborated' the evidence from the inquest, implying that he is both thorough and independent-minded.
   - The fact that he has done this, and the careful and detailed description he gives, make the reader more inclined to accept his story than if it had been told in a sensational way.
   - The use of direct speech gives us the story from his own point of view.

   [Maximum 10 marks]
4. **Look at the mark scheme above (for pp46-47 Practice Questions, Q4) decide which description is closest to your answer and then decide which mark to give yourself. This task is marked for communication and organisation, and for technical accuracy.**

1. **Look at the mark scheme below, decide which description is closest to your answer and then decide which mark to give yourself.**

Marks	Skills
9-10	• You have made accurate and perceptive comments about a wide range of different examples from the text. • You have given a detailed analysis of how the writer uses language and structure to achieve effects and influence readers. • You have used subject terminology accurately to support your comments.
7–8	• You have made accurate comments about a range of different examples from the text. • You have begun to analyse how the writer uses language and structure to influence readers. • You have used subject terminology to support your comments.

You should have included some of the following points in your answer:
- She is 'saddened' making her feelings clear at the start.
- Dislikes the term 'purse pets' and the coverage given to them.
- Uses rhetorical questions.
- Argues that it is not cruel to keep them.
- Says that dogs are dependent on humans and need to be looked after.
- Compares owners of small dogs favourably with those who train dogs to fight.
- Uses an informal tone (abbreviations).
- Acknowledges that the argument is personal and she herself has a small dog.
- Uses anecdotes about celebrities to give a positive argument.

[Maximum 10 marks]

2. **Look at the mark scheme below, decide which description is closest to your answer and then decide which mark to give yourself.**

Marks	Skills
9-10	• You have given a persuasive evaluation of the text and its effects. • You have supported your evaluation with convincing, well selected textual references. • You have shown engagement and involvement, taking an overview of the text to make perceptive comments.
7–8	• You have given a critical evaluation of the text and its effects. • You have supported your evaluation with well selected textual references. • You have shown clear awareness and critical engagement with the text.

You should have included some of the following points in your answer:
- The writer is responding to a fashion which he considers cruel and demeaning to dogs.
- He uses rhetorical devices to express strong opinions.
- He associates love of dogs with being English.
- He sees dogs as noble and sees attempts to breed small dogs as immoral.
- He wants us to feel sorry for the small dogs.
- Some might think his descriptions thought-provoking; others might think them exaggerated and unfair.

[Maximum 10 marks]

3. **Look at the mark scheme below, decide which description is closest to your answer and then decide which mark to give yourself.**

Marks	Skills
9-10	• You have made comparisons that are sustained and detailed. • You have shown clear understanding of the methods used to convey ideas.
7-8	• You have made detailed comparisons. • You have made valid comments on how the ideas are conveyed.

You should have included some of the following points in your answer:
- Both these writers are very passionate about their subject.
- The 'Times' writer attacks those who breed small dogs by making the dogs sound like victims ('all eyes and nerves') but also calls them 'pampered'.
- Hanlon picks up on this but cannot see what's wrong with pampering – she sees it as a sign of love.
- Her tone is chatty and personal, while his is impersonal and authoritative.

[Maximum 10 marks]

4. **Look at the mark scheme below, decide which description is closest to your answer and then decide which mark to give yourself. This task is marked for communication and organisation, and for technical accuracy.**

Communication and Organisation (maximum 12)

11-12	• Your writing shows sophisticated understanding of the purpose and format of the task. • Your writing shows sustained awareness of the reader/intended audience. • You have used an appropriate register, confidently adapted to purpose/audience. • Your content is ambitious, pertinent and sophisticated. • Your ideas are convincingly developed and supported by a range of relevant details.
8-10	• Your writing shows consistent understanding of the purpose and format of the task. • Your writing shows secure awareness of the reader/intended audience. • You have used an appropriate register, consistently adapted to purpose/audience. • Your content is well-judged and detailed. • Your ideas are organised and coherently developed, supported by relevant details.

Vocabulary, sentence structure, spelling and punctuation (maximum 8)

8	• You have used appropriate and effective variations in sentence structure. • Virtually all your sentence construction is controlled and accurate. • You have used a range of punctuation confidently and accurately. • You have spelled almost all words, including complex and irregular words, correctly. • Your control of tense and agreement is totally secure. • You have used a wide range of appropriate, ambitious vocabulary to create precise meaning.
6-7	• You have use varied sentence structure. • Your sentence construction is secure. • You have used a range of punctuation accurately. • You have spelled most words, including irregular words, correctly. • Your control of tense and agreement is secure. • You have used a range of vocabulary with precision.

[Maximum 20 marks]

Pages 60–67 **Revise Questions**

Page 61 Quick Test

1. False.
2. False.
3. False.
4. True.

Page 63 Quick Test

1. Soliloquy.
2. Dialogue.
3. Plot.
4. Theme.

Page 65 Quick Test

1. False.
2. False.
3. True.
4. True.

Page 67 Quick Test

1. Metaphor/rhetorical question.
2. Oxymoron.
3. Rhetorical question.
4. Rhyming couplet.

Pages 68–69 **Review Questions**

1. **Look at the mark scheme on p135 (for pp58-59 Practice Questions, Q1), decide which description is closest to your answer and then decide which mark to give yourself.**
   Your answer should include some of the following points:
   - Most of the passage is a quite straightforward account of the walk, which is what you would expect from a diary entry.
   - It is written in the first person and past tense and just describes what she saw.
   - She often uses simple sentences ('The lake was rough'), and fragments ('A few primroses by the roadside').
   - She does not always used complete sentences ('Saw the plough…') which makes it seem like she's writing notes for herself.
   - The effect of this is to make it seem fresh and immediate.
   - When she describes the daffodils she uses more 'literary' language, personifying them: they 'rested their heads' and 'reeled and danced'.
   - She describes nature in great detail – 'The hawthornes are black and green' – so you can picture it.
   - The simple sentence 'I never saw daffodils so beautiful' emphasises her strong feelings.

   [Maximum 10 marks]
2. **Look at the mark scheme on p135 (for pp58-59 Practice Questions, Q3), decide which description is closest to your answer and then decide which mark to give yourself.**
   Your answer should include some of the following points:
   - Wordsworth seems to be writing for herself, reflecting on her day, whereas Betsy is very aware of her audience.
   - Betsy uses hyperbole, 'complete washout' and 'like the workhouse', for comic effect.
   - She writes in a colloquial way, as she might talk to her friends – 'ropes and stuff'.
   - She also describes other members of the party in a critical yet amusing way (the Camp Commandant…with her whistle round her neck'), while Wordsworth makes no comment about her companions.
   - While Wordsworth clearly gets a lot of pleasure from observing nature, Betsy hates walking round the lake.
   - Wordsworth's writing is serious and descriptive, not saying much about her feelings, but Betsy only thinks about herself.

   [Maximum 10 marks]
3. **Look at the mark scheme on p135 (and above) (for pp58-59, Practice Questions, Q4), decide which description is closest to your answer and then decide which mark to give yourself. This task is marked for communication and organisation, and for technical accuracy.**
   [Maximum 20 marks]

Pages 70–71 **Practice Questions**

For questions 1-3, look at the mark scheme below, decide which description is closest to your answer and then decide which mark to give yourself.

Marks	Skills
13-15	• You have sustained focus on the task, including an overview, and conveyed your ideas consistently and coherently. • You have approached the text sensitively and analysed it critically. • You have shown a perceptive understanding of the text, engaging with a personal response and some originality. • You have included pertinent quotations from the text. • You have analysed and appreciated the writer's use of language, form and structure. • You have used precise subject terminology appropriately.
10-12	• You have sustained focus on the task, including an overview, and conveyed your ideas coherently. • You have approached the text thoughtfully. • You have shown a secure understanding of key aspects of the text, with considerable engagement. • You have included well-chosen quotations from the text. • You have discussed and increasingly analysed the writer's use of language, form and structure. • You have used subject terminology appropriately.

[Maximum 15 marks]

Your answers could include some of the following points:

1. *Romeo and Juliet*
   - Juliet's impatience with the nurse – references to time.
   - Use of the soliloquy.
   - Her thoughts jumping about – use of caesura.
   - Personification of love.
   - Allusions to classical mythology.
   - Contrast of old and young – her belief that the old cannot understand.
   - Imagery of light and dark.
   - Her dependence on the nurse, reflecting social context.
2. *Macbeth*
   - He sees power as good and desirable – 'happy prologues'.
   - He uses a metaphor of music to express how he sees things developing.
   - He immediately has doubts because of the source of the prophecy.
   - Use of the soliloquy.
   - Use of rhetorical questions.
   - The 'horrid' image is the idea of killing the king to gain power.
   - The prophecy has a physical effect on him.
   - Use of sibilance to convey physical state.
3. *Henry V*
   - His immediate reaction is calm and amused.
   - He develops the metaphor of the tennis balls, turning it against the Dauphin.
   - He stresses his status as king, using 'we'.
   - There is a change of tone as he shows anger.
   - Use of rhetorical language, e.g. repetition.

For questions 4-6, look at the mark scheme below, decide which description is closest to your answer and then decide which mark to give yourself.

Marks	Skills
17-20	• You have sustained focus on the task, including an overview, and conveyed your ideas consistently and coherently. • You have approached the text sensitively and analysed it critically. • You have shown a perceptive understanding of the text, engaging with a personal response and some originality. • You have included pertinent quotations from the text. • You have analysed and appreciated the writer's use of language, form and structure. • You have used precise subject terminology appropriately.
13-16	• You have sustained focus on the task, including an overview, and conveyed your ideas coherently. • You have approached the text thoughtfully. • You have shown a secure understanding of key aspects of the text, with considerable engagement. • You have included well-chosen quotations from the text. • You have discussed and increasingly analysed the writer's use of language, form and structure. • You have used subject terminology appropriately.

[Maximum 20 marks]
These questions are also marked for spelling, punctuation and grammar.

Marks	Performance Descriptors
4-5	• You have spelled and punctuated with consistent accuracy. • You have consistently used vocabulary and sentence structure to achieve effective control of meaning.
2-3	• You have spelled and punctuated with considerable accuracy. • You have consistently used a considerable vocabulary and sentence structure to achieve general control of meaning.

[Maximum Marks 5]
Your answers could include some of the following points:

4. *The Merchant of Venice*
   - She is his only daughter and only family.
   - He is protective to the point of locking her up – his main fear is that she marries a gentile.
   - There is no evidence of any affection between them.
   - When she elopes he seems more concerned with the money she has stolen than with her.
   - Her giving of the ring for a monkey indicates how little respect she has for him.
   - The audience's sympathies might change.
5. *Othello*
   - Differences in age and race – the opposition of her father.
   - Her admiration of him and his wooing with stories.
   - Her innocence and naivety.
   - His growing jealousy.
   - How Iago manipulates his feelings.
   - Their deaths and how love leads to tragedy.
6. *Much Ado About Nothing*
   - She is not married and is ambiguous about being single.
   - She is witty and opinionated and happy to express her opinions to men.
   - She does not like being told what to do – but the less assertive Hero can trick her.
   - She has a strong sense of justice and family loyalty.
   - She is dependent on her uncle.
   - She marries but on her own terms.

Pages 72–81 **Revise Questions**

Page 73 Quick Test
1. False. 2. False. 3. True. 4. True.

Page 75 Quick Test
1. Yes. 2. Two. 3. Yes. 4. No.

Page 77 Quick Test
1. Onomatopoeia. 2. Personification. 3. Alliteration. 4. Persona.

Page 79 Quick Test
1. Rhyming couplet. 2. Internal rhyme. 3. Ballad. 4. Free verse.

Page 81 Quick Test
1. Similarity. 2. Difference. 3. Difference. 4. Similarity.

Pages 82–83 **Review Questions**

For mark scheme, see p136 (and above) (pp70-71 Practice Questions, Q1-6). Your answers could include some of the following points.

1. *Othello*
   - They have defied convention and prejudice by marrying.
   - As the husband, Othello takes control.
   - She cannot see the point of being married if she does not live with her husband.

- She uses religious language to describe their love.
- She has fallen in love with his reputation as a soldier.
- Desdemona, unusually, takes the lead in the conversation.
- She shows herself to be determined and assertive when necessary.

2. *Much Ado About Nothing*
   - Beatrice's tone is light-hearted and jokey, although she is talking about a serious matter.
   - The extract is written is prose.
   - She feels that she is different – 'Thus goes everyone in the world but I'.
   - She flirts with Don Pedro, making a joke from the double meaning of 'get' to imply that she would like to marry him.
   - When he asks 'Will you have me, lady?' she makes another joke to show she is not serious.
   - She uses the metaphor of clothes to express the difference in status between her and Don Pedro.
   - She tries to avoid a serious conversation by saying she does not take things seriously – 'born to speak all mirth and no matter'.
   - The last line sums up her ambiguous attitude to life.
3. *The Merchant of Venice*
   - It would seem that Shylock is anxious about Jessica as he had asked for news of her.
   - However, when Tubal gives his news, he is more concerned about the money she has spent than her whereabouts.
   - This is what the Elizabethan audience might expect from a Jew. Modern audiences might think such a stereotype was anti-Semitic.
   - The dramatic exclamation (using a metaphor) 'Thou stick'st a dagger in me' suggests pain.
   - His attention is soon taken by news about Antonio and he uses violent language to show his delight.
   - The revelation about the ring changes our perception again. Shylock cares for his wife's memory, even if Jessica does not.
   - The monkey reflects the animal imagery throughout the play.
4. *Romeo and Juliet*
   - Romeo's love for Juliet can be compared to his feelings for Rosaline.
   - Juliet is taken by surprise by her feelings for Romeo.
   - Their use of a sonnet suggests mutual love.
   - Religious imagery could show the love to be sacred or could suggest it is sacrilegious.
   - In spite of her age, Juliet takes control and makes conditions, wanting to be sure.
   - Both have confidants to share their feelings with.
   - Constant references to 'the stars' suggest their tragedy is inevitable.
   - Although the audience's sympathies are with the couple, some could feel they are in the wrong when they defy their parents.
5. *Macbeth*
   - Macbeth starts off loyal and happy with his status, but the meeting with the witches gives him ideas.
   - The award of the title 'Thane of Cawdor' comes without his seeking it, so he feels he might be able to let fate take its course.
   - His soliloquies show us he is ambitious for power but has a conscience.
   - He gives all the reasons for not killing Duncan and seizing power.
   - Lady Macbeth taunts him and pushes him into killing Duncan.
   - When he gains power he cannot enjoy it because of his conscience and his feelings of vulnerability.
   - He commits more and more terrible acts to keep power, abuses power and ruins his country.
6. *Henry V*
   - Henry is the rightful, anointed king.
   - He is clever politically, e.g. using the Dauphin's insult as an excuse to invade France.
   - He seeks the approval of the church for his actions.
   - He is an effective war leader, planning well and leading from the front.
   - He uses rhetoric to inspire loyalty and affection.

Pages 84–85 **Practice Questions**

1. **a)** First person
   b) Present.
   c) They make us feel as if he is sharing his thoughts and feelings with us.
   d) Among the trees, not stated exactly where. Could be at any time.
   e) Six stanzas of equal length, each of four lines.
   f) It makes it seem as if the hawk is in control and his thoughts are ordered and calm.
   g) It is powerful, solitary bird of prey. It is powerful and violent. It could represent powerful people.
   h) The powerful depend on violence and fear. They do not admit doubt or opposition. They like being in control and know they are right.
   i) 'Creation' and 'foot' are both repeated in the third stanza. The repetition emphasises the importance of what he is saying and his determination to get it across. It draws attention to his arrogance.
   j) It shows the simplicity of his thoughts. Life is straightforward for him. It is as if he is explaining things in simple terms to someone who might not understand what he is saying. It asserts control.
   [2 marks for each point]
2. **a)** First person – includes both singular and plural, as well as the second person singular.
   b) Present.
   c) It is about personal feelings, addressed to the person she shares them with.
   d) To express love to a loved one.
   e) It is a Petrarchan or Italian sonnet, divided into an eight-line octave and a six-line sestet.
   f) It shows the intensity of her love.
   g) Her love is there all time, whether in the day ('sun') or night ('candlelight').
   h) People she loved who have died.
   i) She believes in God and she believes that her love will live on after death.
   j) Her love is very powerful/ it is almost obsessive/ it has changed her life/ it makes her happy.
   [2 marks for each point]
3. **a)** A persona. An old mother.
   b) In a house, probably in a poor rural area, during the course of a day.
   c) Yes. There are four stressed syllables per line, though the number of unstressed syllables varies. The regularity could reflect the routine of her day. In spite of her hard life, it gives the poem a cheerful tone.
   d) Yes. It is in rhyming couplets, regular and simple, reflecting a regular and simple life.
   e) Mostly, it is literal, describing what she sees, though the fire could be taken as a metaphor for life and the stars are personified as they 'blink and peep'.
   f) It is the story of an ordinary old woman's day and her life.
   g) Fire could be a symbol of life. Growing feeble and then cold is an image for old age.
   h) Old age. A woman's role. Death. Work. Envy of the young.
   i) He feels sympathy for the old woman. He sees life as pointless. He is saddened by the passing of time.
   j) All answers are valid.
   [2 marks for each point]

Pages 86–93 **Revise Questions**

Page 87 Quick Test

1. True. **2.** True. **3.** False. **4.** True.

Page 89 Quick Test

All of them.

Page 91 Quick Test

1. Protagonist.
2. Narrator.
3. Dialogue.
4. Stage direction.

Page 93 Quick Test

1. Yes.
2. An act.
3. Where he/she comes from.
4. No.

Pages 94–95 Review Questions

1. **For both parts of the question, look at the mark scheme below, decide which description is closest to your answer and then decide which mark to give yourself. Mark part a) out of 15 and part b) out of 25**

Marks	Skills
13-15 21-25	• You have sustained focus on the task, including an overview, and conveyed your ideas consistently and coherently. • You have approached the text sensitively and analysed it critically. • You have shown a perceptive understanding of the text, engaging with a personal response and some originality. • You have included pertinent quotations from the text. • You have analysed and appreciated the writer's use of language, form and structure. • You have used precise subject terminology appropriately. • You have shown an assured understanding of the relationships between texts and the contexts in which they were written. • (part b) only) You have made critical and illuminating comparisons throughout. • (part b) only) There is a wide ranging discussion of the similarities and differences.
10-12 16-20	• You have sustained focus on the task, including an overview, and conveyed your ideas coherently. • You have approached the text thoughtfully. • You have shown a secure understanding of key aspects of the text, with considerable engagement. • You have included well-chosen quotations from the text. • You have discussed and increasingly analysed the writer's use of language, form and structure. • You have used subject terminology appropriately. • You have shown a secure understanding of the relationships between texts and the contexts in which they were written. • (part b) only) You have made focussed and coherent comparisons throughout. • (part b) only) There is a clear discussion of the similarities and differences.

[Maximum 40 marks]

a) **Your answer might include:**
- The voice is that of a soldier going to war.
- He writes in the future tense.
- Focuses on dying and what it means in war.
- Seems at ease with the idea of dying.
- Sense of patriotism.
- Emotional and perhaps sentimental.
- Literal imagery of nature.
- Idealisation of England.

b) **Your answer is likely to use 'The Manhunt', 'Dulce et Decorum Est', 'A Wife in London' or 'Mametz Wood' for comparison. It might include:**
- Ideas about who is affected by conflict and how – soldiers, relatives, civilians.
- Comparisons dealing with soldiers during and after the conflict.
- Use of language, such as alliteration.
- Comparison of the poems' structure.
- Use of imagery and descriptions of nature.
- Description of suffering.
- Attitudes to death in war.
- The tone of the poems.
- When they were written, which wars inspired them and how they reflect different attitudes to wars.
- The use of the speaker to explore ideas and context.

2. a) **There are 15 marks for part a) and 25 marks for part b) (the comparison). Look at the mark scheme above, decide which description is closest to your answer and then decide which mark to give yourself.**
Your answer to part a) might include comments on:
   - Clare's entirely positive view of nature.
   - Repetition of 'I love'.
   - Use of the sonnet form for a poem about nature.
   - Hope and joy brought about by the season.
   - Use of personification.
   - Listing of all aspects of nature – animals, plants, the weather.
   - The idea of nature being 'happy' and at 'play'.
   - The lack of punctuation, giving a sense of freedom.
   - Use of alliteration and onomatopoeia to create sounds – 'rustle like a wind shook wood'.

[Maximum 15 marks]
Your answer to part b) might include comments on:
- Differing attitudes to nature.
- Difference in focus on one creature / all nature.
- Presence of speaker.
- Use of imagery.
- Use of rhyme.
- Use made of techniques such as alliteration.
- Differences in structure.

[Maximum 25 marks]

Pages 96–97 Practice Questions

Give yourself two marks for each valid point supported by appropriate evidence. The points below are just suggestions. There are many other valid points to be made.

1. *An Inspector Calls*
   - He comes from the 'future' so has the benefit of hindsight.
   - He acts like a real detective, trying to solve a crime.
   - However, he seems more interested in the other characters' attitudes to Eva – and is it really a crime that would be investigated?
   - He is the mouthpiece for the writer, with his speech about the 'future'.
   - He is an outsider.
   - He sometimes shows his impatience with the responses he gets.
2. *Blood Brothers*
   - She is middle-class and well-off.
   - In spite of her money, she is not happy because she cannot have a baby.
   - It is her idea to take one of the babies.
   - She seems to be aware that it will end tragically once Eddie meets Mickey.
   - Her wanting to get away from Mickey looks like snobbery but she is frightened of the secret getting out.
   - She has mental health problems, maybe as a result of the secret.
   - Her actions precipitate the tragic outcome.
3. *The History Boys*
   - He could be seen as the leader of the group – others look up to him.
   - He is sexually active and has an amoral attitude to sex.
   - He is aware of his own attraction and quite vain – he uses it to bestow favours.
   - His language can be very crude but he can also be eloquent.
   - He does not understand why he is attracted to Irwin – although he himself sees everything in sexual terms, it is probably something else.
   - He can adapt easily from one teacher's ways to another's.
   - He realises that he enjoys having power and using it.
4. *The Curious Incident of the Dog in the Night-Time*
   - He is the protagonist. It is the story of him growing up.
   - He is 'different'. Many people would call him 'autistic' but this is not specifically mentioned.
   - He takes things literally and speaks mostly of facts. He does not describe or speculate.
   - The audience knows only what he knows, so we discover things with him.
   - He proves to himself and others that he can cope, but in his own way.
   - Is he the victim or the cause of his family's problems?
5. *A Taste of Honey*
   - She is the protagonist. It is her story.
   - Her relationship with her mother is central – there is an element of role-reversal in it.

- In some ways she is mature for her age and in others naive.
- She might be seen as typical of a girl of her age and class at the time, but her circumstances are unusual.
- She is witty and honest, and shows signs of creativity.
- She is motivated by not wanting to be like her mother.
- Through her eyes we see a world that is generally quite prejudiced and repressive, but she is not part of it.

6. *Lord of the Flies*
   - Simon is inherently good, the opposite of Jack.
   - He is gentle, and kind to the little 'uns.
   - He has the same sort of background as the other boys but, in his case, morality and civilisation are not superficial.
   - He sees what the 'beast' means.
   - His hallucinations are almost mystical and holy.
   - His murder represents the ultimate triumph of evil and savagery.
   - He can be seen as a sacrificial victim, perhaps like Jesus.
7. *Never Let Me Go*
   - Tommy is shown from the start to be different from the others.
   - His fits of temper and lack of 'creativity' mark him out from the others.
   - He does not actively rebel but he does not seem able to conform.
   - For most of the novel Kathy does not understand his attitude but (unlike Ruth) she listens to him.
   - Kathy describes what she sees rather than what she hears when she describes his tantrums.
   - Tommy is interested in finding out about the 'gallery' and other aspects of Hailsham before Kathy is.
   - Like the others, his value to society is only as a donor – but he inspires friendship and love in Kathy.
8. *Anita and Me*
   - Anita, as the title suggests, is the focus of the novel, though not the protagonist.
   - She could be seen as an antagonist, in some ways the opposite of Meena.
   - The changes in Meena's attitude to her show that Meena is growing up.
   - She represents the white working-class culture of Tollington, which the child Meena is part of and yet not part of.
   - Her troubled family helps to make her more sympathetic.
   - She is a leader, looked up to by other children.
   - Her association with Sam brings the community's racism into focus.
9. *The Woman in Black*
   - His position as a lawyer and his careful, thorough manner suggest he is a reliable narrator.
   - In the first chapter he tells us how his experiences have changed him.
   - Emphasises his scepticism but has a sense of adventure.
   - He does not want to appear weak or superstitious: he tries to ignore 'hints' about Eel Marsh House.
   - He is romantic, sensitive and sympathetic.
10. *Oranges are not the Only Fruit*
    - She can be seen as the antagonist.
    - Her presence dominates the novel.
    - Her faith is strong, evangelical and genuine.
    - Everything she says and does is informed by her religion.
    - She has plans for Jeanette and makes her what she is.
    - Her attitude to sex and sexuality.
    - The narrator's feelings about her and what she stands for.

Pages 98–105 **Revise Questions**

Page 99 Quick Test

1. False. **2.** False. **3.** True. **4.** True.

Page 101 Quick Test

1. Yes.
2. An image or idea that recurs in a text.
3. Yes.
4. Yes.

Page 103 Quick Test

No definitive answer – check with your notes/text.

Page 105 Quick Test

1. A variation of English spoken in a particular region.
2. The language of conversation.
3. An object that represents an idea or feeling.
4. Part of the story that takes place at an earlier time.

Pages 106–107 **Review Questions**

Give yourself two marks for each valid point supported by appropriate evidence. The points below are just suggestions. There are many other valid points to be made.

1. *An Inspector Calls*
   - At the time the play is set, women did not have the vote.
   - Eva, the working-class woman, represents different things in different people's eyes. Their ideas of her are shaped by gender as well as class.
   - Mrs Birling fulfils the expected role of a middle-class wife, sitting on committees and giving to charity.
   - Sheila seems to do little but shop and get engaged – but she finds a voice at the end.
   - There is a double standard in terms of sexual morality.
   - The female characters are strong and opinionated.
2. *Blood Brothers*
   - By starting with a tableau of the end, Russell shows the tragedy is inevitable.
   - Mrs Johnstone is very superstitious: for example, she reacts angrily to seeing shoes put upon the table.
   - Mrs Lyons does not believe in superstitions at first but becomes obsessed by trying to escape from fate.
   - The narrator speaks about fate.
   - The characters might think their lack of choice is because of fate, but is it the consequence of their actions?
   - Or is it the result of economics and politics?
3. *The History Boys*
   - Double/triple meaning in title – are the boys making history as well as studying history? Could this have happened only in the past?.
   - As far as the head teacher is concerned, the subject itself is not important. He just wants them to make the school look good.
   - Mrs Lintott's approach to history is conventional and designed to equip pupils to pass exams.
   - Irwin wants them to question everything – a different way of looking at history.
   - However, Irwin's approach is also about passing exams – just different exams. He knows what they want.
   - Irwin's idea that there is 'no need to tell the truth' can be applied to history, politics and to life in general.
   - Irwin ends up playing a part in history as a political adviser.
4. *The Curious Incident of the Dog in the Night-Time*
   - Christopher's family is shown as being unusual, as he lives with his widowed father. Like Christopher, the audience would probably admire his father.
   - Our perceptions are changed when we find Ed has lied and Judy is alive.
   - We learn this when Christopher does, through the sympathetic character of Mrs Alexander.
   - Christopher's relationships with his parents are difficult as he does not like physical contact and does not express emotion. He does not realise this is a problem.
   - We see the strain this has put on his parents in different ways.
   - Judy's letters give a nostalgic account of a happier family, as well as explaining her point of view about the difficulties of family life.
5. *A Taste of Honey*
   - Helen is not interested in love. She is described as a 'semi-whore' and marries Peter for a comfortable life.
   - Jo's relationship with the Boy seems romantic, especially because of his race.
   - Jo does not seem to be too bothered about his not coming back. Perhaps because of her background, she has no idea of long-term relationships.
   - The only relationship that seems loving is with her homosexual friend Geof. Maybe she cannot connect love and sex.
   - The central relationship is that between Jo and Helen – a 'love–hate' relationship.
   - Jo's relationships are all unconventional for the time, but the play is part of the fashion for 'kitchen sink drama', trying to show 'real life' on the stage.
6. *Lord of the Flies*
   - The boys' background – British, public school – suggests they are the epitome of Western civilisation, so their descent into savagery is shocking.
   - They seek organisation and order at first, but they are constructing an idea of order.

- Strong leadership emerges in the form of Jack, showing that the idea of 'leadership' as a force for good is misplaced.
- Civilisation is a thin veneer. Given the opportunity, our instincts are to be savage, even evil.
- The beast acts a symbol of savagery.
- The breakdown of 'civilisation' on the island is no worse than the wars being fought by the apparently civilised world.

7. *Never Let Me Go*
   - The novel centres on Kathy's friendship with Ruth and Tommy, seen through her eyes.
   - Friendship may be more important to them because they do not have families.
   - Their friendships are in many ways like those of any teenagers and young adults, but they are more intense because of their being kept apart.
   - Friendships often turn into sexual relationships. People want to be part of a couple.
   - Kathy notices in the Cottages that behaviour is often copied from television programmes. This might cast doubt on whether any of the clones really do have feelings for each other.
   - The relationship between carer and donor is a form of friendship – Kathy is allowed to choose her donors.
8. *Anita and Me*
   - Meena's family is a novelty in Tollington. As there are no other non-white children, Meena keeps her culture separate.
   - Differences in culture are shown in dress and in food. Meena's mother and Mrs Worrall cook in completely different ways.
   - The cultures are differentiated by language.
   - Meena wants to belong and acts like the other children, exaggerating her accent to be accepted.
   - There is an element of class difference as well as ethnic difference. Meena's family are well educated and middle-class.
   - The visit of Nanima brings Meena closer to her Punjabi culture. She is protective of her grandmother and, by implication, her culture.
   - Meena becomes aware of racism as she matures. When the novel ends she moves away from Tollington and further into her Punjabi culture.
9. *The Woman in Black*
   - The narrator is initially unwilling to believe in the supernatural.
   - The remote locations and the descriptions of landscape and weather create atmosphere.
   - The reactions of local people suggest the presence of the supernatural.
   - Arthur's attempts to rationalise his experiences are unsuccessful.
   - Arthur comes to understand what is happening but has no power against evil forces
10. *Oranges are not the Only Fruit*
   - Being adopted sets Jeanette apart from others.
   - Her mother sees her as a possession, a gift from God.
   - The church gives Jeanette a sense of identity, but her religion sets her apart from other children.
   - The stories of Perceval and Winnet express her need to belong.
   - Her lesbianism results in her being rejected by her church and family.
   - She seems to embrace being different from others.

Pages 108–109 Practice Questions

Look at the mark scheme below, decide which description is closest to your answer and then decide which mark to give yourself.

Marks	Skills
17-20	• You have sustained focus on the task, including an overview, and conveyed your ideas consistently and coherently. • You have approached the text sensitively and analysed it critically. • You have shown a perceptive understanding of the text, engaging with a personal response and some originality. • You have included pertinent quotations from the text. • You have analysed and appreciated the writer's use of language, form and structure. • You have used precise subject terminology appropriately. • You have shown an assured understanding of the relationship between the text and the context in which it was written.
13-16	• You have sustained focus on the task, including an overview, and conveyed your ideas coherently. • You have approached the text thoughtfully. • You have shown a secure understanding of key aspects of the text, with considerable engagement. • You have included well-chosen quotations from the text. • You have discussed and increasingly analysed the writer's use of language, form and structure. • You have used subject terminology appropriately. • You have shown a secure understanding of the relationship between the text and the context in which it was written.

[Maximum 20 marks]

Your answers could include some of the following points:

1. *The Strange Case of Dr Jekyll and Mr Hyde*
   - The extract is in the third person but is seen through the eyes of a maid, distancing it from the narrator.
   - At first the meeting seems innocent and normal.
   - The old man has a 'pretty manner' and 'an innocent and old-world kindness', contrasting with the cruelty of the attacker.
   - There is some mystery about why he has 'accosted' Hyde in the street and why, if he is asking the way, he is pointing.
   - The mention of Hyde's name halfway through alerts the reader to what might happen.
   - The violence builds over a few sentences – from impatiently playing with the cane, to brandishing the cane 'like a madman', to attacking him with the cane.
   - The horror of the attack is underlined by the way he carries on with the attack.
   - The expression 'ape-like fury' makes him seem inhuman.
2. *A Christmas Carol*
   - The extract shows Scrooge refusing to give to charity.
   - His questions show that he thinks the poor are being taken care of and it is none of his business.
   - The replies of the gentleman tell us, as well as Scrooge, how other people are concerned, in contrast with Scrooge.
   - The gentleman mentions 'Christian cheer', reminding us that caring about others is central to Christianity.
   - Scrooge says, 'I wish to be left alone', implying that he is generally solitary and not interested in others.
   - His manner is abrupt and a bit aggressive.
   - His language is quite extreme and shocking, suggesting people should die and 'decrease the surplus population'. He does not think of people as individuals – just statistics.
   - At the end he sets out his philosophy, using the double meaning of 'business' to show both that money is the most important thing for him and that he does not think people like the gentleman should be concerned with others.
3. *Pride and Prejudice*
   - The incident is seen through the eyes of Elizabeth, who overhears it, so the impression we get is the same as hers.
   - The conversation is a private one with his friend, so we can take it to be his true feelings.
   - He is contrasted with Bingley, who is enjoying dancing and is very sociable.

- The fact that he 'detests' dancing suggests he is not much fun, but adding that he has to be 'acquainted' with his partner suggests he does not, like most people, use dancing to meet people.
- The phrase 'such an assembly as this' makes him sound very snobbish and is an insult to the other people there.
- Austen uses Bingley to confirm this impression, calling him 'fastidious'.
- Their judgement of the girls' beauty differs sharply, again to the advantage of Bingley, who finds them 'pleasant' and 'pretty'.
- When Bingley suggests he dance with Elizabeth, Darcy shows himself to be bad-mannered as well as snobbish. The adverb 'coldly' sums up his attitude.
- He damns Elizabeth with faint praise, calling her 'tolerable; but not handsome enough to tempt me', asserting his sense of his own superiority.

4. *War of the Worlds*
   - The first person narrator describes events as he sees them, creating suspense.
   - He has prior knowledge of astronomy and of what has happened on Mars.
   - There is a sense of scientific curiosity about his reaction and he uses scientific terminology, as if writing an academic paper.
   - There is a sense of calm, with none of the fear or panic of later chapters.
   - The other onlookers are also curious, treating it as a day out.
5. *Silas Marner*
   - At the beginning Godfrey's story is separate from Silas's. They come together later.
   - Godfrey's decisions are influenced more by status than by morality.
   - He is portrayed sympathetically and we are given access to his thoughts.
   - He is weak and irresponsible.
   - Eliot is critical of his reliance on luck to get him out of trouble and his reluctance to deal with his problems.
   - He cannot understand why Eppie would not want to be adopted by him.
6. *Jane Eyre*
   - Brontë builds an air of mystery about Rochester before Jane meets him.
   - Their first meeting is dramatic and, while he seems strong, it is she who helps him.
   - The relationship between employer and governess is an odd one. She is neither a servant nor a member of the family.
   - Jane disapproves of a lot of what she sees and hears but accepts Rochester's account of himself.
   - Jane and Rochester both seem to 'earn' each other's love.
   - The fire and the discovery of Blanche turn her world upside down. She has been lied to and betrayed.
   - The first-person narrative allows us to share only Jane's knowledge of Rochester and her feelings about him.
   - Symbolism and imagery are important – fire, the chestnut tree, etc.
   - Rochester's blindness might signify that he can finally see the truth.
   - At the end Jane is in control. It is as if she needs Rochester to be weakened in order to truly love him.

Pages 110–111 **Review Questions**

For mark scheme, see p141 (pp108-109 Practice Questions). Your answers could include some of the following points.

1. *Silas Marner*
   - Godfrey reacts to Dunsey with 'an active expression of hatred'.
   - Dunsey is just as antagonistic, his dislike increased by Godfrey being the elder and more favoured brother.
   - While Godfrey is described as good-natured and well-meaning, Dunsey is sarcastic and a lazy drunk.
   - They are both dependent on their father. Godfrey is worried about his reactions.
   - It is clear that Dunsey has the upper hand in the relationship. He knows Godfrey's secret and is using it to blackmail him.
2. *War of the Worlds*
   - Initially humans are not afraid of the Martians, which leads them into danger.
   - Lack of fear, combined with ignorance, can mean lack of action.
   - Fear is contagious.
   - Some people help each other but most become selfish and even violent.
   - Fear causes some people to act irrationally. Others, like the narrator, think logically.
   - The curate questions his faith and goes mad; the narrator kills the curate to save himself.
   - The narrator and the artilleryman face their fears and plan for the future.
3. *Jane Eyre*
   - Jane comes to his aid. Although he is the master and she the servant, because of his fall he is in a weak position.
   - Jane is the narrator, so we see what she sees and she shares her feelings with us.
   - Her first description of him is plain and unemotional, giving facts about what he is wearing, how tall he is etc., except that his eyes are 'ireful and thwarted', which might suggest his temperament.
   - She does not fall for his looks but points out that he is not handsome or young and, from the point of view of someone writing about her younger self, mocks her own 'theoretical reverence' for such things.
   - She concentrates on what he is not rather than what he is, building an idea of an atypical hero.
   - At the same time she sees this as something they have in common, because she sees herself as unattractive.
   - It is paradoxical that his frown and roughness 'set me at my ease'.
   - Fire and lightning might be associated with passion. Does she want to avoid sexual passion?
4. *The Strange Case of Dr Jekyll and Mr Hyde*
   - Descriptions of London are central. It is a city of wealth and poverty side-by-side.
   - Most events take place in the dark or half-light.
   - The multiple narratives mean that the story is 'distanced' from us. Truth is revealed gradually.
   - The sealed letters add suspense because we know they might contain answers.
   - Many elements are typical of the Gothic tradition.
   - Lots of characters have secrets or do things that are not fully explained.
   - The narrators, Mr Utterson and Dr Lanyon, are logical, professional men, so they are sceptical. If they are afraid, it must be something awful.
   - The physical descriptions of Hyde make him seem almost animal-like.
5. *A Christmas Carol*
   - Scrooge is introduced with a description of his appearance, using imagery, and of how strangers react to him.
   - In the first chapter, he is seen as having no interest in family, through his conversation with his nephew.
   - He expresses his feelings about charity and caring for others in his conversation with the charitable gentlemen.
   - All these encounters are written in quite a comic way, with Dickens as narrator commenting on Scrooge's absurdity.
   - The Ghost of Christmas Past is used to show how Scrooge became like he is, making him think about what might have been and gaining some sympathy for him.
   - The Ghost of Christmas Present takes the idea of 'other people' beyond family and acquaintances, showing Scrooge that he cannot cut himself off from the world.
   - The Ghost of Christmas Yet to Come shows the result of his attitudes.
   - Other characters are used as a contrast with Scrooge, showing love and the 'spirit of Christmas' – his nephew, the Cratchits, Mr Fezziwig.
6. *Pride and Prejudice*
   - Darcy is mostly seen through Elizabeth's eyes. If he is proud, she is prejudiced.
   - His first appearance shows him to be snobbish and unsociable, in contrast with his friend Mr Bingley.
   - Society is very class-conscious. Darcy and Lady Catherine de Burgh are the highest-status characters in the novel. Her attitudes are seen as being shared by him, though it turns out he is not really as snobbish.
   - Some of his 'pride' could be reserve – perhaps the result of his social class or of his own nature.
   - Those who know him best do not see him as proud, while those who criticise him, like Wickham, are not reliable.
   - He is concerned about his reputation and that of his family, which can be seen as proud.
   - His actions, especially with regard to Wickham, show his true nature.
   - In his letter to Elizabeth he admits he did not want Bingley to marry Jane because of the 'connection' but claims this was not because of class but because of the way other family members behaved. Is this pride?

English Language Component 1

Section A

1. **Any five from:**
   - ugly villages of workmen's cottages
   - canals
   - railways
   - churches
   - market places
   - cinemas
   - shops
   - collieries (mines)
   - ash trees

   [5]
2. **Look at the mark scheme on p132 (pp34-35 Practice Questions, Q2), decide which description is closest to your answer and then decide what mark to give it. Your answer should include some of the following points:**
   - The tram pauses in the town and appears happy.
   - It is an 'adventure'.
   - It goes quickly downhill ('reckless swoops').
   - It is cold when the tram stops at the top of the hill.
   - It 'slithers' round the steep drop.
   - It has to keep stopping.
   - It is a long journey (nearly two hours).
   - The journey ends in the city.
   - The city seems sordid. In contrast, the tram is 'jaunty' and fresh.

   [Maximum 5 marks]
3. **Look at the mark scheme on p133 (pp46-47 Practice Questions, Q2), decide which description is closest to your answer and then decide what mark to give it. Your answer should include some of the following points:**
   - The writer writes at first as if he is explaining something to us.
   - Uses the present tense, describing in detail something that is happening now.
   - The phrase 'the spirit of the devil' makes us think of evil.
   - The descriptions of darkness and flames might also have connotations of hell and damnation.
   - There is a sense of excitement in the extended metaphor of the horse race.
   - The metaphor of 'steeplechase' makes the tram seem like a living thing and the experience like being on a horse.
   - There is a contrast between the 'blackness' and 'heart of nowhere', which sound ominous, and the cheerful speech of the people.
   - The paragraph ends with a comic contrast between the danger of the fire and the passengers' down-to-earth colloquial reaction: 'We're stopping where we are. Push on, George.'
   - The writer moves from the general to the particular; from describing the trams as something exotic and fantastical to telling us about particular people on them.

   [Maximum 10 marks]
4. **Look at the mark scheme on p133 (pp46-47, Practice Questions, Q1), decide which description is closest to your answer and then decide which mark to give yourself. Your answer should include some of the following points:**
   - The mood changes at the start of the paragraph 2 with 'the reason for this', which leads into an account of what the trams are actually used for.
   - This contrasts with the fantastical imagery of the first paragraph.
   - He gives the reason for the passengers' behaviour: the bleak weather, which he uses three adjectives to describe.
   - In contrast the tram is 'a haven of refuge'.
   - He mentions that the trams are overcrowded, using hyperbole in the adverb 'desperately'.
   - He continues with hyperbole as he speaks of the 'risk' of going into the 'black gulf' as if it were a life and death situation.
   - At the start of the fourth paragraph he gives a general description of drivers.
   - They are either 'rash young men' or 'delicate': none sound like safe drivers.

   [Maximum 10 marks]
5. **Look at the mark scheme on p133 (pp46-47), Practice Questions, Q3), decide which description is closest to your answer and then decide which mark to give yourself. Your answer should include some of the following points:**
   - The girls are introduced to us as 'fearless young hussies', implying that they do not behave in the way expected of women at the time.
   - He goes on to compare them to non-commissioned officers.
   - Coupled with a description of their unflattering uniform, this may not sound complimentary, but the tone of the description suggests admiration and respect.
   - 'Sang-froid' suggests coolness under pressure.
   - The writer tells us that they are 'rash' and bold. They find their jobs exciting.
   - They are 'perfectly at their ease' when their passengers are shouting and swearing, showing they are not easily shocked or upset.
   - They 'pounce' on youths, suggesting they are like cats or birds of prey: aggressive and in command.
   - The last sentence of paragraph 4 states quite clearly that they are fearless but feared.
   - The short snatch of dialogue at the end shows us Annie interacting with a passenger. She is friendly but blunt with him.
   - The description of her going upstairs 'sturdily' and her 'high boots' reflects her strong character and the idea that she is in charge.

   [Maximum 10 marks]
6. **Look at the mark scheme on p134 (pp46-47, Practice Questions, Q4), decide which description is closest to your answer and then decide which mark to give yourself. This task is marked for communication and organisation, and for technical accuracy.**

   [Maximum 40 marks]
7. **a)** A jewellers or a souvenir stall **[1]**
   b) The Florence Tourist Board **[1]**
   c) Traffic pollution or litter or policing **[1]**
8. **Look at the mark scheme on p135 (pp58-59, Practice Questions, Q1), decide which description is closest to your answer and then decide what mark to give it. Your answer should include some of the following points:**
   - She starts by describing the scene at the Ponte Vecchio.
   - She states what the problem is in a short second paragraph.
   - She uses the words of three local experts to explain the problem.
   - She stresses their expertise by using their titles (Dr and Professor).
   - She reports possible solutions put forward by them.
   - She stresses the history and art of the city and its importance.
   - She contrasts the beauty of the old city with aspects of 1980s life such as pollution and graffiti.
   - She does not put forward a strong personal point of view.

   [Maximum 10 marks]
9. **a)** gold **[1]** **b)** defence **[1]** **c)** wine or fruit **[1]**
10. **Look at the mark scheme on p135 (pp58-59, Practice Questions, Q2), decide which description is closest to your answer and then decide what mark to give it. Your answer should include some of the following points:**
    - In the first paragraph, Dickens uses images of light and richness to describe Florence: 'bright...glittering...like gold!'
    - His exclamations and his use of the second person ('we') make us feel his wonder as if we were there with him.
    - In the second paragraph, he moves into the city and his language reflects both the atmosphere and the architecture.
    - He personifies the buildings, describing 'distrustful windows' and saying they 'Frown, in their old sulky state'.
    - He describes both the beauty of the city, which the tourist sees, and the unpleasant side.
    - He wants to experience more than tourists usually do.
    - He describes the prison as 'squalid' and 'dirty'.
    - He seems fascinated by the more sordid and violent aspects of life in the city.
11. **Look at the mark scheme on p130 (pp44-45, Review Questions, Q3), decide which description is closest to your answer and then decide what mark to give it. Your answer should include some of the following points:**
    - Both writers say the city is beautiful.
    - Dickens describes the view from outside the city and then the centre.
    - Rackham describes tourist places, like the Ponte Vecchio, but says tourists are 'littering' it and also mentions graffiti and 'a very ugly souvenir stall'.
    - Dickens does not say anything about other tourists.

- While Rackham focuses on problems facing the city, Dickens is most interested in the prison and the life of the 'blood-stained' inmates.

[Maximum 4 marks]

12. **Look at the mark scheme on p135 (pp58-59, Practice Questions, Q3), decide which description is closest to your answer and then decide what mark to give it. Your answer should include some of the following points:**
    - Dickens is writing about his personal experience of Florence and the effect it had on him, whereas the purpose of Rackham's article is to examine the 'dilemma' of a city dependent on tourists being ruined by 'mass tourism and potential speculators'.
    - Dickens uses hyperbolic, poetic images to describe the city 'shining in the sun like gold' but also 'stern and sombre'.
    - Rackham starts almost by imitating Dickens as she describes a statue looking 'sternly', but for her this implies a judgement on the tourists, and from then her focus is not on describing the city but on the issues.
    - He describes the 'magnificent' city in detail, whereas she just sketches in a few details about the shops on the Ponte Vecchio.
    - They both look at negative aspects. Dickens contrasts the prison, which is 'foul and dismal' with the 'glittering' city. Rackham writes about the graffiti and pollution spoiling the city.
    - Rackham gives the opinions of others to explain what is happening, while Dickens just describes what he sees.

    [Maximum 10 marks]

13 and 14. Look at the mark scheme on p135-136 (pp58-59, Practice Questions, Q4), decide which description is closest to your answer and then decide which mark to give yourself. These tasks are marked for communication and organisation, and for technical accuracy.

[Maximum 40 marks (20 for each question)]

15–20 For part a) of all questions, look at the mark scheme for Qs 1-3 on pages 70-71, decide which description is closest to your answer and then decide which mark to give yourself. [Maximum mark 15].

For part b) of all questions, look at the mark scheme for Qs 4-6 on pages 70-71, decide which description is closest to your answer and then decide which mark to give yourself.

[Maximum marks 20 + SPG 5]

Your answers could include some of the following points:

15. *Much Ado About Nothing*

    a)
    - Benedick knows Hero has been 'wronged' and her honour questioned.
    - Beatrice sees that the family's honour has been offended.
    - It is part of her love for Hero.
    - Benedick is not part of Hero's family so he is not obliged to defend her.
    - What Beatrice has in mind is 'a man's office' – different ideas of honour for men and women.

    b)
    - Beatrice asks about Benedick at the beginning of the play, showing she is interested.
    - Something happened between them before the play starts but we never know exactly what.
    - They argue and misunderstand each other but their friends think they are suited.
    - Compare/contrast their relationship with the more conventional wooing of Hero by Claudio.
    - Their reactions to Claudio's treatment of Hero.

16. *Macbeth*

    a)
    - Contrast between Macbeth's feelings of guilt and Lady Macbeth's lack of guilt.
    - Lady Macbeth takes control of the situation.
    - The knocking makes him nervous but she reacts in a practical way.
    - She speaks to him as if telling off a child.
    - She may be more ruthless, as she is happy to blame the grooms.

    b)
    - At the start of the play Macbeth is a brave commander.
    - Influence of the witches and Lady Macbeth on him.
    - His murders of Banquo and Macduff's family.
    - His cruelty and tyranny.
    - His heroic defiance and bravery at the end of the play.

17. *Romeo and Juliet*

    a)
    - He falls in love at first sight.
    - The audience might think he has got over Rosaline very quickly.
    - Imagery of light and dark is used to express Juliet's beauty.
    - Religious imagery is introduced.
    - The effect of the soliloquy while the ball continues around him.

    b)
    - Juliet insists on marriage as proof of Romeo's love.
    - Contrast his love for Rosaline and how he expresses it.
    - Marriage seen as a political tool by Capulet.
    - Marriages arranged by parents.
    - Marriage seen as spiritual as well as sexual fulfilment.
    - The Nurse's disregard for the sanctity of marriage as well as for Juliet's feelings.

18. *The Merchant of Venice*

    a)
    - Mercy seen as God-given and natural.
    - Imagery used to express its 'quality'.
    - Mercy contrasted with power, symbolised in the sceptre, but seen as necessary in a ruler.
    - It is not the opposite of justice but 'seasons' it.
    - Use of rhetorical language.

    b)
    - Antonio's treatment of him seen as the norm.
    - Language used to him and of him shows anti-Semitism ('dog').
    - He wants to keep Jessica locked up, away from Christians.
    - Scenes with Jessica and Launcelot show how separate Jewish life is in Venice.
    - Possible audience reactions to his conversion after the trial (differences between modern and Elizabethan perceptions).

19. *Henry V*

    a)
    - Use of rhetorical language, e.g. lists of three, hyperbole.
    - Refers immediately to God, his only authority and the source of his power.
    - Refers to himself in the third person plural ('we'), asserting his superiority.
    - Although he mentions mercy, he gives none, showing he can be ruthless.

    b)
    - They give a sense of the kind of men who would become soldiers.
    - They are portrayed comically.
    - They contribute to the success of the English army.
    - Shakespeare also shows more serious, professional soldiers.
    - He uses characters from different backgrounds and different parts of Britain to create tension, but ultimately they show unity.
    - Henry mingles in disguise with the ordinary soldiers.
    - Victory is seen as victory for the whole nation and by the whole nation.

20. *Othello*

    a)
    - Although he is the villain, Shakespeare gives him soliloquies so we have access to his thoughts.
    - There is no evidence that he is right about Othello and Emilia but the rumour 'will do'.
    - The audience might think he has other reasons, e.g. bitterness and jealousy.

    b)
    - He is introduced as an impressive figure – a successful and admired soldier.
    - He is a man of action and emotion.
    - The audience may feel a range of emotions at the tragic climax of the play.
    - He is brought down by jealousy, his 'fatal flaw'.
    - He also has a degree of 'hubris' or pride, which traditionally brings down heroes.

21. For both parts of the question, look at the mark scheme on page 139 (pp 94-95, Review Questions, Q1), decide which description is closest to your answer and then decide which mark to give yourself. **[Maximum mark 40 (15 for part a) and 25 for part b))].**

    Your answers could include some of the following points:

    a)
    - Use of voices – the poet's voice, the traveller's voice and Ozymandias's voice.
    - Effect of distancing.
    - Legendary/exotic feeling from setting in ancient history and in the desert.
    - Use of sonnet form.

- Powerful symbolism of the decaying statue.
- Literal imagery of the desert.
- Ambiguity/irony in the inscription.

[Maximum 15 marks]

b)

- Comparison with 'Hawk Roosting' – the hawk as a powerful man; the hawk shown at the height of his powers in contrast with Ozymandias; use of the first person.
- The power of nature in 'Hawk Roosting'/'Death of a Naturalist'/'The Prelude'; the use of natural imagery in any of these.
- Romantic sensibility in 'The Prelude'/'London'.
- Sense of powerlessness in 'London'/'A Wife in London'/'The Manhunt'/'Dulce et Decorum Est'; ideas of mortality in all these poems.
- Shelley draws lessons about power where other poets just present it.

[Maximum 25 marks]

22-31 Look at the mark scheme below, decide which description is closest to your answer and then decide which mark to give yourself.

Mark	Skills
29-35	• You have sustained focus on the task, including an overview, and conveyed your ideas consistently and coherently. • You have approached the text sensitively and analysed it critically. • You have shown a perceptive understanding of the text, engaging with a personal response and some originality. • You have included pertinent quotations from the text. • You have analysed and appreciated the writer's use of language, form and structure. • You have used precise subject terminology appropriately.
22-28	• You have sustained focus on the task, including an overview, and conveyed your ideas coherently. • You have approached the text thoughtfully. • You have shown a secure understanding of key aspects of the text, with considerable engagement. • You have included well-chosen quotations from the text. • You have discussed and increasingly analysed the writer's use of language, form and structure. • You have used subject terminology appropriately.

This question is also marked for accuracy in spelling, punctuation and the use of vocabulary and sentence structures [5 marks]
[Maximum 35 + 5 = 40 marks]

Your answer could include some of the following points:

22. *An Inspector Calls*

- Description of Mr Birling in the opening stage directions.
- His physical presence and bombastic style of speech are established in the extract.
- His social position as a rich, self-made man.
- His views on politics, society and the future. The audience knows that his confident assertions about the future are wrong.
- In the extract there is some comedy in his references to the Titanic and the Germans.
- His traditional role in the family and relations with his wife and children.
- His reaction to the Inspector's arrival.
- His contact with Eva Smith and what it tells us about industrial relations.
- The difference hindsight makes to an assessment of his character (both from the 1940s and a modern perspective).

23. *Blood Brothers*

- Narrator makes it sound like the re-telling of a legend or myth.
- Narrator comments on action.
- Narrator enters action as various minor characters.
- Comic effect of narrator's intervention.
- Narrator used to move story forward.
- In the extract the narrator focuses on superstition and fate.
- He watches the scene between the Lyonses, which is 'framed' by his song.
- How the narrator becomes a sinister figure. Does he control as well as comment on the action?
- Narrator as a Brechtian alienation (distancing) technique.

24. *The History Boys*

- Irwin as stereotypical young, keen supply teacher.
- In the extract the boys try to divert him from the subject.
- They are curious about his private life but he does not get involved.
- He reveals his approach to history, connecting different historical figures.
- He wants the boys to be controversial in order to impress at Oxford.
- Headmaster's use of Irwin to get results and to undermine Hector.
- Contrast with Mrs Lintott's approach to history.
- Comparison with Hector's teaching style and ideas.
- His disregard for the truth.
- His sexuality / interest in Dakin and comparisons with Hector's 'groping'.
- Significance of the revelation that he lied about his background.
- His subsequent career as 'spin doctor'.
- His use as a framing device to start the acts from the 'present'.

25. *The Curious Incident of the Dog in the Night-Time*

- She is a Special Needs Teacher – we know little about her beyond this.
- Scenes between her and Christopher show how he reacts to others in school.
- In the extract her lines are short as she asks questions and reacts to what Christopher says.
- She is curious about the dog but wants him to write about it, so perhaps it is just part of the lesson.
- She might seem patronising or helpful or just a teacher doing her job.
- Her role shows us his personality/ character as a 'special need', which is how society sees it. Do we question this?
- She is a sounding board for Christopher's thoughts/ideas/plans.
- She has a professional understanding/ distance which helps her deal with him without the emotional frustrations of his parents.
- She reads out the letters and is therefore a channel through which we hear Judy's point of view.
- She tells him that he cannot live with her because she is not his mother.
- There is sympathy but maybe a lack of emotional attachment – this might make it easier for Christopher to deal with her.

26. *A Taste of Honey*

- In the extract Helen shows irritation at Jo's relationship.
- The ring shows that Jo has romantic feelings for the boy.
- Helen's desire for Jo to learn from her mistakes shows she is not happy with her own life.
- Description of Helen as 'semi-whore' implies casual attitude to sex and society's disapproval.
- Helen more interested in money/ security than love – not certain if she is actually a prostitute.
- Jo has grown up without the usual parental attitudes to sex of the period.
- Unlike Helen she does associate sex with love – she craves affection.
- Characters discuss sexual matters openly, even quite crudely.
- Attitudes to pre-marital sex / single mothers then and now.
- Attitudes to homosexuality then and now.
- A 'kitchen sink drama' – sexual content designed to show 'real working-class life' / shock audiences?

27. *Lord of the Flies*

- The extract focuses on the conch shell. The boys consciously turn this into a symbol.
- It represents ideas about fairness, free speech and the boys' idea of civilisation.
- The Lord of the Flies – the sow's head – symbolising evil and lack of civilisation.
- How they come to worship the Lord of the Flies – its association with the devil through Beelzebub.
- The Beast – an imaginary thing that becomes a powerful symbol.

- Symbolism of place – the forest glade, the mountain, the beach, the island as a whole.
- Piggy's glasses, symbolising intellect and reason, and the conch, symbolising democracy and civilisation, are both destroyed.
- Character can be symbolic of themes/ attitudes.
- Symbols related to the Bible / other literary sources and traditions.
- How the meaning of symbols can change and/or be ambiguous.

28. *Never Let Me Go*
- Tommy is seen through Kathy's eyes.
- The extract focuses on a brief, fairly casual encounter.
- It shows Kathy starting to see Tommy in a different way and take more notice of him.
- He shows concern for Kathy and causes her to be interested in his 'problems'.
- She tries to understand him, giving us anecdotes about him to try to work out why he behaves as he does.
- He is seen as different from other pupils – an outsider, picked on.
- His 'tantrums' seem to come from nowhere, expressions of anger that no-one understands.
- His conversations with Miss Lucy help him and Kathy to understand more about their situation.
- His relationship with Ruth, and Kathy's view of it.
- How he changes as he gets older – what he is like as a donor.
- Kathy's love for him and her feelings after his 'completion'.

29. *Anita and Me*
- The extract shows her admitting to lying to her father and his mild reaction to it.
- She stresses her mother's position as a teacher.
- She loves and looks up to both of them.
- They allow her quite a lot of freedom, which she sometimes abuses.
- She is fascinated by their past lives in India and their love story.
- She sees them as devoted to each other – a love match, not an arranged marriage.
- She idealises them – the only slight implied criticism is that they are a bit pushy and her mother wants to interfere in people's lives.
- The relationship changes a bit after the birth of her brother, when she does not get as much attention.
- They are seen as different from other parents in the village, because of their culture and their class.

30. *The Woman in Black*
- The extract establishes a mood through the description of the weather. It could be seen as pathetic fallacy.
- The narrator, however, claims not to have been sensitive to the atmosphere – 'no 'foreboding'.
- He establishes his young self as being sensible and 'sturdy'.
- The first chapter takes place many years after the main events, establishing his character and his settled family life.
- Kipps decides to write his tale to show what a 'real' ghost story is like.
- His status and profession help to make him a reliable narrator.
- The young Kipps is sceptical but curious. He also has a sense of adventure.
- Readers empathise with Kipps and his personal tragedy.

31. *Oranges are not the Only Fruit*
- Up to this point Jeanette has been educated at home by her mother.
- References to the Bible, religion and prayer are a feature of their normal conversation.
- Mother is seen doing housework, as mothers might be expected to do, but it is juxtaposed with images of religion.
- Mother has passed on her zeal and sense of being different to Jeanette.
- The relationship changes when Jeanette discovers her sexuality and her mother cannot accept it.
- At the end there is a sense that this relationship has made Jeanette and remains the most important in her life.

32-37 Look at the mark scheme below, decide which description is closest to your answer and then decide which mark to give yourself.

Mark	Skills
33-40	• You have sustained focus on the task, including an overview, and conveyed your ideas consistently and coherently. • You have approached the text sensitively and analysed it critically. • You have shown a perceptive understanding of the text, engaging with a personal response and some originality. • You have included pertinent quotations from the text. • You have analysed and appreciated the writer's use of language, form and structure. • You have used precise subject terminology appropriately. • You have shown an assured understanding of the relationship between the text and the context in which it was written.
25-32	• You have sustained focus on the task, including an overview, and conveyed your ideas coherently. • You have approached the text thoughtfully. • You have shown a secure understanding of key aspects of the text, with considerable engagement. • You have included well-chosen quotations from the text. • You have discussed and increasingly analysed the writer's use of language, form and structure. • You have used subject terminology appropriately. • You have shown a secure understanding of the relationship between the text and the context in which it was written

[Maximum 40 marks]

Your answers could include some of the following points:

32. *Jane Eyre*
- The passage starts with 'Unjust!' Jane feels that she does not belong and is used as a scapegoat.
- Her adult narrator's voice analyses her position at Gateshead, seeing it partly as a result of the situation but also as owing to her own nature.
- Even as a child, Jane does not conform to her expected role.
- The Red Room is a powerful symbol of isolation from society, which Jane refers to throughout the novel.
- The description of the room and the weather build a sense of fear and mystery.
- This can be related to the Gothic tradition, although in *Jane Eyre* the supernatural elements are not real – they are the result of a child's fears.
- Jane looks for love and substitute families throughout the novel – at Lowood, at Thornfield, with the Rivers family.
- Her position as governess is neither servant nor family.
- She thinks of herself as different – in her looks and her nature.

33. *Pride and Prejudice*
- The importance of setting – this is Darcy's home and reveals a lot about him.
- Pemberley is described as elegant, tasteful and beautiful. This says something about its owner which surprises Elizabeth.
- The idea of being its mistress appeals to her – she would not marry just for money but she wants a 'good' marriage.
- The presence of the Gardiners reminds her of why she refused Darcy.
- She had already begun to change her feelings after receiving Darcy's letter.
- Now she is given an account of his character by someone who can be seen as reliable and honest.
- The housekeeper maintains he is not proud and has many other good qualities.
- The way he treats and reacts to Wickham are central to Elizabeth's changing feelings. At first she was misled by Wickham. Now she sees Darcy's side. Later, he will prove his love by the way he deals with Wickham and Lydia.
- We are given access to Elizabeth's feelings through Austen's narrative style.

34. The *Strange Case of Dr Jekyll and Mr Hyde*
- Utterson is introduced as a reliable, logical, professional man.
- His profession gives him access to Lanyon, Jekyll and their documents.

- Utterson and Enfield are described as 'dull', making the contrast with the events Enfield describes greater.
- Stevenson uses their walk to describe the contrast between the 'thriving' street and 'sinister' building, like Jekyll and Hyde.
- Use of imagery to create atmosphere.
- Utterson is inquisitive but also discreet – information is gradually revealed to him.
- Even his 'dull' relationship with Enfield has an air of mystery about it.

35. *A Christmas Carol*
- The readers are taken with Scrooge to see an 'ordinary', poor family celebrate Christmas.
- The importance of family life and being with loved ones – contrast with Scrooge's situation.
- Dickens's characteristic use of lists to build descriptions.
- A sense of excitement and anticipation built.
- Bob refers to Tiny Tim's words about Christ.
- A sense throughout that celebration and caring for others go together.
- The ghost shows Scrooge a range of people celebrating Christmas.
- Dickens's use of a popular genre to put across a serious message about society.

36. *War of the Worlds*
- The artilleryman expects the Martians to remain in power and has planned accordingly.
- He sees himself and people like him surviving by living in the wild.
- He expects others will become 'pets' of the Martians or be used for breeding and food.
- The Martians are seen as superior and the humans as animals.
- His vision, although it seems cynical, is similar to what happens in many oppressive regimes.
- Wells shows humans resisting a superior power, panicking and being destroyed.
- The Martians are defeated by nature before we get to see whether he is right about them.

37. *Silas Marner*
- There is a distinction made between religious faith and church practices.
- The church in Lantern Yard is attended by working class people who have a simple faith.
- Their practices are different from the established church but they believe absolutely in them.
- Eliot portrays the drawing of lots as something only ignorant, uneducated people could believe in.
- Silas cannot distinguish between the church and God, leading him to reject God.
- Raveloe's community seems to have a more Christian spirit than Lantern Yard's, shown in the way they support Silas and Eppie.

38. Look at the mark scheme on p139 (pp94-95, Review Questions, Q1 and Q2), decide which description is closest to your answer and then decide which mark to give yourself.
Part a) is marked out of 15 and part b) out of 25.

a) Your answer might include comments on the following:
- He gives a voice to an ordinary soldier.
- Persona's motives for becoming a soldier – poverty, unemployment.
- The ballad form tells a story in a simple, traditional form – appropriate to subject.
- Rhythm and rhyme give it a cheerful tone in contrast with the subject.
- The language is colloquial, the voice working-class.
- His attitude to his enemy – he sees him as the same kind of man.
- References to the 'inn' and 'nipperkin' make it seem homely and everyday.
- Reference to 'traps' places him in the country, perhaps as gamekeeper, perhaps as poacher. He is used to killing animals.
- The nature of the deed contrasts with the friendly language.
- Makes a strong point about war through a naive voice who sees his 'foe' as an individual just like himself.

b) Your answer might include comments on:
- Both are about the past, the voices having returned from war.
- Hardy uses the singular 'I' as a soldier tells an anecdote; Owen uses plural 'we'.
- The use of 'we' makes Owen's experience more general – perhaps the common experience of the soldiers.
- We do not learn anything about the soldiers in 'The Next War' apart from their experience of war.
- Difference in focus – one on killing, the other on suffering.
- Contrast in language – Hardy more colloquial.
- Details of the experience of war in 'The Next War' are more vivid and unpleasant, possibly because of the nature of the war or because of the poet's own experience.
- 'The Next War' personifies death.
- One matter-of-fact, the other emotional.
- Different forms – Hardy's poem is ballad-like, Owen's in the form of a Shakespearean sonnet.
- Why would he use this form to write about war and death?
- Use of imagery in 'The Next War'.
- Difference in tone created by rhythm/metre and language.

[Maximum total marks 40]

Glossary

a

abbreviation a shortened form of a word or phrase
abstract noun a noun which names something you cannot touch or feel, such as an idea or emotion
accent a way of pronouncing words, usually associated with a region or area
act a division of a play
active voice when the subject is the person or thing doing: for example, 'the dog bit the boy'
adjective a word used to describe a noun and add more detail
adverb a word used to describe verbs, often ending in 'ly', such as 'swiftly', 'anxiously'
alliteration repetition of a sound at the beginning of two or more words
alphabetical order the arrangement of information according to the alphabet (A–Z)
ambiguity when something has more than one meaning (adjective – **ambiguous**)
anecdote a short account of an interesting or humorous story, often used to reinforce a point being made
antagonist the person who opposes the protagonist
apostrophe (') punctuation mark used to show possession or omission
archaic old-fashioned, no longer in use
argument a reasoned point of view
article a short piece of writing, usually in a newspaper or magazine
aside a line or lines addressed to the audience while other actors are on stage
associate connect mentally
assonance repetition of a vowel sound within words
atmosphere the tone or mood of the text
attitude a writer's feelings or opinions about something
audience a group of people who hear, watch or read something
authorial voice the writer speaking directly to the reader
authority power or influence, often because of knowledge or expertise (adjective – **authoritative**)
autobiographical describes writing about the author's own experiences
autobiography the story of the author's life

b

ballad a form of poetry that tells a story, usually in quatrains with a regular metre and rhyme scheme
Bildungsroman a novel that tells the story of someone growing up
biography the story of someone's life
blank verse poetry that has a regular metre but does not rhyme
blog a diary or journal published on the internet (short for weblog; **blogger** – a person who writes a blog)
broadsheet a 'serious' newspaper, so-called because they used to be published on large sheets of paper
bullet point a typographical symbol used to introduce an item in a list

c

caesura a pause in a line of poetry, sometimes denoted by a punctuation mark
chapter a division within a book
character a fictional person
chronological order order of time, starting with the earliest event
clause a phrase (group of words) which could stand alone as a sentence, having a main verb and a subject
climax the dramatic high point of a story, usually at the end
colloquial conversational or chatty (noun – **colloquialism**)
colon (:) a punctuation mark used to introduce a list or an explanation
comma (,) a punctuation mark used to separate clauses or items in a list
complex sentence a sentence containing more than one clause (but not a compound sentence)
compound sentence a sentence consisting of two clauses of equal importance, joined by a conjunction
conceit an elaborate or far-fetched simile or (extended) metaphor
conclusion end
concrete noun a noun that names something you can touch or feel (also **common noun**)
conjunction a word used to join two words, clauses or phrases and show the relationship between them: for example, 'and', 'but', 'because'
connective any word or phrase used to join phrases, sentences or paragraphs
connotation a meaning that is suggested by the use of a word or phrase
consonant any letter that is not a vowel
content subject matter; what something contains
context circumstances
contraction making two words into one by leaving out letters and using an apostrophe: for example, 'doesn't', 'I'm', 'who's'
counter-argument an argument that answers one that has already been given
court the people surrounding a king or queen

d

determiner a short word that comes before a noun and helps to define it, including the definite article ('the') and indefinite article ('a')
diagram a plan, sketch, drawing or outline designed to demonstrate or explain how something works
dialect words or phrases particular to a region
dialogue speech between two or more people; conversation
diarist a person who writes a diary
diction the choice of words and phrases used
difference a way in which two or more things are not alike
direct speech the actual words spoken, put in inverted commas
director a person who directs plays
discourse marker a word or phrase that connects sentences or paragraphs
divine right the idea that the right to rule comes from God

e

ellipsis (...) punctuation indicating that something has been left out
embed with reference to a quotation, to place it within sentences so that the whole sentence makes sense
emotive language language used to provoke emotions, such as shock or pity, in readers
end-stopping ending a line of verse with a punctuation mark (also called lineation)
enjambment when lines are not end-stopped but the sense runs on between lines or even stanzas
evidence information referred to in order to support a point being made
exclamation mark (!) a punctuation mark used to denote extreme emotion
explicit open, obvious
exposition setting the scene or giving background information at the beginning of a story

extended metaphor a series of similar metaphors combining to create one image

f

fable a story, often about animals, that gives a moral lesson
feature a newspaper or magazine article that is not a news report
figurative imagery the use of an image of one thing to tell us about another
form a type of writing or the way it is presented
formal language language that is similar to Standard English and used in situations where it is not appropriate to be too conversational
fragment another word for a 'minor sentence', one which does not contain a main verb
free verse poetry that does not have a regular metre or rhyme scheme
full stop (.) a punctuation mark that marks the end of a sentence
function what something is used for

g

genre a kind or type of literature: for example, detective story or romance
gothic genre of writing characterised by gloom and mystery, popular in the 19th century
grammar the study or rules of how words relate to each other

h

headline heading at the top of a newspaper or magazine article
homophone a word that sounds the same as another word but is spelled differently and has a different meaning
hyperbole exaggeration (adjective – **hyperbolic**)

i

iambic pentameter a line of poetry consisting of ten syllables with the stress on every second syllable
identify select; name
image a picture, also used metaphorically of 'word pictures'
imagery when words are so descriptive that they paint a picture in your mind. Imagery is used to allow the reader to empathise or imagine the moment being described.
imply to suggest something that is not expressly stated (noun – **implication**; adjective – **implicit**)
inciting incident an event that starts the action of a story
indent to start writing a little way in from the margin: for example, to start a new paragraph
indirect speech speech that is reported rather than quoted: for example, He said that she was there
infer to deduce something that is not openly stated (noun – **inference**)
informal language conversational language that is spoken between people who are usually familiar with one another
interpret when you infer meaning and explain what you have inferred, you are interpreting implicit information or ideas (noun – **interpretation**)
interval a break during a performance
intrusive narrator a narrator who is outside the action but comments on it
inverted commas (' ') punctuation marks used to indicate quotations, titles, etc.
irony when words are used to imply an opposite meaning, or sarcastic language that can be used to mock or convey scorn (adjective – **ironic**)
isolate separate; place apart
issue a subject being discussed

j

journal a form of diary
journalism writing in a newspaper or magazine

l

literal imagery the use of description to convey mood or atmosphere
location place
lyric a short poem about feelings

m

medium means of communication (plural – **media**)
metaphor an image created by directly comparing one thing to another, such as 'my brother is a little monkey'
metre the pattern of stressed and unstressed syllables in poetry
minor sentence a 'sentence' that does not contain a verb – also known as a 'fragment'
mnemonic a way of remembering information, especially spellings
modal verb a verb that shows the mood or state of another verb: for example, 'could', 'might'
mood the general feeling conveyed (see **atmosphere**)
morality ideas of good and bad behaviour, or right and wrong
motif an idea or image that is repeated at intervals in a text
motivation the reason(s) for doing something
movement a group of writers who share similar ideas about literature and/or write in a similar style
musical theatre a form of drama including music

n

naive narrator a narrator who does not understand what is going on, often a child
narrative story
narrator the person telling a story
non-fiction a text that is mainly based on facts and not made up
noun a naming word

o

object (in grammar) the thing or person to whom something is done (in the active voice)
octave a set of eight lines of verse
omission missing out
omniscient narrator a narrator who is outside the action and knows everything
onomatopoeia the use of a word that sounds like what it describes
opening start, beginning
opinion what someone thinks
oxymoron two contradictory words placed together: for example, 'bitter sweet'

p

paragraph a section of a piece of prose writing, shown by indentation or by leaving a line
parallel phrasing repeating the structure and some of the words, phrases, clauses or sentences
paraphrase to put something in your own words
parenthesis brackets; a word or phrase inserted into a sentence to explain something (plural – **parentheses**)
passive voice where the subject has the action done to him or her: for example, 'the boy was bitten by the dog'
past continuous tense the tense used to convey an action that continued for some time in the past, e.g. 'he was talking for hours'
past perfect tense the tense used to describe events that happened before those being described in the past tense, using 'had'
past tense the tense used to describe something that has happened
pathetic fallacy either a form of personification, giving nature human qualities, or using a description of the surroundings to reflect the mood of a character
perfect tense a form of the past tense, using 'has' or 'have'
period an amount of time
persona a fictional voice used by a poet
personal pronoun a pronoun that stands in for the names of people

personification when an inanimate object or idea is given human qualities
perspective point of view
Petrarchan or Italian sonnet a form of sonnet consisting of an octave and a sestet
playwright a person who writes plays
plot the main events of a story
plural more than one
possession belonging or ownership
preposition a short word showing the relationship of one thing to another: for example, 'to', 'under'
present tense the tense used to describe things happening now
pronoun a short word that replaces a noun ('I', 'you', 'he', 'she', etc.)
proper noun a noun that names an individual person or thing, such as a place or day, and has a capital letter
prose any writing that is not poetry
protagonist the main character, the person whom the story is about
psychology the study of the human mind
pun word play, when words are organised in an amusing way to suggest other meaning

q

quatrain a set of four lines of verse
question mark (?) a punctuation mark used at the end of a question
quotation words or phrases taken directly from the text (verb – **quote**)
quotation marks inverted commas when used around a quotation

r

recipient the person who receives something, especially a letter
refer mention or allude to something (noun – **reference**)
refrain a repeated line or lines, usually at the end of stanzas, in poetry
register the form of language used in particular circumstances
relative pronoun a word such as 'who', 'which' or 'that', used to connect clauses
repetition when words, phrases, ideas or sentences are used more than once – this can be used to highlight key issues and make important sections more memorable
report an account of something that has happened, often in a newspaper
reported speech see **indirect speech**
reverse chronological order ordering events by putting the most recent first and working backwards
review an article that gives an opinion on, for example, a film, play or book
rhetoric the art of speaking (adjective – **rhetorical**)
rhetorical device a language technique used to influence an audience
rhetorical question a question that does not require an answer, used to make the reader think about the possible answer and involve them in the text
rhyme the use of words with the same end sounds to make patterns
rhyming couplet two successive lines of poetry that rhyme
rhythm the beat of the writing, usually in poetry

s

scene a division of a play, often within an act
script the text of a play
semantic field the area from which words and phrases have been taken
semi-colon (;) punctuation mark used to connect clauses, also used in lists
sentiment feeling
sestet a set of six lines of verse
setting where and when the action takes place
Shakespearean or English sonnet a form of sonnet popularised by Shakespeare, consisting of four quatrains and a rhyming couplet
sibilance repetition of 's' sounds
significance what something means or stands for
silent letter a letter within a word which is not pronounced
similarity a way in which two or more things are alike
simile a comparison of one thing to another using the words 'like' or 'as', such as 'the raindrops fell like tears'
simple past tense the form of the past tense usually formed by adding '-ed'
simple sentence a sentence that only contains a main clause
singular one
skim read to read quickly in order to find something in the text
slang informal language, often local and frequently changing
social order where people are 'placed' in society, with some more 'important' than others
soliloquy a speech to the audience, expressing a character's thoughts or feelings (plural **soliloquies**)
sonnet a form of poetry, usually a love poem, of 14 lines
source the origin of something, used by examiners to describe texts used in exams
speech marks inverted commas when used around direct speech
Standard English the variety of English generally accepted as the correct form for writing and formal speech
stanza a section of a poem, often called a verse
strapline a subheading under a headline, which explains or expands on the headline
stress (in poetry) emphasis
subheading used to break up the text and guide the reader through various sections
subject the person or thing that a sentence is about
subordinate clause a clause that contains extra information
summarise give a shortened account of something, retaining the meaning (noun – **summary**)
supernatural not belonging to the natural world; magical
syllable a unit of pronunciation
symbol an object that represents something else: for example, an idea or emotion (adjective – **symbolic**)
synthesis the combining of two or more things (verb – **synthesise**)

t

tabloid a type of newspaper, less serious and easier to read than a broadsheet, traditionally in a smaller format
terminology use of appropriate, often specialised, word
text box a box that contains text
theme subject matter: what the text/poem is about rather than what happens in it
third person he, she, it (singular); they (plural)
tone the overall feel or attitude of the writing
topic sentence a sentence, usually the first in the paragraph, which tells you what the paragraph is about
turning point an event that changes the direction of a story

u

unreliable narrator a narrator who cannot always be trusted

v

verb a doing, thinking, feeling or being word
verse poetry
viewpoint point of view
vocabulary words used
voice the narrator or speaker; his or her characteristic style
volta a turn or change in a poem, especially between the octave and sestet in a Petrarchan sonnet
vowel a, e, i, o, u

Notes

Index

Collins

WJEC Eduqas GCSE 9-1 Revision

English

Language & Literature

English

WJEC Eduqas GCSE 9-1

Workbook

Paul Burns

Contents

Key Technical Skills: Writing

Key Technical Skills: Reading

English Language 1

English Language 2

Shakespeare

Poetry

Post-1914 Prose/Drama

Contents

Key Technical Skills: Writing

Spelling

1 Put the following words into their plural forms:

a) tomato ……………

b) birthday ……………

c) soliloquy ……………

d) family ……………

e) parenthesis …………… [5]

2 Insert the correctly spelled word in each of the following pairs of sentences:

a) Your/you're

…………… not going out like that.

I asked …………… sister to bring it.

b) There/they're/their

…………… are twenty people in the class.

They have all done …………… homework but …………… not sitting in the right places.

c) Where/wear/we're

Turn it off or it will …………… out.

We have no idea …………… it is but …………… going anyway.

d) Past/passed

I …………… him in the street an hour ago.

He walked right …………… me as if I wasn't there.

e) To/too/two

There were only …………… exams …………… sit but that was one …………… many.

f) Practice/practise

If you don't go to the …………… you'll be left out of the team.

If you want to improve you will have to …………… every day. [15]

3 The following passage includes ten incorrect spellings. Find them and circle them, then write the correct spellings below.

> Last nite I went to the cinema with my friend Bob and his farther, Michael. The whole evening was not very succesfull. The cinema was very crouded and we had to sit seperately. Then, it turned out the film was in a forrein langauge and no-one could understand it. I think it was about the enviroment. Afterwards, Michael took us to a resturant were we had pizzas.

……………

……………

……………

……………

…………… [10]

Total Marks …………… / 30

Key Technical Skills: Writing

Punctuation

1 Punctuate the following passage using only commas and full stops. There should be a total of five punctuation marks. You may wish to rewrite the passage to add the punctuation.

> *Great Expectations* one of the best-known novels by Charles Dickens is the story of Pip a boy who grows up in the marshes of Kent at the beginning of the story he meets an escaped convict in the churchyard where his parents are buried

....

....

....

.... [5]

2 Add ten apostrophes, where necessary, to the following passage. You may wish to rewrite the passage to add the apostrophes.

> At about ten o clock, we went to Romios for pizzas. Im not sure what Bobs pizza topping was but I had ham and pineapple. I wish I hadnt because later on I was sick in Michaels car. Its brand new and I thought hed be angry but he wasnt. Were not going there again.

....

....

.... [10]

3 Add a question mark, an exclamation mark, a colon, a semi-colon or parentheses (brackets) to the following clauses so that they make sense:

a) The cat slept quietly on the mat the dog slept noisily on the step.	
b) Who was that masked man nobody knows.	
c) I don't believe it that's the first answer I've got.	
d) Annie deserved the prize she was the best baker by far.	
e) Jane and Elizabeth the two oldest Bennet sisters get married at the end.	

[5]

Total Marks .... / 20

Key Technical Skills: Writing

Sentence Structure

1. Identify whether the sentences below are simple, compound, complex or minor sentences:
   a) I confess that I had my doubts when I reflected upon the great traffic which had passed along the London road in the interval. ....
   b) Very clearly. ....
   c) We all need help sometimes. ....
   d) Mr Collins was punctual to his time, and he was received with great politeness by the whole family. ....
   e) Elizabeth smiled. .... [5]

2. Combine the following sentences to form complex sentences, using the conjunctions **because**, **although** or **until**.
   a) I bought Anna a bunch of flowers. It was her birthday.
   ....
   ....
   b) He did not finish the race. They gave him a certificate.
   ....
   ....
   c) I kept going. I reached the finishing line.
   ....
   .... [3]

3. Use the following sentences to form a complex sentence using a relative pronoun.
   Joey was the oldest cat in the street. He never left the garden.
   ....
   ....
   .... [1]

4. Use the following sentences to form a complex sentence without using a connective:
   I was walking down the street. I realised I had forgotten my phone.
   ....
   ....
   .... [1]

Total Marks .... / 10

Key Technical Skills: Writing

Text Structure and Organisation

1 Rearrange the following paragraphs from 1 to 5 so that the passage makes sense.

a) As a result of this, the student body has decided to appeal to the governors. Jodie has written a letter to every governor, setting out the problems as the students see them. ☐

b) As yet no replies have been received. The increasingly angry students are starting to consider taking 'direct action'. ☐

c) Jodie Collins, a spokesperson for the students, has had several meetings about the issue with the Principal. Ms Rundle apparently listened to the students' points, but later sent an email claiming that nothing can be done because of lack of funds. ☐

d) According to this letter, students' health and safety are at risk. Among other things, toilets are not properly cleaned and standards of hygiene in the kitchen leave a lot to be desired. ☐

e) Students of Summerfield College have expressed concern about the environment they have to work in. They have a number of complaints. ☐

[5]

2 Insert each of these five discourse markers or connectives into the passage so that it makes sense:

nevertheless **when** **subsequently** **in spite of** **however**

(a) .... I read your letter I was shocked by its contents.

(b) .... being a governor of the college, I was completely unaware of the issues that you mention. I have **(c)** .... been in touch with Ms Rundle to express my concern. She **(d)**, ..., has not responded to my letters.

(e) ...., I shall continue to press her for answers. [5]

Total Marks .... / 10

Key Technical Skills: Writing

Standard English and Grammar

1 Insert the correct form of the verb 'to be' or 'to do':

Present tense

a) You .... a great singer.

b) They .... trying hard.

Simple past

c) We .... waiting for you.

d) He .... what they told him to do.

Perfect

e) She .... my friend for years.

f) They .... all their exams now.

Simple past + past perfect

g) We .... happy because we .... all the exercises. [7]

2 Which of the following is correct in Standard UK English? Circle the correct word.

a) The defendant **pleaded/pled** guilty.

b) He's one of the **only/few** people who can do that.

c) He has **got/gotten** two coffees. [3]

3 Change the following dialogue to Standard English:

Jo:	Hey. How are you guys doing? ....
Arthur:	Good. Real good. ....
Jo:	Wanna drink? ....
Arthur:	Can I get two coffees? ....
Jo:	Sure. Where are you sat? .... [5]

4 Rewrite the following passage in Standard English:

> I was stood in the street when Frankie come over. I give him a smile and opened me gob to speak. I was gonna ask him how he done in math. I never said nothing. Soon as I seen him I knew he done good.

....

....

....

.... [5]

Total Marks .... / 20

Identifying Information and Ideas 1

1 Read the passage below:

> The tower of St Peter's church was, until very recently, the tallest building in the town. On a clear day, it can still be seen from miles away. However, it is now overshadowed by a brutal example of modern architecture. Built two years ago, and twice as high as the church tower, the Kingsley Tower dominates the surrounding landscape.

Look at the statements below. Which of them are explicitly stated in the text? Tick the correct answers.

a) The church tower used to be the tallest building in town. ☐

b) Everyone hates the new building. ☐

c) The Kingsley Tower is taller than the church tower. ☐

d) The writer does not like modern architecture. ☐ [2]

2 Read the passage below:

List five things that we learn about the old gentleman's appearance.

> It was by the Green Dragon that the old gentleman travelled. He was a very nice looking old gentleman, and he looked as if he were nice, too, which is not at all the same thing. He had a fresh-coloured, clean-shaven face, and white hair, and he wore rather odd-shaped collars and a top hat that wasn't exactly the same kind as other people's. Of course the children didn't see all this at first. In fact, the first thing they noticed about the old gentleman was his hand.
>
> From *The Railway Children* by E. Nesbit

[5]

Total Marks .... / 7

Key Technical Skills: Reading

Identifying Information and Ideas 2

1 Read the passage and answer the questions below.

> Work experience is an established part of today's school calendar. All Year 10 pupils in all schools have to do it. But why? I decided to ask around and found the general opinion amongst the adults I asked was that it would prepare young people for the world of work. I have to say, though, that none of them sounded terribly convinced and I got the distinct impression that they were just following the party line.
>
> Assuming the object of the exercise is to prepare us for the world of work, does it? My placement was in my uncle's office. He is a solicitor and the rationale behind the placement was that I had expressed an interest in studying Law. That sounds logical. But what did I learn? I learned that you should dress smartly and be punctual. I learned how to answer the telephone politely. I learned that solicitors drink an awful lot of coffee. I could have found out all of that just by having a chat with my uncle.

a) In which school year is work experience compulsory?

.... [1]

b) In the writer's opinion, do adults say what they really think about work experience?

.... [1]

c) What job does the writer's uncle do?

.... [1]

d) Name one thing the writer did while on work experience.

.... [1]

e) Did the writer find the experience valuable?

.... [1]

Total Marks .... / 5

Synthesis and Summary

Summary

1 Reduce each of the following sentences to five words to give the necessary information without losing sense.

a) Stunning trees stand like soldiers behind the shed.	
b) Charlotte Green, the girl with blonde hair, ate Lydia's chocolate.	
c) I demand that you tell me now who did it.	

[3]

2 Read this statement from the witness to a crime.

> I was walking down our street – Arbuckle Lane – at nine o'clock on Monday. I know it was nine o'clock because I was worried about being late for work and I looked at my watch. As I passed number eighteen, the big house with the yellow front door where Mrs Lightbody used to live, I heard a noise, so I stopped and turned around. There were two men on the step and one of them had something in his hand, which he was using to break the glass in the door. I shouted out and they turned. One of them was tall, about six foot, with a grey beard – he reminded me of someone on the television – and the other one was stocky with curly black hair. When they saw me the tall man dropped something and they both ran. It gave me quite a turn.

If you were investigating the crime, which FIVE of the following pieces of information would be relevant to solving it? Tick the correct answers.

a) Mrs Lightbody lived at number eighteen. ☐

b) One of the men was six foot tall. ☐

c) He used something to break the glass in the door. ☐

d) The witness was worried about being late. ☐

e) The witness lives in Arbuckle Lane. ☐

f) The tall man dropped something. ☐

g) One man had curly black hair. ☐

h) It was nine o'clock. ☐ [5]

3 On a separate piece of paper, write a summary of the statement. Aim for 70 words or fewer. [12]

Total Marks .... / 20

Synthesis and Summary

1 Read the two passages below.
Pick out as many differences as you can between the two girls' experiences of school and write them in the table below or on a separate piece of paper.

Mary Jane: I grew up on a farm near Barrow. My parents were not at all happy about me going to school, but they were told it was the law and I had to go. They couldn't see the point of it. But I loved school and I never missed a day. The school was a low stone building in the centre of the village. There were two huge rooms, one for the juniors and one for the infants. There were forty pupils in my class and we sat in rows, facing the teacher. We worked really hard all day, except for playtime, and we were not allowed to speak at all unless spoken to. Miss Murdishaw was very strict. We did like her, though, and she only gave you the cane if you were very naughty.

Sarah: I would never have gone to school at all if I'd had my way. But I was never allowed to stay off. 'Education, education, education', my mum used to say, 'that's what you need in life. Miss a day's school and you'll regret it'. My first school was in the village near where we lived. There were twenty-four children in our class and we used to sit around tables in groups of six. All my group did was talk, talk, talk all day long. I don't think we did much work at all. The teacher just wandered around the room smiling at us and telling us everything we did was brilliant. She never punished anyone really, not even telling them off. I think she thought we all loved her, but I certainly didn't.

Mary Jane	Sarah

[10]

2 Now sum up the differences between the girls' experiences of school, writing in proper sentences.

[4]

Total Marks .... / 14

Key Technical Skills: Reading

Referring to the Text

1 Match each statement (**a–c**) with its paraphrase (**d–f**):

a) The modern apartments are situated close to all amenities.

b) Six o'clock struck on the bells of the church that was so conveniently near to the solicitor's dwelling, and still he was digging at the problem.

c) She suggested liaising outside the church at 18.05. I said yes.

d) The lawyer was still trying to work it out in the evening.

e) The flats are up-to-date and near shops and transport.

f) We agreed to meet at about six o'clock by the church.

[3]

2 The following sentences all include quotations from *Macbeth* which have not been set out correctly. Set them out correctly, using colons and/or quotation marks where appropriate.

a) Macbeth refers to the prophecies as happy prologues.	
b) He tells us that one of them has come true I am Thane of Cawdor.	
c) Macbeth asks how the prophecies can be evil when the witches have told the truth If ill, Why hath it given me earnest of success/Commencing in a truth?	

[6]

3 The following sentences are an example of the use of PEE. Identify the point, the evidence and the explanation.

Frankenstein's response is negative from the start. Referring to the experiment as a 'catastrophe' and his creation as a 'wretch' suggests that he has rejected the creature and will not try to find any good in it.

Point	
Evidence	
Explanation	

[3]

Total Marks .... / 12

Key Technical Skills: Reading

Analysing Language 1

1 How would you describe the register of the following sentences?

Choose from:

formal

technical

dialectical

colloquial

a) 'Appen he were took badly but he'll be all reet. ....

b) It may be that the gentleman was feeling ill. It is, however, likely that he will recover.

....

c) Me mate wasn't feeling too good but he's OK now. ....

d) The patient suffered a brief episode of disequilibrium, which could be a symptom of a number of chronic conditions.

.... [4]

2 Read the passage below and identify the word class (part of speech) of the highlighted words:

> Since the party, she had been more **eager** than ever, and had planned many ways of making friends **with** him; **but** he had not been seen lately, and Jo began to think he had gone away, when she one day spied a brown face at an upper **window**, looking **wistfully** down into their garden, where Beth and Amy **were snowballing** one another.
>
> From *Little Women* by Louisa May Alcott

a) eager		**b)** with	
c) but		**d)** window	
e) wistfully		**f)** were snowballing	

[6]

3 **a)** The passage above is only one sentence. What sort of sentence is it? ....

b) Give an example from the passage of a proper noun. ....

c) Is the clause 'he had not been seen lately' in the active or passive voice? ....

d) What tense is 'had planned' in the first line? ....

e) In what 'person' is the narrative written? .... [5]

Total Marks .... / 15

Key Technical Skills: Reading

Analysing Language 2

1 State whether each of the following sentences contains a metaphor or a simile and describe the effect of the comparison.

	Metaphor or simile?	What is its effect?
a) He ran like the wind.		
b) An army of insects invaded the kitchen.		
c) Her heart was as cold as ice.		

[6]

2 Read the passage below. Find an example of each of the techniques listed in the table below.

> Time was not on their side. The fire fizzed and crackled around them as the brave Brown brothers entered the building. Inside, great flames came in waves.

a) personification	
b) onomatopoeia	

[2]

3 Read the passage below, from *The Hound of the Baskervilles* by Arthur Conan Doyle.

> October 16th – A dull and foggy day, with a drizzle of rain. The house is banked with rolling clouds, which rise now and then to show the dreary curves of the moor, with thin, silver veins upon the sides of the hills, and the distant boulders gleaming where the light strikes upon their wet faces. It is melancholy outside and in. The baronet is in a black reaction after the excitements of the night. I am conscious myself of a weight at my heart and a feeling of impending danger – ever-present, which is the more terrible because I am unable to define it.
>
> And have I not cause for such a feeling?

What impressions does the writer create of the narrator's thoughts and feelings?

You must refer to the language used in the text to support your answer. [5]

(Write your answer on a separate piece of paper.)

Total Marks .... / 13

Key Technical Skills: Reading

Analysing Form and Structure

1 Here is the opening of a short story (*The Count and the Wedding Guest* by O. Henry).

> One evening when Andy Donovan went to dinner at his Second Avenue boarding-house, Mrs Scott introduced him to a new boarder, a young lady, Miss Conway. Miss Conway was small and unobtrusive. She wore a plain, snuffy-brown dress, and bestowed her interest, which seemed languid, upon her plate. She lifted her diffident eyelids and shot one perspicuous, judicial glance at Mr Donovan, politely murmured his name, and returned to her mutton. Mr Donovan bowed with the grace and beaming smile that were rapidly winning for him social, business and political advancement, and erased the snuffy-brown one from the tablets of his consideration.

a) What do we learn about the story's setting?

.... [2]

b) What is your first impression of Miss Conway?

.... [2]

c) What is the effect of the phrase 'shot one perspicuous, judicial glance'?

.... [2]

d) What does the description of Andy Donovan's response tell us about him?

.... [2]

e) What do you think might happen next?

.... [2]

2 Match the endings **a–c** with the descriptions **x–z**.

Endings		Descriptions
a) Honour the charge they made! Honour the Light Brigade, Noble six hundred!		**x)** This ending draws a lesson from the story.
b) …the wishes, the hopes, the confidence, the predictions of the small band of true friends who witnessed the ceremony, were fully answered in the perfect happiness of the union.		**y)** This ending might inspire the reader.
c) 'Was I not right?' said the little Mouse. Little friends may prove great friends.		**z)** A happy ending, leaving the reader satisfied.

[3]

Total Marks .... / 13

English Language 1

Reading Literature 1

1 Read the extracts below and state which is narrated by:

A naive/unreliable narrator	
An omniscient narrator	
A reliable first-person narrator	
An intrusive narrator	

[8]

A She told me to pray every day, and whatever I asked for I would get it. But it warn't so. I tried it. Once I got a fish-line but no hooks. It warn't any good to me without hooks. I tried for hooks three or four times, but somehow I couldn't make it work.

From *The Adventures of Huckleberry Finn* by Mark Twain

B The extract from my private diary which forms the last chapter has brought my narrative up to the 18th of October, a time when these strange events began to move swiftly towards their terrible conclusion.

From *The Hound of the Baskervilles* by Sir Arthur Conan Doyle

C As John Bold will occupy much of our attention, we must endeavour to explain who he is, and why he takes the part of John Hiram's beadsmen.

From *The Warden* by Anthony Trollope

D Mr James Duffy lived in Chapelizod because he wished to live as far as possible from the city of which he was a citizen and because he found all the other suburbs of Dublin mean, modern and pretentious.

From *Dubliners* by James Joyce

Total Marks .... / 8

English Language 1

Reading Literature 2

1 Look at the quotations in the table. In the third column (or on a separate piece of paper) enter **how we learn about character**, choosing from:

a) Narrator's description

b) What the character says

c) What others say about/to the character

d) What the character does

e) How others react to the character

In the fourth column (or on a separate piece of paper) say **what we learn about the character**.

Character	Quotation	How we learn about the character	What we learn
Hyde's housekeeper *The Strange Case of Dr Jekyll and Mr Hyde*	She had an evil face, smoothed by hypocrisy; but her manners were excellent.		
Magwitch *Great Expectations*	'Hold your noise!' cried a terrible voice […] 'Keep still, you little devil, or I'll cut your throat.'		
Darcy *Pride and Prejudice*	[Darcy] was looked at with great admiration for about half the evening, till his manners gave a disgust which turned the tide of his popularity.		
Mrs Reed *Jane Eyre*	Mrs Reed, impatient of my now frantic anguish and wild sobs, abruptly thrust me back and locked me in…		
Victor Frankenstein *Frankenstein*	'My dear Victor,' cried he, 'what, for God's sake, is the matter? Do not laugh in that manner. How ill you are!'		

[15]

Total Marks .... / 15

English Language 1

Creative Writing 1

Imagine you have been set the following creative writing task:

Write a story about someone who wins a huge amount of money on the lottery.

Use the following questions and points to help you create a plan for your writing.

1 Character and Voice

a) What person will you write in? If first person, is the narrator also the protagonist?

b) What kind of register will the narrator use?

Now make notes on your protagonist's:

c) gender

d) age

e) appearance

f) background

g) relationships

h) way of speaking

i) interests

j) opinions [10]

2 Place and Time

a) Where does it start?

b) Does the setting change during the story?

c) When is it set – now, in the past or in the future?

d) How long does the story take?

e) Will it be written in chronological order? [5]

3 Structure

On a separate piece of paper, make notes on your:

a) exposition

b) inciting incident

c) turning point(s)

d) climax

e) coda (ending) [5]

Total Marks / 20

English Language 1

Creative Writing 2

You have decided to describe:

a character in your story **and** a scene where part of your story takes place.

1 Give a name to:

Your character ....

The place .... [2]

2 **The Five Senses**

Using an adjective and a noun for each, in the table below jot down at least two things you can sense:

Sense	Character	Scene
a) see		
b) hear		
c) smell		
d) taste	Not applicable	
e) touch/feel		

[10]

3 **Big to Small**

Make notes on the scene/person from:

	Character	Scene
a) long distance		
b) middle distance		
c) close up		

[6]

4 **Imagery**

Write down an appropriate:

	Character	Scene
a) simile		
b) metaphor		

[2]

Total Marks .... / 20

English Language 2

Reading Non-fiction

1 Read the following short texts and use the table below to list differences in the writers' points of view and how they are expressed.

A

It's easy to miss Little Mickledon. It's a tiny village, with no shop or pub, nestling in a valley surrounded by fields of grazing sheep. It's a bit like stepping back in time to the Olde England of yore. It's charming and tranquil, cut off from 'civilization' by having no broadband and no mobile phone signal. But for visitors to Alf and Maisie's delightful bed and breakfast, that's a big attraction. 'People come here to relax', beams Maisie, 'and to rediscover a sense of inner peace and calm.'

B

The Bideaway B & B, Little Mickledon, was a massive disappointment. We were promised peace and quiet, sure, but we didn't expect to be totally cut off from the modern world. Be warned. There's no broadband and we couldn't get a mobile signal. When we complained – not our only complaint: the rooms were grubby and the breakfast pitiful – the hippy owners just shrugged their shoulders.

	Text A	Text B
What is the writer's attitude to Little Mickledon?		
What is the writer's opinion of the B & B?		
What impression do you get of the writer?		
How would you describe the general tone and style?		
Comment on language features.		

[20]

Total Marks .... / 20

English Language 2

Transactional/Persuasive Writing

1. Imagine you have been asked to give your opinion on the statement 'Work Experience is a complete waste of time and should be abolished'.

   Use the table below to list five arguments in favour of abolishing work experience (pro) and five against it (con).

Pros	Cons

[10]

2. The statement above was made in an article in your local newspaper. Decide whether you agree or disagree with it and write **the opening paragraph** of a letter to the newspaper expressing your view.

[5]

3. Now write **the opening paragraph** of an article for a teenage magazine expressing your views on the same statement.

[5]

Total Marks .... / 20

Shakespeare

Context and Themes

1 Think about the Shakespeare play you have studied and write a sentence to explain how each of the following aspects of social and historical context is reflected in it.

a) The play's setting — **Example: *Romeo and Juliet* is set in Italy, a country associated with romance and feuding families.**

b) History and politics

c) Religion

d) Society

e) Gender roles

f) Cultural context

[12]

2 Think about the play you have studied and write a sentence explaining how each of the following themes is reflected in it.

a) Marriage — Example: **In *Romeo and Juliet* Capulet sees it as his right and duty to choose Juliet's husband, but Romeo and Juliet see marriage as an expression of love.**

b) Appearance and reality

c) Power

d) Revenge

e) Loyalty and betrayal

f) Parents and children

[12]

Total Marks .... / 24

Shakespeare

Characters, Language and Structure

1 Choose at least three characters from the play you have studied and find quotations (either something they say or something other characters say) which you feel tell us something about their characters.

Enter the characters' names and appropriate quotations, together with a brief explanation of what you think each quotation tells us, in a table like the one below on a separate piece of paper.

For example, if you have studied *The Merchant of Venice* you could start with:

Character	Quotation	What it tells us
Portia	If I live to be as old as Sybilla, I will die as chaste as Diana unless I be obtained by the manner of my father's will. (Act 1 Scene 2).	Portia reveals her sense of duty and love for her father, as well as her strength of character, using classical references which show her level of education.

[12]

2 Below are some quotations from Shakespeare which demonstrate his use of the following literary techniques: metaphor, oxymoron, pathetic fallacy / personification, rhetorical question.

For each quotation, state which technique is being used and explain its effect.

a) O brawling love, O loving hate (*Romeo and Juliet*, Act 1 Scene 1)

b) But since I am a dog, beware my fangs. (*The Merchant of Venice*, Act 3 Scene 3)

c) Can this Cock-pit hold/ the vasty fields of France? (*Henry V*, Prologue)

d) Rough quarries, rocks and hills, whose heads touch heaven. (*Othello*, Act 1 Scene 3)

	Technique	Effect
a)		
b)		
c)		
d)		

[12]

Total Marks .... / 24

Poetry

Context and Themes

Context

Think about the social, historical and cultural context of the poems you have studied.

1. Match these descriptions of the context of poems to the appropriate poems.
   - **a)** This poem is rooted in the poet's Irish heritage. ....
   - **b)** The poem's language reflects the speaker's Asian heritage. ....
   - **c)** The poet uses a Petrarchan sonnet to express her feelings. ....
   - **d)** In this Romantic poem the poet learns from nature. ....
   - **e)** This poem is inspired by the finding of soldiers' remains in a field.
     .... [5]

Themes

Now think about themes and ideas touched on in the poems you have studied.

2. Which poems touch on the following aspects of the main theme (love and relationships)? Try to find at least two for each. You may list the same poem under more than one heading:

a) The power of nature	
b) The beauty of nature	
c) City life	
d) Romantic love	
e) The experience of combatants (soldiers)	
f) The effect of war on non-combatants	
g) Childhood	
h) Memories	

[16]

Total Marks .... / 21

Poetry

Language, Form and Structure

1 Below are some lines taken from poems which demonstrate poets' use of various language choices and literary techniques.

a) How do I love thee? Let me count the ways! (Sonnet 43)

b) The slap and pop were obscene threats. Some sat
Poised like mud grenades, their blunt heads farting. ('Death of a Naturalist')

c) Our summer made her light escape ('As Imperceptibly as Grief')

d) The mind-forged manacles I hear: ('London')

e) And sure as shooting arrows to the heart,
Astride a dappled mare, legs braced as far apart ('Cozy Apologia')

f) the wind
Is ruining their courting-places

That are still courting-places ('Afternoons')

g) She walks in beauty, like the night
Of cloudless climes and starry skies, ('She Walks in Beauty')

Some of the techniques below are used in more than one of these quotations, and some quotations include more than one technique. State which techniques are being used and explain their effect. You may prefer to write your answers on a separate piece of paper.

alliteration archaic language assonance caesura end-stopping enjambment metaphor pathetic fallacy/personification repetition rhyming couplet simile onomatopoeia

	Technique	Effect
a)		
b)		
c)		
d)		
e)		
f)		
g)		

[36]

Total Marks .... / 36

Poetry

Unseen Poetry

1 Read the poem below and answer the questions that follow. (Use a separate piece of paper if necessary.)

Storm in the Black Forest, D. H. Lawrence

Now it is almost night, from the bronzey soft sky
jugfull after jugfull of pure white liquid fire, bright white
tipples over and spills down,
and is gone
and gold-bronze flutters bent through the thick upper air.

And as the electric liquid pours out, sometimes
a still brighter white snake wriggles among it, spilled
and tumbling wriggling down the sky:
and then the heavens cackle with uncouth sounds.

And the rain won't come, the rain refuses to come!

This is the electricity that man is supposed to have mastered
chained, subjugated to his use!
supposed to!

a) Where and when is it set? ....

....

b) Is there a strong regular rhythm or rhyme scheme? If so, what effect does it have? If not, what effect does this have? ....

c) Give an example of alliteration and explain its effect. ....

....

d) Give an example of assonance and explain its effect. ....

....

e) Give an example of the use of metaphor and explain its effect. ....

....

f) Explain the poet's repeated use of 'and'. ....

....

g) What is the significance of the final line 'supposed to!'? ....

....

h) What do you think the poem is really about? ....

i) How does the storm make the poet feel? ....

j) How does the poem make you feel? .... [20]

Total Marks .... / 20

2 Read this poem. (Note that this poem is one stanza.)

The Vixen, John Clare

Among the taller wood with ivy hung,
The old fox plays and dances round her young.
She snuffs and barks if any passes by
And swings her tail and turns prepared to fly.
The horseman hurries by, she bolts to see,
And turns agen, from danger never free.
If any stands she runs among the poles
And barks and snaps and drives them in the holes.
The shepherd sees them and the boy goes by
And gets a stick and progs the hole to try.
They get all still and lie in safety sure,
And out again when everything's secure,
And start and snap at blackbirds bouncing by
To fight and catch the great white butterfly.

Re-read the poem on page 179 and compare the two poems using the chart below.

	'Storm in the Black Forest'	'The Vixen'
Setting (time and place)		In the woods on what seems to be a typical day for the vixen.
What happens in the poem		
Structure		
Rhythm and rhyme		
Vocabulary/register		
Use of sound		
Imagery		
Themes and poet's attitude		

[32]

Total Marks .... / 32

Post-1914 Prose/Drama

Context and Themes

1 Think about the social, historical and cultural context of the post-1914 text you have studied.

a) Write a paragraph describing the 'world' of the post-1914 text you have studied. Include information about when and where it is set, the lifestyle of the characters, their attitudes and the attitudes of society in general.

[5]

b) Write a paragraph explaining how this world differs from the world you live in today.

[5]

c) Now think about when the text was written, its genre and form, and its intended audience. Write a paragraph about how these elements are reflected in the text.

[5]

2 **a)** In the table below, or on a separate piece of paper, write down some themes that occur in the text you have studied. Try to find four. [4]

b) Now write a sentence or two about each theme, for example:

hypocrisy	In *An Inspector Calls* the Birlings are a respectable middle-class family who seem to embody the moral and social values of the time. The inspector's investigation reveals their failure to live up to these values.

[8]

Total Marks .... / 27

Post-1914 Prose/Drama

Characters, Language and Structure

Characters

1. Identify the main characters in your novel and draw up and complete a chart for each like the one below:

Name	
Background	
Personality	
Relationships	
Motivation	
Function	

[24]

Language and Structure

2. If you have studied a novel, answer the following questions (**a–e**).

a) How would you describe the narrator? ....

b) How would you describe the register used by the narrator? ....

c) Have you noticed anything interesting about the way in which any of the characters speak? ....

d) How is your text divided? ....

e) Give an example of the use of figurative language from your text. ....

....

If you have studied a play, answer these questions (**f–j**):

f) What, if anything, do we learn from the stage directions? ....

....

g) Do any of the characters speak directly to the audience? If so, which ones and why?

....

h) Are there any interesting differences between the ways in which characters speak?

....

i) How is the play divided? ....

j) Give an example of the use of figurative language from your text.

....

.... [10]

Total Marks .... / 34

Nineteenth-Century Prose

Context and Themes

1 Look at these statements about life in the nineteenth century and write a sentence or two saying whether and how each one is reflected in the novel you have studied.

a) Christianity was part of the fabric of life and writers could assume their readers shared Christian ideas and values.

Example: **In *Silas Marner*, the moral values are those of Christianity. Virtues such as humility, self-sacrifice and love win out over vices like selfishness, greed and dishonesty.**

b) Nineteenth-century Britain was a rich country but many people were extremely poor.

c) Nineteenth-century women had far fewer rights than men and a more limited role in society.

d) The nineteenth century was a time of discovery, adventure and scientific advances.

e) Nineteenth-century writers wrote about both personal feelings and moral responsibility.

[10]

2 **a)** On a separate piece of paper, write down some themes that occur in the novel you have studied. Try to find five. Here are some examples to get you started:

Pride and Prejudice	social class
Silas Marner	redemption
A Christmas Carol	poverty
Jane Eyre	integrity
War of the Worlds	fear
The Strange Case of Dr Jekyll and Mr Hyde	hypocrisy

[5]

b) Now write a sentence or two about each of these themes, for example:

In *Pride and Prejudice* awareness of social class can lead to misunderstanding and unhappiness, as well as being a source of humour. [10]

Total Marks .... / 25

Nineteenth-Century Prose

Characters, Language and Structure

1 Identify the main characters in your novel and draw up a chart for each like the one below:
Try to complete charts for five characters.

Name	
Background	
Personality	
Relationships	
Motivation	
Function	

[25]

2 Below are five quotations from nineteenth-century novels (**a–e**) and five descriptions of their use of language (**v–z**). Match each quotation to the appropriate description.

a) It is a truth universally acknowledged that a single man in possession of a good fortune must be in want of a wife. *Pride and Prejudice*, Chapter 1	**v)** The writer uses pathetic fallacy to create a mood.
b) To see the dingy cloud come drooping down, obscuring everything, one might have thought that nature lived hard by and was brewing on a large scale. *A Christmas Carol*, stave 1	**w)** The first-person narrator uses a short, simple sentence for impact.
c) The gold had asked that he should sit weaving longer and longer, *Silas Marner*, chapter 14.	**x)** The author uses irony to amuse the reader, making a statement that is clearly not true.
d) 'This'll tike us rahnd Edgeware?' asked the driver, *War of the Worlds*, chapter 16	**y)** The writer uses personification, making an idea more real by writing as if it were a person.
e) Reader, I married him. *Jane Eyre*, Chapter 38	**z)** The writer uses non-standard English to reflect the origins of the speaker.

[10]

Total Marks .... / 35

WJEC Eduqas

GCSE ENGLISH LANGUAGE

COMPONENT 1

20th Century Literature Reading and Creative Prose Writing

PRACTICE PAPER

1 hour 45 minutes

INSTRUCTIONS TO CANDIDATES

Use black ink or black ball-point pen.

Answer **all** questions in Section A.

Select **one** title to use for your writing in Section B.

Write your answers on separate pieces of paper.

You are advised to spend your time as follows:

Section A-about 10 minutes reading
-about 50 minutes answering the questions

Section B-about 10 minutes planning
-about 35 minutes writing

INFORMATION FOR CANDIDATES

Section A (Reading): 40 marks

Section B (Writing): 40 marks

The number of marks is given in brackets at the end of each question or part-question.

Practice Exam Papers

SECTION A: 40 marks

Read carefully the passage below. Then answer **all** *the questions that follow it.*

This extract is the opening of 'The Invisible Man', a short detective story by G. K. Chesterton, first published in 1911.

In the cool blue twilight of two steep streets in Camden Town, the shop at the corner, a confectioner's,[1] glowed like the butt of a cigar. One should rather say, perhaps, like the butt of a firework, for the light was of many colours and some complexity, broken up by many mirrors and dancing on many gilt and gaily-coloured cakes and sweetmeats. Against this one fiery glass were glued the noses of many gutter-snipes,[2] for the chocolates were all wrapped in those red and gold and green metallic colours which are almost better than chocolate itself; and the huge white wedding-cake in the window was somehow at once remote and satisfying, just as if the whole North Pole were good to eat. Such rainbow provocations could naturally collect the youth of the neighbourhood up to the ages of ten or twelve. But this corner was also attractive to youth at a later stage; and a young man, not less than twenty-four, was staring into the same shop window. To him, also, the shop was of fiery charm, but this attraction was not wholly to be explained by chocolates; which, however, he was far from despising.

He was a tall, burly, red-haired young man, with a resolute face but a listless manner. He carried under his arm a flat, grey portfolio of black-and-white sketches, which he had sold with more or less success to publishers ever since his uncle (who was an admiral) had disinherited him for Socialism, because of a lecture which he had delivered against that economic theory. His name was John Turnbull Angus.

Entering at last, he walked through the confectioner's shop to the back room, which was a sort of pastry-cook restaurant, merely raising his hat to the young lady who was serving there. She was a dark, elegant, alert girl in black, with a high colour and very quick, dark eyes; and after the ordinary interval she followed him into the inner room to take his order.

His order was evidently a usual one. 'I want, please,' he said with precision, 'one halfpenny bun and a small cup of black coffee.' An instant before the girl could turn away he added, 'Also, I want you to marry me.'

The young lady of the shop stiffened suddenly, and said: 'Those are jokes I don't allow.'

The red-haired young man lifted grey eyes of an unexpected gravity

'Really and truly, 'he said, 'it's as serious – as serious as the halfpenny bun. It is expensive, like the bun; one pays for it. It is indigestible, like the bun. It hurts.'

The dark young lady had never taken her dark eyes off him, but seemed to be studying him with almost tragic exactitude. At the end of her scrutiny, she had something like the shadow of a smile, and she sat down in a chair.

'Don't you think,' observed Angus absently, 'that it rather cruel to eat these halfpenny buns? I shall give up these brutal sports when we are married.'

The young lady rose from her chair and walked to the window, evidently in a strong but not unsympathetic cogitation[3]. When at last she swung round again with an air of resolution, she was bewildered to observe that that the young man was carefully laying out on the table various objects from the shop window. They included a pyramid of highly coloured sweets, several plates of sandwiches, and the two decanters containing that mysterious port and sherry which are peculiar to pastry-cooks. In the middle of this neat arrangement he had carefully let down the enormous load of white sugared cake which had been the huge ornament of the window.

'What on earth are you doing?' she asked.

'Duty, my dear Laura,' he began.

'Oh, for the Lord's sake, stop a minute,' she cried, 'and don't talk to me in that way. I mean what is all that?'

'A ceremonial meal, Miss Hope,'

'And what is that?' she asked impatiently, pointing to the mountain of sugar.

'The wedding cake, Mrs Angus,' he said.

[1] *confectioner* – a maker or seller of sweets and pastries

[2] *gutter-snipes* – 'street' children

[3] *cogitation* – thinking

Read lines 1–8.

A1 List five things that can be seen through the window of the confectioner's shop. **[5]**

Read lines 8–12.

A2 How does the writer show how attractive the shop window is to the young man?

You must refer to the language used in the text to support your answer, using relevant subject terminology. **[5]**

Read lines 13–21.

A3 What impressions do you get of John Turnbull Angus from these lines?

You must refer to the language used in the text to support your answer, using relevant subject terminology. **[10]**

Read lines 22–34.

A4 How does the writer build the reader's interest in the relationship between Angus and the young lady in these lines?

You should write about:

- what happens in these lines to build the reader's interest
- the writer's use of language and structure
- the effects on the reader

You must refer to the text to support your answer, using relevant subject terminology. **[10]**

Read from line 35 to the end.

A5 'There is something mysterious and intriguing about the young lady and her reaction to Angus.' How far do you agree with this view?

You should write about:

- your own thoughts and feelings about how Laura is presented here and in the passage as a whole
- how the writer has created these thoughts and feelings.

You must refer to the text to support your answer. **[10]**

SECTION B: 40 marks

In this section you will be assessed for the quality of your ***creative prose writing*** *skills.*

24 marks are awarded for communication and organisation. 16 marks are awarded for vocabulary, sentence structure, spelling and punctuation.

You should aim to write about 450-600 words.

Choose one of the following titles for your writing: **[40]**

Either,

(a) Looking through the Window.

Or,

(b) A Big Decision.

Or,

(c) Write a story which begins:

I never expected much to happen while I was serving coffee to strangers.

Or,

(d) Write about a person who made a big impression on you.

WJEC Eduqas

GCSE ENGLISH LANGUAGE

COMPONENT 2

19th and 21st Century Non-fiction Reading and Transactional / Persuasive Writing

PRACTICE PAPER

2 hours

INSTRUCTIONS TO CANDIDATES

Use black ink or black ball-point pen.

Answer **all** questions in Sections A and B

Write your answers on separate pieces of paper.

You are advised to spend your time as follows:

Section A-about 10 minutes reading
-about 50 minutes answering the questions

Section B-spend 30 minutes on each question
-about 5 minutes planning
-about 25 minutes writing

INFORMATION FOR CANDIDATES

Section A (Reading): 40 marks

Section B (Writing): 40 marks

The number of marks is given in brackets at the end of each question or part-question.

SECTION A: 40 marks

*Answer **all** the following questions.*

The extract below is a newspaper article by Alfie Witherspoon.

SAVE OUR LIBRARY

Local writer joins the fight against closure

By our Arts and Education Correspondent, Alfie Witherspoon

The campaign to save King's Park Library from closure has the backing of an array of local talent. Children's writer Mandy Frobisher says that without the library she would never have become a writer.

'I can't tell you how much that library meant to me,' she told me. 'It gave me a refuge, a place to do my homework, access to centuries of learning and a lifelong love of literature. It made me who I am. Why should today's children be deprived of the opportunities which our generation took for granted?'

Actor Steve Gomez agrees wholeheartedly. 'When I was growing up, the library was the centre of our community. People from all walks of life and all ages used it. They still do. If it closes, there'll be a black hole at the heart of King's Park.' Steve may not mean this literally, but other locals are concerned about what will happen to the building itself, a purpose-built, generously proportioned, roomy building beautifully decorated in the style of the Edwardian Arts and Crafts movement.

Campaigners have high hopes that the backing of Mary and Steve, and other well-known local figures, will help to publicize their campaign and maybe even persuade the Mayor and council to change their minds.

However, a spokesperson for the council claims that the facts simply don't justify keeping the library open. Statistics show that there are now fewer than 300 regular borrowers, almost all of them pensioners, and that number is falling all the time. Figures for people using the references facilities are equally depressing, with only a handful of knowledge-seekers using the facilities each day.

Nevertheless, campaign leader Councillor Laurel Tompkins says she will continue to fight the closure 'every inch of the way'. According to her, the savings to be made by shutting King's Park and five other local libraries are 'a drop in the ocean'. She acknowledges the government has made cuts in its funding – and that King's Park isn't the thriving, populous area it once was – but is convinced that it is not worth devastating the community for a comparatively small saving. 'And when new research is showing that one in three children in the UK does not own a book,' she adds, 'how can the Mayor deprive our kids of the chance of borrowing one and being turned on to reading for life?'

The following text is a letter to The Times, written in 1891, about a vote on the issues of public libraries in the London district of Marylebone. Under the Public Libraries Act, people had to vote in favour of public libraries before they could be built by a local council. This letter is from representatives of a group that was running free libraries without public funding.

PUBLIC LIBRARIES IN MARYLEBONE: TO THE EDITOR OF *THE TIMES*

Sir,– May we be allowed, through your columns, to appeal to the ratepayers[1] of Marylebone to record their votes at the end of the present week in favour of the adoption of the Public Libraries Acts, and thus secure for this large and wealthy parish the inestimable social advantages of good libraries, free to all classes, in every district?

We do not make this appeal in order to expatiate upon these advantages, because, with free libraries springing up in all directions, they are generally admitted. We would rather remind Marylebone of the work which our voluntary association has accomplished during the last three years – a work which must, in all probability, be brought to an end within the next year or so, unless the financial burden of maintaining the existing voluntary libraries be transferred from our association to the ratepayers at large.

The history of the Marylebone Free Library movement is briefly this:– An effort was made in 1887 to obtain sufficient funds, £20,000, to erect a handsome central library, which should not only be a permanent Jubilee[2] memorial, but also serve as a stimulus to the inhabitants of Marylebone to adopt the Public Libraries Acts. The movement failed, only about £7,000 being promised, and an appeal to the ratepayers the following year failed also, not so much from opposition as from apathy on the part of the inhabitants. Our association, in no wise daunted, decided to establish small local reading rooms and libraries in two of the most populous parts of the parish, in the hope that by these object-lessons demonstration amounting to proof would be given both of a great social need and a successful means of meeting it. We have not been mistaken in our calculations. The library in Lisson-grove, opened in 1889, has been an extraordinary success. The space is limited, and accommodation plain and insufficient, but notwithstanding these drawbacks no less than 219,000 persons of all sorts and conditions have used the news and reading room and the reference and lending libraries during the past year. A carefully selected library of 4,000 volumes has attracted 1,200 borrowers, whilst the demand increases daily. Our second library in Mortimer-street, nearly opposite the Middlesex Hospital, was only opened nine months ago and is on a smaller scale. Its success, however, is proportionately greater. Funds, and funds only, are required to enable the association to multiply these useful institutions. One library is £300 in debt, and the funds of the second are running low. Unfortunately, many of our actual and also many of our would-be subscribers feel that the very success of our movement relieves them of individual responsibility. That which exists, they say, for the good of all should be paid for by all, more especially when the maximum amount imposed upon each ratepayer by the 1d. rate[3] is so trifling. During the past few years no less than 28 metropolitan and suburban districts, some poor, some rich, have adopted the Public Libraries Acts. Others are about to follow, and our association hopes that Marylebone will be of the number. Much want of knowledge and indifference still exist on the subject of free libraries, and we therefore appeal to you to give publicity to our case, and thus contribute to success at the poll.

We beg, Sir, to remain yours obediently,

JOHN R. HOLLOND Chairman

FRANK DEBENHAM Treasurer

Marylebone Public Libraries Association, 18 Baker-street. March 4.

[1] *ratepayers* – people who pay 'rates' or local taxes, the equivalent of Council Tax today
[2] *Jubilee* – the golden jubilee of Queen Victoria had taken place in 1887
[3] *1d. rate* – a one -penny tax; local councils could increase rates by up to a penny per pound for libraries and museums.

Read the newspaper article by Alfie Witherspoon.

A1 **(a)** What audience does Mandy Frobisher write for? **[1]**

(b) How many people regularly borrow books from the library? **[1]**

(c) How many libraries is the Council proposing to close? **[1]**

A2 What do you think of the campaign to save King's Park Library as described in the article?

You should comment on:

- what both campaigners and their opponents say
- how they say it

You must refer to the text to support your comments. **[10]**

To answer the following questions you will need to read the letter to *The Times*.

A3 **(a)** What are the writers trying to persuade readers of the newspaper to do? **[2]**

(b) What do they mean by saying the advantages of libraries are 'generally admitted'? **[1]**

A4 How do the writers of the letter try to persuade people to support their point of view?

You should comment on:

- what they say to influence readers
- their use of language and tone
- the way they present their argument. **[10]**

To answer the following questions you will need to use both texts.

A5 What are the main differences between King's Park Library now and the two Marylebone libraries in 1891? **[4]**

A6 Both the texts are about public libraries. Compare the following:

- the writers' attitudes to libraries
- how they put across these attitudes.

You must use the texts to support your comments and make clear which text you are referring to. **[10]**

SECTION B: 40 marks

Answer questions B1 ***and*** *B2.*
In this section you will assessed for the quality of your writing skills.

For each question, 12 marks are awarded for communication and organisation; 8 marks are awarded for vocabulary, sentence structure, spelling and punctuation.

Think about the purpose and audience of your writing.

You should aim to write about 300-400 words for each task.

B1 The council has announced that it is planning to close your local library.

Write a letter to the local newspaper giving your views. **[20]**

B2 Your school supports a different charity each term. Your form has chosen this term's charity and has asked you to write an article for the school magazine or website about your plans to raise money.

Write your article.

You could include:

- details of your chosen charity and an explanation of why you have chosen it and why others should support it
- details of your plans for money-raising activities. **[20]**

WJEC Eduqas

GCSE ENGLISH LITERATURE

COMPONENT 1

Shakespeare and Poetry

PRACTICE PAPER

2 hours

Section A

Question

1 *Macbeth*
2 *Romeo and Juliet*
3 *Henry V*
4 *The Merchant of Venice*
5 *Much Ado About Nothing*
6 *Othello*

Section B

Question

7 Poetry

INSTRUCTIONS TO CANDIDATES

Answer two questions: one from Section A (questions 1-6) **and** Section B (question 7).

INFORMATION FOR CANDIDATES

Each section carries 40 marks.

You are advised to spend your time as follows:

Section A - about one hour

Section B - about one hour

The number of marks is given in brackets at the end of each question or part-question.

5 marks are given for accuracy in spelling, punctuation and the use of vocabulary and sentence structures in Section A, question part (b).

Practice Exam Papers

SECTION A: Shakespeare

Answer on one text only.

1. ***Macbeth***

*Answer **both** part (a) **and** part (b).*

You are advised to spend about 20 minutes on part (a) and about 40 minutes on part (b).

(a) Read the extract below.

Look at how Macbeth speaks and behaves here. What does it tell the audience about his state of mind at this point in the play? Refer closely to details from the extract to support your answer. **[15]**

MACBETH I have almost forgot the taste of fears.
The time has been my senses would have cooled
To hear the night-shriek, and my fell of hair
Would at a dismal treatise rise and stir
As life were in't. I have supped full with horrors.
Direness, familiar to my slaughterous thoughts,
Cannot once start me.

Enter Seyton

Wherefore was that cry?

SEYTON The Queen, my lord, is dead.

MACBETH She should have died hereafter.
There would have been a time for such a word.
Tomorrow, and tomorrow, and tomorrow
Creeps in this petty pace from day to day
To the last syllable of recorded time,
And all our yesterdays have lighted fools
The way to dusty death. Out, out, brief candle.
Life's but a walking shadow, a poor player
That struts and frets his hour upon the stage,
And then is heard no more. It is a tale
Told by an idiot, full of sound and fury,
Signifying nothing.

***(b)** Write about how Shakespeare presents the relationship between Macbeth and Lady Macbeth at different points in the play. **[25]**

**5 of this question's marks are allocated for accuracy in spelling, punctuation and the use of vocabulary and sentence structures.*

2. ***Romeo and Juliet***

*Answer **both** part (a) **and** part (b).*

You are advised to spend about 20 minutes on part (a) and about 40 minutes on part (b).

(a) Read the extract below.

Look at how Romeo and Juliet speak and behave here. What does it tell the audience about their relationship at this point in the play? Refer closely to details from the extract to support your answer. **[15]**

JULIET Wilt thou be gone? It is not yet near day.
It was the nightingale, and not the lark,
That pierced the fear-full hollow of thine ear.
Nightly she sings on yon pomegranate tree.
Believe me, love, it was the nightingale.
ROMEO It was the lark, the herald of the morn,
No nightingale. Look, love, what envious streaks
Do lace the severing clouds in yonder east.
Night's candles are burnt out, and jocund day
Stands tiptoe on the misty mountain tops.
I must be gone and live, or stay and die.
JULIET Yon light is not daylight; I know it, I.
It is some meteor that the sun exhaled
To be to thee this night a torchbearer
And light thee on thy way to Mantua.
Therefore stay yet. Thou need'st not be gone.

***(b)** Write about how Shakespeare presents Romeo's feelings towards Juliet in the play as a whole. **[25]**

**5 of this question's marks are allocated for accuracy in spelling, punctuation and the use of vocabulary and sentence structures.*

3. *Henry V*

*Answer **both** part (a) **and** part (b).*

You are advised to spend about 20 minutes on part (a) and about 40 minutes on part (b).

(a) Read the extract below.

Look at how the characters speak and behave here. How would an audience respond to this part of the play? Refer closely to details from the extract to support your answer. **[15]**

BARDOLPH On,on,on,on,on! To the breach, to the breach!.

NIM Pray thee corporal, stay. The knocks are too hot, and for mine own part, I have not a case of lives. The honour of it is too hot, that is the very plainsong of it.

PISTOL 'The plainsong' is most just, for humours do abound. Knocks
Go and come God's vassals drop and die,
[*sings*]And sword and shield
In bloody field
Doth win immortal fame.

BOY Would I were in London. I would give all my fame for a pot of ale, and safety.

PISTOL [*sings*] And I
If wishes would prevail with me
My purpose should not fail with me
But thither would I hie.

BOY [*sings*]As duly
But not as truly
As bird doth sing on bough.
[*Enter Captain Fluellen and beats them in*]

FLUELLEN God's plud! Up to the breaches, you dogs! Avaunt you cullions!

PISTOL Be merciful, great duke, to men of mould.
Abate thy rage, abate thy manly rage,
Abate thy rage, great duke. Good bawcock, bate
Thy rage. Use lenity, sweet chuck.

NIM These be good humours!
[*Fluellen begins to beat Nim*]
Your honour runs bad humours.
Exeunt all but the boy

BOY As young as I am, I have observed these three swashers. I am boy to them all three, but all they three, though they should serve me, could not be man to me, for indeed three such antucs do not amount to a man,

***(b)** Write about how an audience might react to King Henry's speeches at different points in the play. **[25]**

**5 of this question's marks are allocated for accuracy in spelling, punctuation and the use of vocabulary and sentence structures.*

4. ***The Merchant of Venice***

*Answer **both** part (a) **and** part (b).*

You are advised to spend about 20 minutes on part (a) and about 40 minutes on part (b).

(a) Read the extract below.

Look at how Antonio and Shylock speak and behave here. How does Shakespeare present Shylock as an outsider at this point in the play? Refer closely to details from the extract to support your answer. **[15]**

SHYLOCK Jailer, look to him. Tell me not of mercy.
This is the fool that lent the money gratis.
Jailer, look to him.
ANTONIO Hear me yet, good Shylock.
SHYLOCK I'll have my bond. Speak not against my bond.
I have sworn an oath that I will have my bond.
Thou called'st me a dog before thou hadst a cause,
But since I am a dog, beware my fangs.
The Duke shall grant me justice. I do wonder,
Thou naughty jailer, that thou art so fond
To come abroad with him at his request.
ANTONIO I pray thee hear me speak.
SHYLOCK I'll have my bond. I will not hear thee speak.
I'll have my bond, and therefore speak not me more.
I'll not be made a soft and dull-eyed fool
To shake the head, relent, and sigh, and yield
To Christian intercessors. Follow not.
I'll have no speaking. I will have my bond.

***(b)** How does Shakespeare explore ideas about justice and mercy in the play as a whole? **[25]**

**5 of this question's marks are allocated for accuracy in spelling, punctuation and the use of vocabulary and sentence structures.*

5. ***Much Ado About Nothing***

*Answer **both** part (a) **and** part (b).*

You are advised to spend about 20 minutes on part (a) and about 40 minutes on part (b).

(a) Read the extract below.

Look at how the characters speak and behave here. What does it tell the audience about the relationship between Beatrice and Benedick at this point in the play? Refer closely to details from the extract to support your answer. **[15]**

LEONATO	Faith, niece, you tax Signor Benedick too much. But he'll be meet with you, I doubt it not.
MESSENGER	He hath done good service, lady, in these wars.
BEATRICE	You had musty victual, and he hath holp to eat it. He is a very valiant trencherman, he hath an excellent stomach.
MESSENGER	And a good soldier too, lady.
BEATRICE	And a good soldier to a lady, but what is he to a lord?
MESSENGER	A lord to a lord, a man to a man, stuffed with all honourable virtues.
BEATRICE	It is so, indeed. He is no less than a stuffed man. But for the stuffing – well, we are all mortal.
LEONATO	You must not, sir, mistake my niece. There is a kind of merry war betwixt Signor Benedick and her. They never meet but there's a skirmish of wit between them.

***(b)** Write about how Shakespeare presents ideas about honour in the play as a whole. **[25]**

**5 of this question's marks are allocated for accuracy in spelling, punctuation and the use of vocabulary and sentence structures.*

6. ***Othello***

*Answer **both** part (a) **and** part (b).*

You are advised to spend about 20 minutes on part (a) and about 40 minutes on part (b).

(a) Read the extract below.

Look at how Othello speaks and behaves here. How would an audience respond to this part of the play? Refer closely to details from the extract to support your answer. **[15]**

OTHELLO Soft you, a word or two before you go.
I have done the state some service and they know't;
No more of that: I pray you in your letters,
When you shall these unlucky deeds relate,
Speak of them as they are; nothing extenuate,
Nor set down aught in malice; then must you speak
Of one that loved not wisely but too well:
Of one not easily jealous, but being wrought,
Perplexed in the extreme; of one whose hand,
Like the base Indian, threw a pearl away,
Richer than all his tribe; of one whose subdued eyes,
Albeit unused to the melting mood.
Drops tears as fast as the Arabian trees
Their medicinal gum; set you down this,
And say besides, that in Aleppo once,
Where a malignant and turbaned Turk
Beat a Venetian, and traduced the state,
I took him by the throat the circumcised dog,
And smote him thus.
He stabs himself
LODOVICO O bloody prevail!
GRATIANO All that's spoke is marred.
OTHELLO I kissed thee ere I killed thee, no way but this,
Killing myself, to die upon a kiss.

***(b)** Write about how an audience might react to the character of Iago at different points in the play. **[25]**

**5 of this question's marks are allocated for accuracy in spelling, punctuation and the use of vocabulary and sentence structures.*

SECTION B: Poetry

7. *Answer **both** part (a) **and** part (b).*

You are advised to spend about 20 minutes on part (a) and about 40 minutes on part (b).

(a) Read the poem *London* by William Blake. In this poem Blake writes about human suffering. Write about the ways in which he presents human suffering in this poem. **[15]**

(b) Choose **one** other poem from the anthology in which the poet also writes about suffering.

Compare the presentation of suffering in your chosen poem to the presentation of suffering in *London*. **[25]**

In your answer to part (b) you should compare:

- the content and structure of poems – what they are about and how they are organised;
- how the writers create effects, using appropriate terminology where relevant;
- the contexts of the poems and how these might have influenced the ideas in them.

***London* by William Blake**

I wander through each chartered street,
Near where the chartered Thames does flow,
And mark in every face I meet
Marks of weakness, marks of woe.

In every cry of every man,
In every infant's cry of fear,
In every voice, in every ban,
The mind-forged manacles I hear:

How the chimney-sweeper's cry
Every black'ning church appals
And the hapless soldier's sigh
Runs in blood down palace walls.

But most through midnight streets I hear
How the youthful harlot's curse
Blasts the new-born infant's tear,
And blights with plague the marriage hearse.

WJEC Eduqas

GCSE ENGLISH LITERATURE

COMPONENT 2

Post-1914 Prose/Drama, 19th Century Prose and Unseen Poetry

PRACTICE PAPER

2 hours and 30 minutes

Section A

Questions

1 *An Inspector Calls*
2 *Blood Brothers*
3 *The History Boys*
4 *The Curious Incident of the Dog in the Night-Time*
5 *A Taste of Honey*
6 *Lord of the Flies*
7 *Never Let Me Go*
8 *Anita and Me*
9 *The Woman in Black*
10 *Oranges are not the Only Fruit*

Section B

Questions

11 *The Strange Case of Dr Jekyll and Mr Hyde*
12 *A Christmas Carol*
13 *Jane Eyre*
14 *Pride and Prejudice*
15 *Silas Marner*
16 *War of the Worlds*

Section C

Question

17 *Unseen Poetry*

Instructions to Candidates

Answer **one** question in Section A (questions 1-10), **one** question in Section B (questions 11-16) **and** Section C (question 17).

Information for Candidates

Each section carries 40 marks.

You are advised to spend your time as follows:
Section A - about 45 minutes
Section B - about 45 minutes
Section C - about one hour

The number of marks is given in brackets at the end of each question or part-question.
5 marks are allocated for accuracy in spelling, punctuation and the use of vocabulary and sentence structures in Section A.

Practice Exam Papers

SECTION A: Post-1914 Prose/Drama

Answer one question only from this section.

1. *An Inspector Calls*

You are advised to spend about 45 minutes on this question.

You should use the extract referred to below and your knowledge of the whole text to answer the question.

Write about the significance of Eva Smith and how she is presented in *An Inspector Calls.*

In your response you should:
- refer to the extract and the play as a whole
- show your understanding of the characters and events in the play. **[40]**

5 of this question's marks are given for accuracy in spelling, punctuation, sentence structure and vocabulary

Re-read Act 1 from

INSPECTOR: I'd like some information, if you don't mind, Mr Birling.

to

INSPECTOR: It's the way I like to work. One person and one line of inquiry at a time. Otherwise, there's a muddle.

2. *Blood Brothers*

You are advised to spend about 45 minutes on this question.

You should use the extract referred to below and your knowledge of the whole text to answer the question.

Write about how Russell uses Mickey and Edward to explore ideas about social class in *Blood Brothers.*

In your response you should:
- refer to the extract and the play as a whole
- show your understanding of the characters and events in the play. **[40]**

5 of this question's marks are given for accuracy in spelling, punctuation, sentence structure and vocabulary

Re-read Act 1 from

MICKEY (off): Does Eddie live here?

to

MRS LYONS: Because, because you're not the same as him. You're not, do you understand?

3. ***The History Boys***

You are advised to spend about 45 minutes on this question.

You should use the extract referred to below and your knowledge of the whole text to answer the question.

Write about how Bennett presents different attitudes to history in *The History Boys*.

In your response you should:
- refer to the extract and the play as a whole
- show your understanding of the characters and events in the play. **[40]**

5 of this question's marks are given for accuracy in spelling, punctuation, sentence structure and vocabulary

> **Re-read Act 2 from**
>
> *IRWIN: If you want to learn about Stalin study Henry VIII.*
>
> **to**
>
> *IRWIN: God is dead. Shit lives.*

4. ***The Curious Incident of the Dog in the Night-Time***

You are advised to spend about 45 minutes on this question.

You should use the extract referred to below and your knowledge of the whole text to answer the question.

Write about how Stephens presents the character of Judy as a mother in *The Curious Incident of the Dog in the Night-Time.*

In your response you should:
- refer to the extract and the play as a whole
- show your understanding of the characters and events in the play. **[40]**

5 of this question's marks are given for accuracy in spelling, punctuation, sentence structure and vocabulary

> **Re-read Act 2 from**
>
> *JUDY: Dear Christopher. I said that I wanted to explain to you why I went away when I had time to do it properly.*
>
> **to**
>
> *JUDY: And then I had to walk you all the way home, which took hours because I knew you wouldn't go on the bus again.*

5. ***A Taste of Honey***

You are advised to spend about 45 minutes on this question.

You should use the extract referred to below and your knowledge of the whole text to answer the question.

Write about the character of Jo and how she is presented in *A Taste of Honey.*

In your response you should:

- refer to the extract and the play as a whole
- show your understanding of the characters and events in the play. **[40]**

5 of this question's marks are given for accuracy in spelling, punctuation, sentence structure and vocabulary

Re-read Act 1 from

Jo: Won't be long now. Who lives here besides us, Helen. Any young people?

to

Jo: It's nice to see a few flowers, isn't it?

6. ***Lord of the Flies***

You are advised to spend about 45 minutes on this question.

You should use the extract referred to below and your knowledge of the whole text to answer the question.

How does Golding present ideas about the breakdown of civilisation in *Lord of the Flies*?

In your response you should:

- refer to the extract and the novel as a whole
- show your understanding of the characters and events in the novel. **[40]**

5 of this question's marks are given for accuracy in spelling, punctuation, sentence structure and vocabulary

Re-read Chapter 8 from

The forest near them burst into uproar.

to

Then the three of them turned and trotted away.

7. ***Never Let Me Go***

You are advised to spend about 45 minutes on this question.

You should use the extract referred to below and your knowledge of the whole text to answer the question.

Write about the guardians and how they are presented in *Never Let Me Go.*

In your response you should:
- refer to the extract and the novel as a whole
- show your understanding of the characters and events in the novel. **[40]**

5 of this question's marks are given for accuracy in spelling, punctuation, sentence structure and vocabulary

Re-read Chapter 3 from

Tommy had heard all this before, but there was something about Miss Lucy's manner that made him keep listening hard.

to

'Anyway, when she said all this, she was shaking.'

8. ***Anita and Me***

You are advised to spend about 45 minutes on this question.

You should use the extract referred to below and your knowledge of the whole text to answer the question.

Write about how racism is presented in *Anita and Me.*

In your response you should:
- refer to the extract and the novel as a whole
- show your understanding of the characters and events in the novel. **[40]**

5 of this question's marks are given for accuracy in spelling, punctuation, sentence structure and vocabulary

Re-read Chapter 5 from

I had expected aggression, some name calling, the kind of hissed comments I occasionally endured from the young lads on the council estate near my school, the school where mama taught.

to

Mama said, 'Wipe your nose,' and handed me a tissue and we went inside.

9. ***The Woman in Black***

You are advised to spend about 45 minutes on this question.

You should use the extract referred to below and your knowledge of the whole text to answer the question.

How does Hill write about supernatural events in *The Woman in Black*?

In your response you should:

- refer to the extract and the novel as a whole
- show your understanding of the characters and events in the novel. **[40]**

5 of this question's marks are given for accuracy in spelling, punctuation, sentence structure and vocabulary

Re-read 'The Funeral of Mrs Drablow' from

At last he said in a low voice, 'I did not see a young woman,'

to

'No!' He almost shrieked.

10. ***Oranges are not the Only Fruit***

You are advised to spend about 45 minutes on this question.

You should use the extract referred to below and your knowledge of the whole text to answer the question.

How does Winterson present ideas about identity and belonging in *Oranges are not the Only Fruit?*

In your response you should:

- refer to the extract and the novel as a whole
- show your understanding of the characters and events in the novel. **[40]**

5 of this question's marks are given for accuracy in spelling, punctuation, sentence structure and vocabulary

Re-read 'Joshua' from

The Awful Occasion was the time my natural mother had come to claim me back.

to

She never spoke of what had happened and neither did I.

SECTION B: 19th-Century Prose

*Answer **one** question only from this section.*

11. ***The Strange Case of Dr Jekyll and Mr Hyde***

You are advised to spend about 45 minutes on this question.

You should use the extract referred to below and your knowledge of the whole novel to answer this question.

Write about how Stevenson uses Jekyll's transformation to explore ideas about good and evil in the novel.

In your response you should:

- refer to the extract and the novel as a whole;
- show your understanding of characters and events in the novel;
- refer to the contexts of the novel. **[40]**

Re-read Chapter 8 ('The Last Night') from

'That's it!' said Poole. 'It was this way. I came suddenly into the theatre from the garden. It seems he had slipped out to look for this drug or whatever it is; for the cabinet door was open, and there he was at the far end of the room digging among the crates…'

to

'…No, sir, that thing in the mask was never Doctor Jekyll – God knows what it was but it was never Doctor Jekyll; and it is the belief of my heart that there was murder done.'

12. ***A Christmas Carol***

You are advised to spend about 45 minutes on this question.

You should use the extract referred to below and your knowledge of the whole novel to answer this question.

How does Dickens write about social problems in the novel?

In your response you should:

- refer to the extract and the novel as a whole;
- show your understanding of characters and events in the novel;
- refer to the contexts of the novel. **[40]**

Re-read Stave (Chapter) 3 from

'Forgive me if I am not justified in what I ask,' said Scrooge, looking intently at the Spirit's robe, 'but I see something strange, and not belonging to yourself, protruding from your skirts. Is it a foot or a claw?'

to

Are there no prisons?' said the Spirit, turning on him for the last time with his own words. 'Are there no workhouses?'

13. ***Jane Eyre***

You are advised to spend about 45 minutes on this question.

You should use the extract referred to below and your knowledge of the whole novel to answer this question.

Write about how Brontë presents the character of Mr Rochester and Jane's changing feelings towards him.

In your response you should:

- refer to the extract and the novel as a whole;
- show your understanding of characters and events in the novel;
- refer to the contexts of the novel. **[40]**

Re-read Chapter 15 from

And was Mr Rochester now ugly in my eyes?

to

Suppose he should be absent spring, summer, and autumn: how joyless sunshine and fine days will seem!

14. ***Pride and Prejudice***

You are advised to spend about 45 minutes on this question.

You should use the extract referred to below and your knowledge of the whole novel to answer this question.

How does Austen write about attitudes to marriage in the novel?

In your response you should:

- refer to the extract and the novel as a whole;
- show your understanding of characters and events in the novel;
- refer to the contexts of the novel. **[40]**

Re-read Chapter 20 from

'An unhappy alternative is before you, Elizabeth. From this day you must be a stranger to one of your parents. – Your mother will never see you again if you do not marry Mr Collins, and I will never see you again if you do.'

to

A'But I tell you what, Miss Lizzy, if you take it into your head to go on refusing every offer of marriage in this way, you will never get a husband at all – and I am sure I do not know who is to aintain you when your father is dead.'

15. ***Silas Marner***

You are advised to spend about 45 minutes on this question.

You should use the extract referred to below and your knowledge of the whole novel to answer this question.

Write about Silas's relationship with Eppie and how it is presented in the novel.

In your response you should:

- refer to the extract and the novel as a whole;
- show your understanding of characters and events in the novel;
- refer to the contexts of the novel. **[40]**

Re-read Chapter 12 from

When Marner's sensibility returned, he continued the action which had been arrested, and closed his door…

to

-that there was a human body, with the head sunk low into the furze, and half-covered with the shaken snow.

16. ***War of the Worlds***

You are advised to spend about 45 minutes on this question.

You should use the extract referred to below and your knowledge of the whole novel to answer this question.

Write about how Wells presents the reactions of different characters to the invasion at different points in the novel.

In your response you should:
- refer to the extract and the novel as a whole;
- show your understanding of characters and events in the novel;
- refer to the contexts of the novel. **[40]**

Re-read Book 1, Chapter 13 from

I do not clearly remember the arrival of the curate…

to

'Killed!' he said, staring about him. 'How can God's ministers be killed?'

SECTION C: Unseen Poetry

17. Answer **both** part (a) **and** part (b).

You are advised to spend about 20 minutes on part (a) and about 40 minutes on part (b).

Read the two poems, *Death the Leveller* by James Shirley and *Requiem* by Robert Louis Stevenson. In both these poems the poets write about their feeling about death.

(a) Write about *Death the Leveller* and its effect on you. **[15]**

You may wish to consider:

- what the poem is about and how it is organised;
- the ideas the poet may have wanted us to think about;
- the poet's choice of words, phrases and images and the effects they create;
- how you respond to the poem.

Death the Leveller, James Shirley

The glories of our blood and state
Are shadows, not substantial things;
There is no armour against Fate;
Death lays his icy hand on kings:
Sceptre and Crown
Must tumble down,
And in the dust be equal made
With the poor crookèd scythe and spade.

Some men with swords may reap the field,
And plant fresh laurels where they kill:
But their strong nerves at last must yield;
They tame but one another still:
Early or late
They stoop to fate,
And must give up their murmuring breath
When they, pale captives, creep to death.

The garlands wither on your brow,
Then boast no more your mighty deeds!
Upon Death's purple altar now
See where the victor-victim bleeds.
Your heads must come
To the cold tomb:
Only the actions of the just
Smell sweet and blossom in their dust.

(b) Now compare *Death the Leveller* and *Requiem*. **[25]**

You should compare:

- what the poems are about and how they are organised;
- the ideas the poets may have wanted us to think about;
- the poets' choice of words, phrases and images and the effects they create;
- how you respond to the poems.

Requiem, Robert Louis Stevenson

Under the wide and starry sky,
Dig the grave and let me lie.
Glad did I live and gladly die,
And I laid me down with a will.

This be the verse you gave for me:
Here he lies where he longed to be;
Home is the sailor, home from the sea,
And the hunter home from the hill.

Answers

Key Technical Skills: Writing – pages 156–160

Page 156: Spelling

1. a) tomatoes b) birthdays
   c) soliloquies d) families
   e) parentheses **[maximum 5]**
2. a) **You're** not going out like that. I asked **your** sister to bring it.
   b) **There** are twenty people in the class. They have all done **their** homework but **they're** not sitting in the right places.
   c) Turn it off or it will **wear** out. We have no idea **where** it is but **we're** going anyway.
   d) I **passed** him in the street an hour ago. He walked right **past** me as if I wasn't there.
   e) There were only **two** exams **to** sit but that was one **too** many.
   f) If you don't go to the **practice** you'll be left out of the team. If you want to improve you will have to **practise** every day.
   [1] for each correct answer up to a maximum of **[15]**
3. Last **night** I went to the cinema with my friend Bob and his **father**, Michael. The whole evening was not very **successful**. The cinema was very **crowded** and we had to sit **separately**. Then, it turned out the film was in a **foreign language** and no-one could understand it. I think it was about the **environment**. Afterwards, Michael took us to a **restaurant** **where** we had pizzas.
   [1] for each correct answer up to a maximum of **[10]**

Page 157: Punctuation

1. *Great Expectations,* **[1]** one of the best-known novels by Charles Dickens**,** **[1]** is the story of Pip**,** **[1]** a boy who grows up in the marshes of Kent. At **[1]** the beginning of the story he meets an escaped convict in the churchyard where his parents are buried. **[1]** **[maximum 5]**
2. At about ten o'clock **[1]**, we went to Romio's **[1]** for pizzas. I'm **[1]** not sure what Bob's **[1]** pizza topping was but I had ham and pineapple. I wish I hadn't **[1]** because later on I was sick in Michael's **[1]** car. It's **[1]** brand new and I thought he'd **[1]** be angry but he wasn't **[1]**. We're **[1]** not going there again. **[maximum 10]**
3. **a)** The cat slept quietly on the mat; the dog slept noisily on the step. **b)** Who was that masked man? Nobody knows. **c)** I don't believe it! That's the first answer I've got. **d)** Annie deserved the prize: she was the best baker by far. **e)** Jane and Elizabeth (the two oldest Bennet sisters) get married at the end.
   [1] for each correct answer up to a maximum of **[5]**

Page 158: Sentence Structure

1. a) complex b) minor c) simple
   d) compound e) simple
   [maximum of **[5]**
2. a) I bought Anna a bunch of flowers **because** it was her birthday. **[1]**
   b) He did not finish the race **although** they gave him a certificate. **[1]**
   a) and b) could be written with the conjunctions at the beginning of the sentence, but you would then need to add a comma after the first clause.
   c) I kept going **until** I reached the finishing line. **[1]**
3. Joey, who was the oldest cat in the street, never left the garden. **[1]**
4. Walking down the street, I realised I had forgotten my phone. **[1]**

Page 159: Text Structure and Organisation

1. a) 3
   b) 5
   c) 2
   d) 4
   e) 1 **[maximum 5]**
2. a) When
   b) In spite of
   c) subsequently
   d) however
   e) Nevertheless **[maximum 5]**

Page 160: Standard English and Grammar

1. a) are b) are c) were d) did
   e) has been f) have done g) were...had done
   [maximum 7]
2. a) pleaded b) few c) got
   [maximum 3]
3. Jo: Hello. How are you? **[1]**
   Arthur: Well. Very well, thank you. **[1]**
   Jo: Do you want (*or* would you like) a drink? **[1]**
   Arthur: May I have two coffees, please? **[1]**
   Jo: Of course. Where are you sitting? **[1]**
4. I was **standing** in the street when Frankie **came** over. **[1]** I gave him a smile and opened **my mouth** to speak. **[1]** I was **going to** ask him how he **did** in **maths** (*or* **mathematics**). **[1]** I **did not say anything**. **[1]** **As** soon as I **saw** him I knew he **had done well**. **[1]**

Key Technical Skills: Reading – pages 161–168

Page 161: Identifying Information and Ideas 1

1. a, c **[maximum 2]**
2. **Any five from**: He was very nice looking. He had a fresh-coloured face. He was clean shaven. He had white hair. He wore odd-shaped collars. He wore a top hat. **[maximum 5]**

Page 162: Identifying Information and Ideas 2

1. a) Year 10 b) No
   c) Solicitor d) Answered the telephone
   e) No **[maximum 5]**

Page 163: Synthesis and Summary

1. **a)** Trees stand behind the shed. **[1]** **b)** Charlotte Green ate Lydia's chocolate. **[1]** **c)** Tell me who did it. **[1]**
2. b, c, f, g, h **[maximum 5]**
3. The summary below is a suggestion only. You should have included details of where and when it happened, and a description of the men.
   [1] for each point up to a maximum of **[12]**.

   At nine o'clock on Monday I was in Arbuckle Lane. As I passed number eighteen, I heard a noise. There were two men on the step. One was breaking the glass in the door with something in his hand. I shouted and they turned. One was about six foot, with a grey beard. The other was stocky with curly black hair. The tall man dropped something and they ran.

Page 164: Synthesis and Summary

1.

Mary Jane	Sarah
Parents did not see the point of school	Mother thought education important
Loved going to school	Did not like going to school
40 in a class	24 in class
(Everyone) worked hard	Did not do much work
Teacher very strict	Teacher never told anyone off
Sat in rows	Sat in groups
Not allowed to talk	Talked all the time
Liked the teacher	Did not like the teacher
Respected the teacher	Did not respect the teacher
Appreciated/valued school	Did not appreciate/value school

[1] for each pair up to a maximum of **[10]**

2. Look at the mark scheme below, decide which description is closest to your answer and then decide what mark to give it up to a maximum of **[4]**.

Marks	Skills
4	• You have shown clear understanding of both texts. • You have synthesised evidence from texts. • You have used a range of relevant detail from both texts.
3	• You have shown some understanding of both texts. • You have shown clear connections between texts. • You have used relevant detail from both texts.

Page 165: Referring to the Text

1. a–e, b–d, c–f **[maximum 3]**
2. **a)** Macbeth refers to the prophecies as 'happy prologues'. **[2]**
   b) He tells us that one of them has come true: 'I am Thane of Cawdor.' **[2]**
   c) Macbeth asks how the prophecies can be evil when the witches have told the truth:

If ill,
Why hath it given me earnest of success
Commencing in a truth? **[2]**

3.

Point	Frankenstein's response is negative from the start.
Evidence	Referring to the experiment as a 'catastrophe' and his creation as a 'wretch'
Explanation	suggests that he has rejected the creature and will not try to find any good in it.

[maximum 3]

Page 166: Analysing Language 1

1. **a)** dialectical (also colloquial) **b)** formal
   c) colloquial **d)** technical **[maximum 4]**
2. **a)** adjective **b)** preposition
   c) conjunction **d)** (concrete) noun
   e) adverb **f)** verb **[maximum 6]**
3. **a)** complex **b)** Jo, Beth or Amy
   c) passive **d)** past perfect
   e) third person **[maximum 5]**

Page 167: Analysing Language 2

1. **a)** Simile. It suggests he ran extremely quickly as the wind travels quickly. **[2]** **b)** Metaphor. It suggests that there are a lot of insects and that they are dangerous, violent and organised. **[2]** **c)** Both. 'Heart' is a metaphor for her feelings/emotions. Describing it as cold or frozen suggests that she feels nothing. **[maximum 6]**
2. **a)** Time **b)** fizzed/crackled **[maximum 2]**
3. Look at the mark scheme below, decide which description is closest to your answer and then decide what mark to give it up to a maximum of **[5]**.

Marks	Skills
5	• You have made accurate and perceptive comments about the text. • You have analysed the effects of the choice of language. • You have used well-considered subject terminology accurately.
4	• You have given accurate impressions. • You have begun to analyse the choice of language. • You have used relevant subject terminology appropriately.

Page 168: Analysing Form and Structure

1. Up to **[2]** for any reasonable answer to each question up to a maximum of **[10]**.
   a) A boarding house / in a city / a place where single people rent rooms / Second Avenue (New York / America).
   b) 'Small and unobtrusive' / dressed plainly / shy / does not draw attention to herself / not interested in what's going on.
   c) Does not fit with the previous description of her / a change in mood / shows an interest in Andy / shows that she is sharp or intelligent / suggests she is judging him.
   d) He is polite or well-mannered / he has charm / he is starting a successful career / he is shallow or superficial / he is not interested in Miss Conway.
   e) She does something to make herself noticed / they get to know each other / they fall in love / they argue / it turns out that they know each other / any other reasonable conjecture.
2. a–y, b–z, c–x

[1] for each up to a maximum of **[3]**

English Language 1 – pages 169–172

Page 169: Reading Literature 1

1.

A naive/unreliable narrator	A
An omniscient narrator	D
A reliable first-person narrator	B
An intrusive narrator	C (also omniscient)

[2] for each up to a maximum of **[8]**

Page 170: Reading Literature 2

[1] for each correct answer in 'How we learn' and up to **[2]** for a reasonable explanation in 'What we learn' up to a maximum of **[15]**.

1.

Character	How we learn	What we learn
Hyde's housekeeper:	a)	She is a bad person / she cannot be trusted / she is polite.
Magwitch:	b)	He is aggressive / rough / frightening.
Darcy:	e)	People are generally impressed by him when they first meet him but quickly change their minds because of the way he behaves.
Mrs Reed:	d)	She is bad-tempered / aggressive / cruel / uncaring.
Victor Frankenstein:	c)	He is behaving strangely / he is sick / he is hysterical. He worries his friend.

Page 171: Creative Writing 1

The following answers are examples of the sort of thing you might write. Your own answers might be completely different. **[1]** for each reasonable answer.

1. **a)** First person; yes. **b)** Formal, using Standard English. **c)** Female **d)** 82 **e)** Small, neat, well-dressed **f)** Grew up on a farm and married a farmer, now living in a bungalow in a village **g)** A widow, with two children who live abroad, friendly with the neighbours but no close friends **h)** Speaks in a Cornish accent but uses Standard English **i)** walking and bird watching **j)** keeps her opinions to herself but hates being told what to do. **[maximum 10]**
2. **a)** In the village post office. **b)** Yes, she goes abroad. **c)** Now. **d)** A year. **e)** Yes (except for some memories in flashback). **[maximum 5]**
3. **Exposition**: Doris leads a quiet life in a small village with her two cats. **Inciting incident**: She wins the lottery. She decides to visit her children but not tell them she's a millionaire. **Turning point**: She goes to see her daughter in France, who is too busy to be bothered. She books her a ticket to Australia. In Australia her son lets her stay but after a while he puts her in a horrible home. **Climax**: She buys the nursing home, improves the lives of its patients and returns home, where she spends the rest of her money on herself and on charities. **Coda/ending**: Doris is living happily in the village with her cats and a man she met in the nursing home. She has spent all her money and not given any to her children. **[maximum 5]**

Page 172: Creative Writing 2

The following answers are examples of the sort of thing you might write. Your own answers will be completely different. **[1]** for each reasonable answer up to a maximum of **[20]** overall.

1. **a)** Arnold Spence
   b) A fairground in Australia.
2. **Character – a)** grey hair/woollen cardigan **b)** Scottish accent/cough **c)** aftershave/cough sweets **d)** not applicable **e)** rough hands/soft wool.
   Scene – a) Gaudy rides, milling crowds. **b)** Screeching child, loud dance music. **c)** Spicy sausage, burning wood. **d)** Tangy mustard, sweet toffee. **e)** Sticky candyfloss, slimy mud.
3. **Character – a)** a group of elderly people gathered around the television **b)** straight-backed smartly dressed gentleman **c)** startlingly white dentures.
   Scene – a) A blur of swirling colours and harsh noises. **b)** Candy-striped stall; fluffy toys piled high. **c)** Blue nylon fur, plastic brown eyes.
4. **Character – a)** like a leopard amongst domestic cats **b)** a whirlwind of activity.
   Scene – a) The crowd rumbled and rolled like a storm-tossed ship. **b)** An explosion of excited laughter.

English Language 2 – pages 173–174

Page 173: Reading Non-fiction

1. Up to **[2]** for each answer similar to the following up to a maximum of **[20]**:

	Text A	Text B
What is the writer's attitude to Little Mickledon?	Likes it. Finds it 'charming and tranquil'.	Does not like the peace and quiet: 'totally cut off'.
What is the writer's opinion of the B & B?	Finds it 'delightful' and gives positive impression of the owners.	Finds it a 'disappointment', criticises several aspects and does not like owners' attitude.
What impression do you get of the writer?	Someone who likes peace and quiet. Someone who focuses on positive aspects.	Someone who likes to be in touch. Someone who likes to criticise / likes to find fault.
How would you describe the general tone and style?	Positive/ enthusiastic/vague	Negative/critical/ honest
Comment on language features.	Uses words like 'relax', 'calm' and 'tranquil' to give an impression of peace and quiet. Uses archaic words/ spellings (Olde, yore) and puts quotation marks round 'civilization'.	Colloquial – addresses readers with imperative ('Be warned'). Uses adjectives to give an unflattering picture: 'grubby', 'pitiful', 'hippy'.

(Continued)

Page 174: Persuasive/Transactional Writing

1. The following are only suggestions. There are many other points you could make. **[1]** for each up to a maximum of **[10]**.

Pros	Cons
Studying for exams is much more important.	It helps you understand the importance of things like punctuality and politeness.
The work being done is not interesting or meaningful.	It helps you choose your future career.
Students on work experience are just free labour.	You can learn new skills.
In the time you cannot get a realistic idea of what the work is like.	You might make contacts which would lead to paid employment.
You've got the rest of your life to experience work.	You get to meet a wide range of people.

2. **[1]** for each of the following up to a maximum of **[5]**:
   - opening with 'Dear Sir' or 'Dear Editor'
   - setting out the opening correctly
   - using a formal tone
   - clearly stating the purpose of your letter
   - putting your point of view strongly and clearly
   - using a rhetorical or literary device
   - accurate spelling and punctuation.
3. **[1]** for each of the following up to a maximum of **[5]**:
   - using an intriguing/amusing headline
   - using a strapline
   - using an appropriate informal tone
   - clearly stating the purpose of your article
   - putting your point of view strongly and clearly
   - using a rhetorical or literary device
   - accurate spelling and punctuation.

Shakespeare – pages 175–176

Page 175: Context and Themes

1. Up to **[2]** for each reasonable answer up to a maximum of **[12]**.
2. Up to **[2]** for each reasonable answer up to a maximum of **[12]**.

Page 176: Characters, Language and Structure

1. **[2]** for each quotation and **[2]** for a reasonable interpretation up to a maximum of **[12]**.
2. **[1]** for each correct answer and up to **[2]** for a reasonable explanation similar to the suggestions below up to a maximum of **[12]**.
   a) Oxymoron. Its use suggests confusion about love and how the themes of love and hate are intertwined in the play. **b)** Metaphor. The speaker (Shylock) picks up on an insulting comparison and extends it to warn that he can 'bite.' **c)** Rhetorical question. The chorus asks whether it is

possible to recreate the war in a theatre. He is challenging the audience and hoping to prove that the answer is 'yes'.

c) Pathetic fallacy / personification.

Othello makes the rocks and hills seem alive, making his description more vivid and impressive.

Poetry – pages 177–180

Page 177: Context and Themes

1. **a)** 'Death of a Naturalist' **[1]** **b)** 'Living Space' **[1]** **c)** Sonnet 43 **[1]** **d)** Excerpt from 'The Prelude' **[1]** **e)** 'Mametz Wood' **[1]**
2. The following answers are suggestions. You may have listed other poems. **[1]** for each title listed appropriately, up to a maximum of **[16]**.
   a) 'The Prelude'; 'Hawk Roosting'; Death of a Naturalist'.
   b) 'To Autumn'; 'The Prelude'; 'As Imperceptibly as Grief'; 'She Walks in Beauty'.
   c) 'Living Space'; 'London'; 'A Wife in London'.
   d) Sonnet 43; 'Cozy Apologia'; 'The Manhunt'; 'She Walks in Beauty'.
   e) 'Dulce et Decorum Est'; 'The Soldier'; 'The Manhunt; 'London'; 'Mametz Wood'.
   f) 'The Manhunt'; 'A Wife in London'.
   g) 'Death of a Naturalist'; 'The Prelude'; 'Afternoons'.
   h) 'Afternoons'; 'Death of a Naturalist'; 'The Prelude'; Sonnet 43.

Page 178: Language, Form and Structure

1. **[1]** for each technique identified and **[1]** for each reasonable explanation (the explanations below are suggestions only), up to a maximum of **[36]**.
   a) Caesura, archaic language. The use of 'thee' makes it sound almost religious. The caesura makes the reader stop as the poet stops to think. **[4]**
   b) Onomatopoeia, simile, caesura, enjambment. Onomatopoeia gives a 'sound picture' of the comic brutality of the frogs. The simile associates them with war, making them the enemy. The combination of caesura and enjambment means the poem is broken up in an irregular, disturbing way. **[8]**
   c) Personification. This makes the season sound like a young girl who only stays briefly. **[2]**
   d) Alliteration, metaphor. Manacles are used to restrain prisoners. Blake's metaphor says that they are made in the mind. Whether the minds of those who are oppressed or those who are oppressing is not clear. The alliteration emphasises his point and gives an almost numbing sound. **[4]**
   e) Alliteration (sibilance), simile, rhyming couplet, end-stopping. The sibilance reflects the gentle feelings described, contrasting with the traditional simile of 'arrows' to denote the pain of love. The rhyming couplets reflect the simplicity of the feeling and the end-stopping shows confidence in the feeling expressed. **[8]**
   f) Repetition/enjambment. The sentence runs across two stanzas, showing how things continue. This is emphasised by the repetition of the phrase 'courting-places'. The wind is seen almost as a person, deliberately spoiling things. **[6]**
   g) Alliteration, simile/personification. The woman is associated with the beauty of nature and the mystery of the night. The alliteration conveys a calm, gentle feeling. This feeling is reinforced by the use of enjambment. **[6]**

Page 179: Unseen Poetry

1. Up to **[2]** for each answer similar to those below. Other answers might be equally valid.
   a) It is set in a forest during a storm.
   b) No, it is irregular (free verse). The lack of regular patterns reflects the unpredictability of the storm.
   c) 'Cackle with uncouth sounds' conveys the harshness of the sounds described. It could be called onomatopoeia.
   d) In 'white liquid fire, bright white' the 'i's are sharp and quick, like the lightning.
   e) Describing the lightning as a 'white snake' adds a sense of danger as well as painting a vivid picture.
   f) By adding a lot of details in this simple way, the poet builds a sense of the way the storm continues and shows no sign of stopping.
   g) The repetition of this phrase and the shortness of the line give it greater impact, emphasising that humans may think they have harnessed the power of electricity but they cannot really tame nature.
   h) The power and wonder of nature – the insignificance of humans – the arrogance of humans.
   i) He is in awe of nature – he is excited and perhaps frightened by the storm – it makes him feel insignificant – it makes him realise that humans are not really powerful.
   j) Any answer rooted in the text. **[maximum 20]**

Page 180: Unseen Poetry

2. The answers below are suggestions. There may be other valid responses. Up to **[2]** for every box filled in with a reasonable response, up to a maximum of **[32]**.

	'Storm in the Black Forest'	'The Vixen'
Setting (time and place)	In a forest during a storm.	In the woods on what seems to be a typical day for the vixen.
What happens in the poem	The poet describes the stages of a violent storm and how it never seems to end, making him think about man and nature.	The poet describes the behaviour of a vixen and her cubs, and how she reacts to danger.
Structure	Four stanzas of unequal lengths (one of only one line) and lines of different lengths, giving a sense of unpredictability.	One stanza of 14 lines, describing what happens in a controlled way. 14 lines, as in a sonnet, but not sonnet structure.
Rhythm and rhyme	No regularity – again reflecting the storm.	Iambic pentameter – smooth and regular. Rhyming couplets – simple structure, each couplet describing one small action.
Vocabulary/register	Language of richness (bronzey), danger (snake), movement (wriggling) and science (electric) combine to convey awe and wonder.	Everyday, straightforward language.

Use of sound	Alliteration and assonance used to suggest the sounds of the storm.	Sounds made by vixen conveyed by onomatopoeia. Alliteration in line 13.
Imagery	Metaphor and personification used to give vivid impression of the power of the storm.	Literal imagery: the poem describes the scene.
Themes and the poet's attitude	The power of nature; the arrogance of man; the wonder of nature. The last stanza draws a 'lesson' from the experience. He is excited and frightened by nature and impressed by its power. He feels humans are comparatively powerless, though they think they are powerful.	Tension between nature and man; motherhood; the beauty of nature. He is impressed by the vixen's care for her cubs. He sees the danger posed by humans from her point of view. The ending gives a positive, hopeful view of life.

Post-1914 Prose/Drama – pages 181–182

Page 181: Context and Themes

Below are examples of the kind of answer you might have given. Up to **[5]** for each reasonable answer similar to these, depending on how full your answer is.

1. a) *An Inspector Calls* is set shortly before the First World War, in 1912, in a 'large city' in the Midlands. The family is middle-class and wealthy, Mr Birling being a self-made man who has married someone from a higher social class. They are 'comfortable' and smug but the Inspector reveals the dark underside of their world.

b) The world of *Never Let Me Go* seems to be just like the real world of just a few years ago. However, there are aspects of this world which are not real (as far as we know). Breeding people to provide spare parts is not something that is done officially now, although there are cases of people having children to provide genetic material for existing children who are sick.

c) *Blood Brothers* was originally written to be performed for schools and youth groups on Merseyside. This is reflected in the simple plot, the characters and the issues. It later became a musical. The use of songs to express feelings or advance the plot reflects the tradition of musical theatre.

2. a) **[1]** for each theme up to a maximum of **[4]**.

b) Up to **[2]** for each reasonable answer up to a maximum of **[8]**.

Page 182: Characters, Language and Structure

1. **[1]** for every box completed with a reasonable answer up to a maximum of **[24]**.
2. Up to **[2]** for each reasonable answer up to a maximum of **[10]**.

Nineteenth-Century Prose – pages 183–184

Page 183: Context and Themes

1. Up to **[2]** for each reasonable answer up to a maximum of **[10]**.
2. **a)** **[1]** for each reasonable answer up to a maximum of **[5]**.
b) Up to **[2]** for each reasonable answer up to a maximum of **[10]**.

Page 184: Characters, Language and Structure

1. **[1]** for every box completed with a reasonable answer up to a maximum of **[25]**.
2. a–x, b–v, c–y, d–z, e–w **[2]** for each correct answer up to a maximum of **[10]**

Practice Exam Papers – pages 185–216

Page 186 English Language Component 1

Section A: Reading

A1
- mirrors
- cakes
- sweetmeats
- chocolates
- wedding cake.

[1] for each up to a maximum of **[5]**

A2 Look at the mark scheme below, decide which description is closest to your answer and then decide what mark to give it up to a maximum of **[5]**.

Marks	Skills
5	• You have made accurate and perceptive comments about what makes the shop window attractive. • You have analysed the effects of the choice of language. • You have used well-considered subject terminology accurately.
4	• You have made accurate comments about what makes the shop window attractive. • You have begun to analyse the choice of language. • You have used relevant subject terminology appropriately.

You might have included some of the following points in your answer:

- The word 'rainbow' is used to show how colourful it is; it has connotations of happiness (sun after rain).
- It is 'natural' for the window to attract children – maybe adults as well.
- There may be an implication that he is child-like in his wonder.
- 'Fiery charm' suggests warmth and passion.
- The attraction is not just the sweets, hinting that there is something or someone else attracting him to the shop.
- Litotes (ironic understatement) is used to tell us that the chocolates are still part of the attraction: he 'was far from despising' them.

A3 Look at the mark scheme below, decide which description is closest to your answer and then decide which mark to give yourself up to a maximum of **[10]**

Marks	Skills
9–10	• You have made accurate and perceptive comments about the text. • You have given a detailed analysis of how the writer uses language to achieve effects. • You have chosen an appropriate range of examples. • You have used well-considered subject terminology accurately to support your comments.
7–8	• You have made accurate comments about the text. • You have begun to analyse how the writer uses language to achieve effects. • You have chosen appropriate examples. • You have used relevant subject terminology accurately to support your comments.

In your answer you might have made some of the following points:

- The writer gives his background, establishing something about his character and what he does.
- There is a physical description – 'Tall, burly, red-haired', three adjectives giving a clear picture.
- There is a contradiction between his 'resolute face' and his 'listless manner'.
- His face makes him seem determined, but he behaves in a relaxed way.
- He is an artist – he has sketches with him – and makes some money (but not a lot) from them.
- He comes from a rich family but will not inherit their money.
- He is involved in politics (Socialism).
- He is polite to the young lady in the shop.
- The statement that he 'merely' raises his hat suggests that he might be expected to be friendlier towards her.

A4 Look at the mark scheme below, decide which description is closest to your answer and then decide which mark to give yourself up to a maximum of **[10]**.

Marks	Skills
9–10	• You have made accurate and perceptive comments about the text. • You have given a detailed analysis of how the writer uses language and the organisation of events (structure) to achieve effects. • You have chosen an appropriate range of examples. • You have used well-considered subject terminology accurately to support your comments.
7–8	• You have made accurate comments about how details are used. • You have begun to analyse how the writer uses language and the organisation of events (structure) to achieve effects. • You have chosen appropriate examples. • You have used relevant subject terminology accurately to support your comments.

In your answer you might have made some of the following points:

- Their first encounter is casual yet polite, as we might expect from a customer and a waitress.
- The short sentence 'His order was evidently a usual one' establishes him as a 'regular' and the visit to the shop as part of his routine.
- At this stage the woman has not been given a name. We do not know how well he knows her.
- His casual proposal comes as a surprise – it could be a joke or it could be serious.
- She takes control by saying she doesn't 'allow' such remarks.
- She seems to see the proposal as a joke – the reader would probably agree.
- The man suddenly looks serious, changing the tone and suggesting it is not a joke.
- However, his comparison of love to a bun is comical.
- Her reaction is intriguing. She is 'studying' and seems 'tragic', giving a serious turn to the story.
- The 'shadow of a smile' suggests she is interested, as does sitting down. It is now clear this is not just a customer/waitress relationship.
- Angus remains frivolous but returns to the subject of marriage.
- There is contrast between what they say and the looks they give each other.

A5 Look at the mark scheme below, decide which description is closest to your answer and then decide which mark to give yourself up to a maximum of **[10]**.

Marks	Skills
9–10	• You have persuasively evaluated the text and its effects. • You have used convincing, well-selected examples from the text to explain your views. • Your response shows engagement and involvement, taking an overview and making comments on the text as a whole. • You have explored with insight how the writer has created thoughts and feelings.
7–8	• You have critically evaluated the text and its effects. • You have used well-selected examples from the text to explain your views. • Your response shows critical awareness and clear engagement with the text. • You have explored how the writer has created thoughts and feelings.

In your answer you may have mentioned some of the following points:

- We are not told what she is thinking about except that she is 'not unsympathetic' – so perhaps she returns his feelings.
- The revelation of what she thinks or feels is delayed by his actions.
- She continues to try to do her job – there is tension between this and her relationship with Angus.
- He calls her 'dear Laura', showing that there is some kind of friendship/relationship between them.
- However, she tells him not to talk 'like that': it is not clear whether she thinks he is being over-friendly.
- She is exasperated with him and his manner, but she tries to stay in control of the situation. She has, so far, been the object of the young man's attention but towards the end of the passage the focus is much more on her.
- There is a feeling we might now learn what she has been thinking about and how she feels about Angus.

Page 189 English Language Component 1

Section B: Writing

Look at the mark scheme below, decide which description is closest to your answer and then decide which mark to give yourself. This task is marked for communication and organisation, and for technical accuracy.

Communication and Organisation (maximum 24)

Marks	Skills
20–24	• Your writing is fully coherent and controlled. Plot and characterisation are developed with detail, originality and imagination. • Your writing is clearly and imaginatively organised. The narrative is sophisticated and fully engages the reader's interest. • You have used structure and grammatical features ambitiously to give the writing cohesion and coherence. • You have communicated ambitiously and consistently to convey precise meaning.
15–19	• Your writing is clear and controlled. Plot and characterisation show convincing detail, and some originality and imagination. • Your writing is clearly organised. The narrative is purposefully shaped and developed. • You have used structure and grammatical features to give the writing cohesion and coherence. • You have communicated with some ambition to convey precise meaning.

Vocabulary, sentence structure, spelling and punctuation (maximum 16)

Marks	Skills
14–16	• You have used appropriate and effective variations in sentence structure. • Virtually all your sentence construction is controlled and accurate. • You have used a range of punctuation confidently and accurately. • You have spelled almost all words, including complex and irregular words, correctly. • Your control of tense and agreement is totally secure. • You have used a wide range of appropriate, ambitious vocabulary to create precise meaning.
11–13	• You have used varied sentence structure. • Your sentence construction is secure. • You have used a range of punctuation accurately. • You have spelled most words, including irregular words, correctly. • Your control of tense and agreement is secure. • You have used a range of ambitious vocabulary with precision.

Page 193 English Language Component 2

Section A: Reading

A1 a) children **[1] b)** under 300 **[1] c)** six **[1]**

A2 Look at the mark scheme below, decide which description is closest to your answer and then decide what mark to give it up to a maximum of **[10]**.

Marks	Skills
9–10	• You have given a persuasive evaluation of the text and its effects. • You have supported your evaluation with convincing, well-selected textual references. • You have shown engagement and involvement, taking an overview of the text to make perceptive comments.
7–8	• You have given a critical evaluation of the text and its effects. • You have supported your evaluation with well selected textual references. • You have shown clear awareness and critical engagement with the text.

You should have included some of the following points in your answer:

- The campaign has support from well-known people, including a writer.
- Frobisher says going to the library made her a writer.
- She and Gomez use persuasive arguments about the value of the library to the community.
- This aspect of the library's role is mentioned several times.
- The campaigners also refer to the importance of reading.
- The opposing argument is put for balance.
- The statistics about library use are quite convincing.
- More space is given to campaigners than opponents – and their actual words are reported.
- The impression is given that the campaign has a lot of support and the campaigners are very passionate and committed.

A3 (a) Support their campaign for public libraries **[1]** by voting for them **[1]**. **(b)** Most people understand why libraries are a good idea. **[1]**

A4 Look at the mark scheme below, decide which description is closest to your answer and then decide which mark to give it up to a maximum of **[10]**.

Marks	Skills
9–10	• You have made accurate and perceptive comments about a wide range of different examples from the text. • You have given a detailed analysis of how the writer uses language and structure to achieve effects and influence readers. • You have used subject terminology accurately to support your comments.
7–8	• You have made accurate comments about a range of different examples from the text. • You have begun to analyse how the writer uses language and structure to influence readers. • You have used subject terminology to support your comments.

You should have included some of the following points in your answer:

- The tone is extremely polite and to a modern reader might even seem sycophantic, the writers signing off with 'We beg, Sir, to remain yours obediently'.
- They start with a question, which explains what they want in a very polite way.
- In the second paragraph they say what they are not going to do, giving the idea that people already agree with them.
- They give a long explanation, in the past tense, of the history of their libraries.
- They use statistics as evidence to impress the reader of their 'success', a word they keep repeating.
- The whole letter has a polite tone (for example, the use of modal verbs: 'May we be allowed'; 'We would').
- The use of long, complex sentences also makes the tone seem reasonable and polite.

A5 Look at the mark scheme below, decide which description is closest to your answer and then decide what mark to give it up to a maximum of **[4]**.

Marks	Skills
4	• You have shown clear understanding of both texts. • You have synthesised evidence from texts. • You have used a range of relevant detail from both texts.
3	• You have shown some understanding of both texts. • You have shown clear connections between texts. • You have used relevant detail from both texts.

You might have included some or all of the following points:

- In 1891 the libraries in Marylebone are new, although the buildings they are in are unsuitable, one being 'plain and insufficient'.
- The King's Cross library, which was built over 100 years ago, is 'roomy' and 'generously proportioned'.
- The number of people using this library is falling, reflecting the fact that the area is not 'thriving'.
- In Marylebone in 1891, where the libraries are 'in two of the most populous parts of the parish', 'the demand increases daily'.
- The libraries in Marylebone are not funded by the council. King's Park is run by the council but the council does not want it.
- They also say it is only really pensioners who use it, whereas the Marylebone libraries are used by 'persons of all sorts and conditions'.

A6 Look at the mark scheme below, decide which description is closest to your answer and then decide which mark to give it up to a maximum of **[10]**.

Marks	Skills
9–10	• You have made comparisons that are sustained and detailed. • You have shown clear understanding of the methods used to convey ideas.
7–8	• You have made detailed comparisons. • You have made valid comments on how the ideas are conveyed.

You should have included some of the following points in your answer:

- The two texts have different purposes. The article's is to report on the campaign to save the library and the letter's is to persuade people to support public libraries.
- The article includes both direct and reported speech from several people who are trying to keep the library open and who use emotive language, such as 'heart' and 'devastating', together with personal anecdotes, clichés ('drop in the ocean') and rhetorical techniques such as rhetorical questions ('how can the Mayor…?') to persuade.
- The letter also uses rhetorical techniques but is more subtle. The letter starts by saying what it is NOT going to do, implying confidence that the argument for public libraries has been won.
- The letter's tone is calm and measured, its arguments backed by evidence. This is similar to the way the council spokesperson in the newspaper article puts her case.
- Witherspoon is reporting the views of others while Debenham and Hollond give their own point of view.

Page 194 English Language Component 2

Section B: Writing

B1 and B2 Look at the mark scheme below, decide which description is closest to your answer and then decide which mark to give yourself. This task is marked for communication and organisation, and for technical accuracy.

Communication and Organisation (maximum 12)

Marks	Skills
11–12	• Your writing shows sophisticated understanding of the purpose and format of the task. • Your writing shows sustained awareness of the reader/intended audience. • You have used an appropriate register, confidently adapted to purpose/audience. • Your content is ambitious, pertinent and sophisticated. • Your ideas are convincingly developed and supported by a range of relevant details.
8–10	• Your writing shows consistent understanding of the purpose and format of the task. • Your writing shows secure awareness of the reader/intended audience. • You have used an appropriate register, consistently adapted to purpose/audience. • Your content is well-judged and detailed. • Your ideas are organised and coherently developed, supported by relevant details.

Vocabulary, sentence structure, spelling and punctuation (maximum 8)

Marks	Skills
8	• You have used appropriate and effective variations in sentence structure. • Virtually all your sentence construction is controlled and accurate. • You have used a range of punctuation confidently and accurately. • You have spelled almost all words, including complex and irregular words, correctly. • Your control of tense and agreement is totally secure. • You have used a wide range of appropriate, ambitious vocabulary to create precise meaning.
6–7	• You have used varied sentence structure. • Your sentence construction is secure. • You have used a range of punctuation accurately. • You have spelled most words, including irregular words, correctly. • Your control of tense and agreement is secure. • You have used a range of vocabulary with precision.

Page 196 English Literature Component 1

Section A: Shakespeare

For all questions, look at the mark scheme below, decide which description is closest to your answer and then decide which mark to give yourself up to a maximum of **[15]** for part **a)** and **[20]** for part **b)**.

Marks	Skills
a) 13–15 **b)** 17–20	• You have sustained focus on the task, including an overview, and conveyed your ideas consistently and coherently. • You have approached the text sensitively and analysed it critically. • You have shown a perceptive understanding of the text, engaging with a personal response and some originality. • You have included pertinent quotations from the text. • You have analysed and appreciated the writer's use of language, form and structure. • You have used precise subject terminology appropriately.
a) 10–12 **b)** 13–16	• You have sustained focus on the task, including an overview, and conveyed your ideas coherently. • You have approached the text thoughtfully. • You have shown a secure understanding of key aspects of the text, with considerable engagement. • You have included well-chosen quotations from the text. • You have discussed and increasingly analysed the writer's use of language, form and structure. • You have used subject terminology appropriately.

Part **(b)** is also marked for spelling, punctuation, vocabulary and sentence structure **[maximum 5]**.

Marks	Skills
4–5	• You have spelled and punctuated with consistent accuracy. • You have consistently used vocabulary and sentence structure to achieve effective control of meaning.
2–3	• You have spelled and punctuated with considerable accuracy. • You have consistently used a considerable vocabulary and sentence structure to achieve general control of meaning.

Your answers could include some of the following points.

1. *Macbeth*

(a)
- Macbeth is seen here preparing for battle; he is a soldier again.
- Speaking in soliloquy, he says he has no fear.
- He is aware of what he has done.
- Ambiguity in 'she should have died hereafter'.
- Repetition of 'tomorrow' and imagery used to describe time.
- Imagery conveys one man's insignificance and the pointlessness of life.

(b)
- Lady Macbeth may be more ruthless than Macbeth, blaming the guards for Duncan's murder.
- She persuades him to murder Duncan.
- She embraces evil; he knows he is doing wrong.
- He discusses his guilt; hers seems not to affect her until the sleepwalking scene.
- As a woman she only has power through him, but she dominates him and taunts him about his role as a man.

2. *Romeo and Juliet*

(a)
- Juliet's desire for Romeo to stay, pretending it is still night.
- Imagery of light and dark – they can only be together in the dark.
- The marriage is consummated and so is a real marriage – important later in the play.
- Romeo's use of nature imagery/personification.
- Imagery reflects the enormity of their passion.
- Awareness of danger – love and death.

(b)
- Contrast with his love for Rosaline.
- His soliloquies expressing his feelings.
- The sonnet used to express mutual love
- The imagery he uses to express his feelings.
- Portrayal of his love and their relationship in the balcony scene.
- His commitment to her and his actions after their marriage.
- Association of love and death.
- Marriage as holy – spiritual and sexual fulfilment.
- Nurse's disregard for the sanctity of marriage as well as for Juliet's feelings.

3. *Henry V*

(a)
- Contrast of comic scene/characters with previous scene.
- Characters once associated with Falstaff and Henry in his youth, but now rejected by Henry.
- Boy's rejection of them echoes this.
- They are inspired by Henry's speech, repeating 'the breach' and are determined to fight.
- They sing and fight, behaving as if they are in a tavern, not on a battlefield.
- Fluellen is wild and violent – a stereotypical Welshman of the time.

(b)
- He can be ruthless as well as statesmanlike.
- He can also be clever and diplomatic.
- He inspires his men before Agincourt.
- He is seen as a war leader and a successful king.
- A more human/ordinary side is seen in his interactions with soldiers and his wooing of Katherine.

4. *The Merchant of Venice*

(a)
- He sees Antonio as a 'fool' for lending without interest, recalling that moneylenders had to be outsiders.
- He has no interest in appearing merciful as society might expect.
- Repetition of 'my bond' shows anger.
- He recalls his former treatment by Antonio.
- Calling him a dog implies Jews are seen as less than human.
- The jailer has allowed Antonio to 'come abroad' – Antonio, the insider, is not seen as a criminal.

(b)
- The Doge's role in the trial. Can it be fair?
- Shylock's demands for justice and his 'bond'.
- Portia's speech about mercy.
- The failure of Portia's appeal to Shylock and what this says about him.
- Is the outcome of the trial just?
- How far would differences in Elizabethan and modern attitudes influence an audience's reaction to the trial?

5. *Much Ado About Nothing*

(a)
- Benedick has not yet appeared, but we anticipate a clash and/or romance with Beatrice.
- Beatrice asks if he is with Don Pedro, indicating an interest in him.
- Something happened the last time they met but we never know exactly what.
- Contrast between the messenger's account of Benedick as a 'good soldier' and Beatrice's.
- She does not seem to want to hear anything good about him.
- Leonato's reference to a 'merry war' makes us expect battles of wits – but is there real dislike or is it all a joke?

(b)
- Different definitions of 'honour': chastity; reputation; family responsibilities.
- Claudio does not behave honourably to Hero though he rejects her because he thinks she has lost her honour.
- Benedick is not obliged to defend Hero but doing so shows his love for Beatrice.
- It also shows that he understands 'honour' as being a matter of right and wrong, not loyalty to friends.
- Honour is associated with the court and the aristocracy. Claudio has not behaved as a man of his class is expected to.

6. *Othello*

(a)
- The audience may still be shocked by the killing of Desdemona.
- After attacking Iago, Othello is calm.
- He does not want to make excuses: 'nothing extenuate'.
- He blames his passion and his love.
- He still has pride in his achievements.
- Audience members may feel a range of emotions.

(b)
- Iago is the opposite of Othello, but Othello is still quick to believe his wife is unfaithful.
- Because of his soliloquies the audience is drawn into Iago's plans.
- As they progress we see the effects of his dishonesty and ruthlessness.

- He is reminiscent of the 'devils' of medieval plays, who spoke to the audience about their villainy.
- His motives are not always clear – Jealousy? Revenge? Racism?
- His relationship with Emilia can be compared to Othello and Desdemona's marriage.

Page 202 English Literature Component 1

Section B: Poetry

1. For both parts of the question, look at the mark scheme below, decide which description is closest to your answer and then decide which mark to give yourself. Mark part **(a)** out of **15** and part **(b)** out of **25**.

Marks	Skills
(a) 13–15 **(b)** 21–25	• You have sustained focus on the task, including an overview, and conveyed your ideas consistently and coherently. • You have approached the text sensitively and analysed it critically. • You have shown a perceptive understanding of the text, engaging with a personal response and some originality. • You have included pertinent quotations from the text. • You have analysed and appreciated the writer's use of language, form and structure. • You have used precise subject terminology appropriately. • You have shown an assured understanding of the relationships between texts and the contexts in which they were written. • (part b) only) You have made critical and illuminating comparisons throughout. • (part b) only) There is a wide ranging discussion of the similarities and differences.
(a) 10–12 **(b)** 16–20	• You have sustained focus on the task, including an overview, and conveyed your ideas coherently. • You have approached the text thoughtfully. • You have shown a secure understanding of key aspects of the text, with considerable engagement. • You have included well-chosen quotations from the text. • You have discussed and increasingly analysed the writer's use of language, form and structure. • You have used subject terminology appropriately. • You have shown a secure understanding of the relationships between texts and the contexts in which they were written. • (part b) only) You have made focussed and coherent comparisons throughout. • (part b) only) There is a clear discussion of the similarities and differences.

Your answer might include:

(a)
- The poet witnesses the suffering but is not personally involved.
- Suffering is both physical and psychological.
- Regularity of form, metre and rhyme.
- Ballad form – return to simple forms in Romantic movement.
- Effect of use of repetition.
- Suffering caused by the powerful – others are victims.
- Urban setting, in the context of the industrial revolution and the growth of cities.
- Angry tone.
- The politics of the French Revolution and their influence on Romanticism shown here.

(b)
- Possible comparison with 'Living Space', focussing on suffering in an urban environment and the powerlessness of ordinary people.
- Compare with 'Dulce et Decorum Est' or 'The Manhunt' where suffering is the result of war.
- Compare ideas of power with 'Hawk Roosting' or 'Ozymandias'.
- Compare the use of regular form with 'Ozymandias' or 'Hawk Roosting'
- Compare the use of an outsider observing suffering to 'A Wife in London'/ 'Mametz Wood'.
- Contrast with the personal involvement of the poet in 'Dulce et Decorum Est' or the persona in 'The Manhunt'.

Page 204 English Literature Component 2

Section A: Post-1914 Prose/Drama

22–31. Look at the mark scheme below, decide which description is closest to your answer and then decide which mark to give yourself.

Marks	Skills
29–35	• You have sustained focus on the task, including an overview, and conveyed your ideas consistently and coherently. • You have approached the text sensitively and analysed it critically. • You have shown a perceptive understanding of the text, engaging with a personal response and some originality. • You have included pertinent quotations from the text. • You have analysed and appreciated the writer's use of language, form and structure. • You have used precise subject terminology appropriately.
22–28	• You have sustained focus on the task, including an overview, and conveyed your ideas coherently. • You have approached the text thoughtfully. • You have shown a secure understanding of key aspects of the text, with considerable engagement. • You have included well-chosen quotations from the text. • You have discussed and increasingly analysed the writer's use of language, form and structure. • You have used subject terminology appropriately.

This question is also marked for accuracy in spelling, punctuation and the use of vocabulary and sentence structures. **[5 marks]**

Marks	Skills
4–5	• You have spelled and punctuated with consistent accuracy. • You have consistently used vocabulary and sentence structure to achieve effective control of meaning.
2–3	• You have spelled and punctuated with considerable accuracy. • You have consistently used a considerable vocabulary and sentence structure to achieve general control of meaning.

[Maximum 35 + 5 = 40 marks]

Your answers could include some of the following points.

1. *An Inspector Calls*
   - Eva Smith as a representative of the working class.
   - Is she one person or several people? In the extract the Inspector refers to 'several names'.

- He gives shocking details of her death, invoking horror and sympathy.
- The Inspector establishes her connection to the Birlings in the extract, but Arthur Birling is dismissive.
- To him she is just one of 'several hundred young women'.
- The Inspector shows the photo to the Birlings separately.
- She is involved with all the Birlings.
- The situations she is in are almost stereotypical.
- The Birlings' treatment of her reveals their characters and attitudes.

2. *Blood Brothers*
   - The fact of their being brothers demonstrates the importance of class in their futures.
   - They behave and speak differently. This is shown clearly in the extract.
   - Some of the tension in the extract comes from class differences, but some from the situation and Edward's mother's reactions.
   - Irony in 'you're not the same as him'.
   - Edward has opportunities that Mickey does not have.
   - Is it just money or is there more to class?
   - There does not seem to be any social mobility in the play.
   - The differences between them are quite crudely drawn.
   - The two boys are not different in nature – their differences are the result of upbringing.
3. *The History Boys*
   - In the extract Irwin is shown as television presenter/popular historian.
   - His language is deliberately shocking, as are the points he makes.
   - His focus on the toilets could be seen as making history more real or as appealing to the lowest common denominator.
   - It is history as entertainment.
   - Why has Bennett made the choice to have all the boys studying history (unlikely in real life)?
   - Is it just a way of passing exams?
   - Mrs Lintott and Irwin have different approaches. Irwin wants to question everything.
   - Is this any better than accepting everything?
   - The idea that there is 'no need to tell the truth'.
   - Irwin's subsequent career involves him in making history.
4. *The Curious Incident of the Dog in the Night-Time*
   - Christopher accepts his father's version of events, as does the audience at first.
   - His desire to solve the mystery leads him to the truth.
   - Judy speaks through letters.
   - Her version of events is very different.
   - In the extract she makes calm reasonable points about why Christopher is better off with his father.
   - She then tells a long anecdote, showing what it was like to take him out.
   - She is using this to justify her actions – would she gain the audience's sympathy here?
   - She gives the other side of living with Christopher, admitting she could not cope.
   - She presents a nostalgic view of family life.
   - In the end she returns and commits to Christopher.
5. *A Taste of Honey*
   - The mother–daughter relationship is central.
   - In the extract the writer establishes a relationship that is more like a friendship.
   - Jo is more like the adult, looking after Helen.
   - The story about Helen's ex-boyfriend shows that Jo has romantic crushes on men.
   - Reference to the flowers shows a creative side/a longing for something different.
   - She argues with her mother about everything and resents their way of life.
   - She knows nothing about her father and is worried by what her mother tells her about him.
   - There is a role-reversal, Jo seemingly more mature than Helen.
   - Jo is critical of her mother but puts up with her.
   - Jo is motivated by not wanting to be like her mother.
   - She feels she can do without her but in the end has no-one else.
6. *Lord of the Flies*
   - Golding's characters are English public schoolboys, representatives of the 'civilised' world.
   - At first they behave as they would expect adults to, electing a leader and making rules.
   - Rivalries, fights, etc. are usual in schools but here they get out of hand.
   - The role of Jack and the hunters.
   - In the extract, words like 'tribe' and 'savages' are used to describe the hunters.
   - Jack is naked apart from paint and a belt.
   - They are starting to enjoy killing rather than just killing for food.
   - Jack and his 'tribe' have rejected the civilisation created on the island by Ralph and others.
   - The symbolism of the conch and the beast.
   - Changes in the way the boys speak.
   - Stages in the escalation of violence: killing the pig, Piggy, Simon.
   - What happens at the end? Has civilisation broken down or have we just learned how superficial the idea is?
7. *Never Let Me Go*
   - They are called guardians, not teachers. What is the difference?
   - In some ways they act like conventional teachers, but some things they do – such as the 'sex lectures' or the gallery – are odd.
   - They know about the children's future but only give little bits of information.
   - They are part of the system and controlled by the system.
   - Miss Geraldine is the most popular guardian and is a stereotype of the popular female teacher.
   - Miss Lucy's talks with Tommy show her doubts about the school. She is 'idealistic'.
   - In the extract Miss Lucy talks on the surface like a teacher speaking to a pupil but there is something mysterious and disturbing about what she says.
   - Here Tommy starts to realise the guardians may not be what they seem.
   - Her 'shaking' is disturbing. She is angry but not at Tommy – so what is she angry about?
   - Miss Emily's views are ambiguous. She works within society as it is.
8. *Anita and Me*
   - Some of the neighbours' behaviour is casual, even unknowing, racism.
   - The dog's name causes Meena to question racist language: 'it's like a swear word'.
   - Sam's behaviour at the fete is more openly racist – Meena feels personally hurt.
   - Meena's mother and her friends talk about English people in a way that could be thought racist.
   - In the extract, racist language is used against Meena's mother.
   - This is a shock to Meena but not to her mother.
   - She realises it is part of everyday life for her family and explains how it makes her feel.
   - Racist violence against Aunty Usha is reported and Sam's racism culminates in beating up Mr Bhatra.
   - The reference to 'Paki bashing' suggests an acceptance of racism which Meena has not been aware of.
   - First-person narrative gives empathy to Meena and the reader shares her growing awareness.
   - References to *To Kill a Mockingbird*, and the marked similarity of the ending to that novel's ending.
9. *The Woman in Black*
   - In the extract Arthur sees a woman in the graveyard.
   - He explains away what he sees to himself.

- Mr Jerome's reaction is unexpected as it shows that he is afraid.
- Mr Jerome does not discuss the woman with Arthur, leaving him puzzled. Readers would question Arthur's 'logical' explanation.
- The narrator has been introduced as being intelligent, sensible and sceptical.
- The sense of the supernatural is built through rumours.
- The use of unexplained noises, building to unexplained sights.
- Atmospheric descriptions of the landscape.
- Solving the mystery and understanding the woman's motives does not prevent her from harming Arthur Kipps.
- Sense that supernatural forces cannot be defeated or appeased.

10. *Oranges Are not the Only Fruit*
- The extract focuses on the visit of her natural mother.
- This is of huge significance but is not described in detail.
- Readers are left wondering what exactly has been said.
- It is told almost 'by the way' as a flashback in a chapter about other events.
- The reactions of both Jeanette and her mother are equally emotional.
- Why does Jeanette accept that it should be left in the past?
- Jeanette's identity initially comes from her adopted mother and her religion.
- As she grows up she finds a sense of identity through education and relationships.
- The fairy tale/fantasy elements of the novel are about searching for meaning and identity.

Page 209 English Literature Component 2

Section B: 19th-Century Prose

Look at the mark scheme below, decide which description is closest to your answer and then decide which mark to give yourself up to a maximum of **[40]**.

Marks	Skills
32–40	• You have sustained focus on the task, including an overview, and conveyed your ideas consistently and coherently. • You have approached the text sensitively and analysed it critically. • You have shown a perceptive understanding of the text, engaging with a personal response and some originality. • You have included pertinent quotations from the text. • You have analysed and appreciated the writer's use of language, form and structure. • You have used precise subject terminology appropriately. • You have shown an assured understanding of the relationship between the text and the context in which it was written.
24–31	• You have sustained focus on the task, including an overview, and conveyed your ideas coherently. • You have approached the text thoughtfully. • You have shown a secure understanding of key aspects of the text, with considerable engagement. • You have included well-chosen quotations from the text. • You have discussed and increasingly analysed the writer's use of language, form and structure. • You have used subject terminology appropriately. • You have shown a secure understanding of the relationship between the text and the context in which it was written.

[Maximum 40 marks]

Your answers could include some of the following points:

11. *The Strange Case of Dr Jekyll and Mr Hyde*
- The story is told by Poole, introducing another narrator.
- Another piece of the jigsaw for Utterson and the reader.
- Poole very close to Jekyll but is convinced it is not Jekyll.
- Poole's reaction is one of fear, his hair standing up – feels he has seen something evil.
- Compares the man he saw to a rat – Hyde is often compared to animals. He is also referred to as 'it', as if he is no longer human.
- Jekyll has physically shrunk – 'more of a dwarf' – matching other descriptions of Hyde.
- Stevenson is building up gradually to a full description of transformation.
- Utterson and others assume Hyde is a separate person. They see Jekyll as 'good'.
- Consider Dr Lanyon's narrative and his reaction.
- Consider Jekyll's own narrative and his motivation – to separate good and evil.
- The story shows that this is impossible – what else does it say about good and evil?

12. *A Christmas Carol*
- Here Dickens uses shock and horror, surprising the reader at the end of the chapter.
- The two children are personifications of Ignorance and Want (poverty).
- The language used to describe them is vivid and repulsive.
- However, the description is not very much exaggerated – it is what very poor children would look like.
- The ghost uses them as a warning of what might happen if poverty and lack of education are not dealt with – revolution.
- Dickens uses Scrooge's transformation to explore ideas about responsibility.
- Using the Christmas ghost story, a popular form, Dickens gets his messages across in an entertaining way.
- Being charitable and socially responsible is part of the spirit of Christmas – it does not stop you enjoying yourself.
- This chapter shows a wide range of people at Christmas, many poor.
- The Cratchits are used to show what life is like for poor families and how easy it could be to improve their lives.

13. *Jane Eyre*
- As narrator Jane shares the feelings she had at the time with the reader.
- Here she analyses her feelings, which she does throughout the novel.
- She opens with a rhetorical question and answers it.
- She analyses Rochester's character, calling him 'proud, sardonic, harsh' but also listing his good qualities.
- She is concerned with morality. It is important for her to think he is no longer immoral.
- It is now clear that she is in love with him, a feeling that has been developing throughout the novel.
- Jane rescues Rochester on several occasions – almost as if he has to be less powerful for her to love him.
- Symbolism of the fire and Rochester's attitude to Jane after it.
- His marriage to Bertha and his deception – Jane's reasons for leaving Thornfield.
- Jane's return to Thornfield and their mutual love.

14. *Pride and Prejudice*
- Contrast in reactions of Mr and Mrs Bennet.
- Elizabeth's reasons for rejecting Mr Collins.
- Ironic/comic tone of passage.
- Use of dialogue to convey attitudes of Mr and Mrs Bennet and their characters.
- Serious point given to unlikely character to make in a comic way. Who will maintain her if she is not married?
- Contrast Elizabeth's refusal with Charlotte Lucas's acceptance of Mr Collins.
- Marriage must be for love but must also make sense financially and socially.

- Other examples of marriage: Mr and Mrs Bennet, Lydia and Wickham, Jane and Bingley.
- Marriage of Elizabeth and Darcy as an ideal.

15. *Silas Marner*
- Silas's condition means he has not seen the child arrive and we see the discovery through his eyes.
- At first, he thinks it is his missing gold, the most important thing in his life.
- When he sees the child, he thinks it might be his dead sister, stirring feelings of love.
- The word 'mystery' is used at first in a religious sense, relating to the idea of a 'Power' sending her.
- At the end it is a mystery to be solved as he starts to think logically.
- He tries to help her but his 'dull bachelor mind' is not used to children.
- Eppie helps him to rediscover feelings (and the faith) he had lost.
- She brings him closer to the community as others offer to help.
- She replaces gold in his affections.
- He is rewarded when she chooses him over her natural father.

16. *War of the Worlds*
- The curate, like others, tries to make sense of the invasion.
- He sees it as a punishment from God, referring to the Bible and wondering what he and others have done to deserve it.
- His biblical language contrasts with the mundane details of suburban life in Weybridge (the Sunday school etc.)
- The narrator, while not rejecting God, rejects this idea using logic and humour: 'He is not an insurance agent'.
- Like many others, the curate feels helpless and is astonished that one of 'God's ministers' has been killed.
- The narrator's reaction changes as he experiences the invasion.
- He observes curiosity, panic, defiance and despair.
- Contrast the artilleryman's considered view with the curate's.

Page 215 English Literature Component 2

Section C: Unseen Poetry

17. Look at the mark scheme below, decide which description is closest to your answer and then decide which mark to give yourself. Part **a)** is marked out of **15** and part **b)** out of **25**. Total maximum mark **[40].**

Marks	Skills
(a) 13–15 **(b)** 21–25	• You have sustained focus on the task, including an overview, and conveyed your ideas consistently and coherently. • You have approached the text sensitively and analysed it critically. • You have shown a perceptive understanding of the text, engaging with a personal response and some originality. • You have included pertinent quotations from the text. • You have analysed and appreciated the writer's use of language, form and structure. • You have used precise subject terminology appropriately. • You have shown an assured understanding of the relationships between texts and the contexts in which they were written. • (part b) only) You have made critical and illuminating comparisons throughout. • (part b) only) There is a wide ranging discussion of the similarities and differences.
(a) 10–12 **(b)** 16–20	• You have sustained focus on the task, including an overview, and conveyed your ideas coherently. • You have approached the text thoughtfully. • You have shown a secure understanding of key aspects of the text, with considerable engagement. • You have included well-chosen quotations from the text. • You have discussed and increasingly analysed the writer's use of language, form and structure. • You have used subject terminology appropriately. • You have shown a secure understanding of the relationships between texts and the contexts in which they were written. • (part b) only) You have made focussed and coherent comparisons throughout. • (part b) only) There is a clear discussion of the similarities and differences.

Your answer might include comments on the following:

a)
- Poem in three regular stanzas.
- Impact of short rhyming couplet in lines 5 and 6 of each stanza.
- It starts with a grand, general statement and then gives examples.
- The third stanza addresses the reader directly.
- Death is a 'leveller' because it is the same for everyone and all are equal.
- Personification of Death ('his icy hand').
- Identification of classes of people by things associated with them ('Sceptre and Crown', 'scythe and spade') – called 'metonymy' in literary criticism.
- The poem reads like a warning.
- The language reflects decay: 'dust', 'wither'.
- There are many words associated with surrender and powerlessness: 'tumble', 'yield', 'stoop', 'captives'.
- For most of the poem the tone is negative – it seems as if no human activity is worthwhile as it all ends in death.
- The last two lines give hope of a kind, an idea that 'the just' can leave something behind.

b)
- The first is about death in general, the second about the death of an individual.
- Stevenson speaks of how he would like to be remembered; Shirley implies no-one will be remembered.
- Stevenson expresses contentment with both life and death. Shirley's view of death is not comforting.
- Both focus on what remains; the grave; the dust.
- Rhythm, rhyme and alliteration give Stevenson's poem a cheerful tone. Shirley's is more ponderous, with a heavy beat.
- Both have stanzas of equal length, but Shirley's are more complex, as is what he is saying.
- The rhyme schemes are also regular in both poems – again, Stevenson's is simpler.
- Both poets use the second person, 'you', but for Stevenson 'you' seems to be a loved one, while for Shirley it is anyone who reads the poem.
- Stevenson's idea of death being like coming home contrasts with Shirley's focus on the 'cold tomb'.
- Shirley's poem reads like a warning, inspiring fear and guilt, whereas Stevenson seeks to comfort the reader.

Notes

Notes

Collins GCSE Revision

Visit the website to view the complete range and place an order:

www.collins.co.uk/collinsGCSErevision

ACKNOWLEDGEMENTS

The author and publisher are grateful to the copyright holders for permission to use quoted materials and images.

Cover, p.1, p.153 © Shutterstock.com/Stocksnapper, © Shutterstock.com/amiloslava

All other images © Shutterstock.com

P.30 *Nineteen Eighty-Four* by George Orwell (Copyri © George Orwell, 1949)

P.76, 77, 178 *Death of A Naturalist* by Seamus Heaney New and Selected Poems 1966-1967 (2002) Reprinted permission of the publishers, Faber and Faber Ltd.

P.77 Hawk Roosting' from *Bestiary* by Ted Hughes (2014) Reprinted by permission of the publishers, Faber and Faber

P.91, 93, 124, 205 © Simon Stephens, 2004, *The Curio Incident of the Dog in the Night-Time*. Reprinted by permission of Methuen Drama Bloomsbury Publishin

P.91, 123, 205 *The History Boys* by Alan Bennett (200 Faber and Faber Ltd.

P.92, 124, 206 *Lord of the Flies* by William Golding (1954) Faber and Faber Ltd.

P.92, 125, 207 *Anita and Me* by Meera Syal, Flaming (1997) © Meera Syal

P.92, 125, 207 *Never Let Me Go* by Kazuo Ishiguro (2 Reprinted by permission of the publishers, Faber an Faber Ltd.

P.93, 123, 204 © Willy Russell, 2001, *Blood Brothers*. Reprinted by permission of Methuen Drama Blooms Publishing Plc.

P.115 'Florence' by Joyce Rackham, from *The Times* October 1982)

P.123, 204 From AN INSPECTOR CALLS by J.B. Priestl (Penguin Books, 2001) Copyright © J.B. Priestley, 19

P.124, 206 © Shelagh Delaney, 1982, *A Taste of Honey*. Reprinted by permission of Methuen Drama Bloomsbury Publishing Plc.

P.125, 208 *The Woman in Black* by Susan Hill (1983)

P.126, 208 *Oranges are Not the Only Fruit* by Jeanet Winterson (1985)

P.178 Cozy Apologia. Copyright © 2004 by Rita Dov from COLLECTED POEMS: 1974-2004 by Rita Dove. by permission of W. W. Norton & Company, Inc.

Every effort has been made to trace copyright holders and obtain their permission for the use copyright material. The author and publisher wi gladly receive information enabling them to rec any error or omission in subsequent editions. All facts are correct at time of going to press.

Published by Collins

An imprint of HarperCollins*Publishers* Ltd

1 London Bridge Street,
London, SE1 9GF

9780008292010

First published 2018

10 9 8 7 6 5 4 3 2 1

British Library Cataloguing in Publication Data.

A CIP record of this book is available from the British Library.

Author: Paul Burns
Commissioning Editors: Clare Souza and Kerry Ferg
Editor and Project Manager: Katie Galloway
Cover Design: Sarah Duxbury and Paul Oates
Inside Concept Design: Sarah Duxbury and Paul C
Text Design and Layout: Jouve India Private Limi
Production: Natalia Rebow
Printed in the UK, by Martins The Printers

6 EASY WAYS TO ORDER

1. Available from www.collins.co.uk
2. Fax your order to 01484 665736
3. Phone us on 0844 576 8126
4. Email us at education@harpercollins.co.u
5. Post your order to: Collins Education, FREEPOST RTKB-SGZT-ZYJL, Honley HD9 6QZ
6. Or visit your local bookshop.